THE
INDUSTRIAL COLOUR BAR
IN SOUTH AFRICA

The
Industrial Colour Bar
in South Africa

G. V. DOXEY

SENIOR LECTURER IN COMMERCE AND APPLIED ECONOMICS
UNIVERSITY OF THE WITWATERSRAND

CAPE TOWN   LONDON   NEW YORK
OXFORD UNIVERSITY PRESS
1961

Oxford University Press, Amen House, London, E.C.4

GLASGOW   NEW YORK   TORONTO   MELBOURNE   WELLINGTON
BOMBAY   CALCUTTA   MADRAS   KARACHI   KUALA LUMPUR
CAPE TOWN   IBADAN   NAIROBI   ACCRA

⊛ SET AND PRINTED IN 11 ON 12 PT. TIMES BY
RUSTICA PRESS, PTY., LTD., WYNBERG, CAPE

Acknowledgements

I T WOULD BE INVIDIOUS for me to set out a list of people to
whom I am indebted in the writing of this book, for such
a list could not be exhaustive and I have benefited in one
way or another from the knowledge and advice of a great
number of people of all races, both in academic and official
circles and in the sphere of industry and commerce.

I should, however, like to place on record the value I attach
to my association firstly with the Department of Economics of
the University of Cape Town, under Professor H. M. Robertson,
and secondly, over the past two years, with Sir Theodore
Gregory, whose penetrating and scholarly approach to South
African problems has at all times been stimulating and
informative.

I should also like to express my appreciation of the help and
encouragement given to me by my wife which has been more
than she would, herself, admit.

JOHANNESBURG
JANUARY 1960

Contents

ACKNOWLEDGEMENTS   V

INTRODUCTION   ix

1 THE COUNTRY, ITS PEOPLES
     AND ITS BEGINNINGS   1

The South African dilemma—Historical
background prior to 1870—The Coloured
people—The Indian population—The pre-
industrial society.

2 THE AGE OF DIAMONDS   12

The beginning of industrialism—The impact
of the discoveries—Migration to the diamond-fields—The character of the early
diggings—The impact of amalgamation upon
the labour market—Illicit diamond buying—The compound system—The resulting
pattern.

3 THE IMPACT OF GOLD   39

Discoveries—The problems of mining—The
determining factors in the labour market—
The problems of labour—New sources of
labour.

4 THE SPREAD OF INDUSTRIALIZATION
     [PART ONE] THE DIVERSIFICATION
     OF THE ECONOMY AND THE WHITE
     COMMUNITY   65

The agents of change—The development of
secondary industry—The group approach—
The composition of the labour force: whites
—The problem of the Poor White—The
challenge to industry.

5 THE SPREAD OF INDUSTRIALIZATION
     [PART TWO] THE PART PLAYED BY
     THE NON-WHITE POPULATION   85

The Africans—Coloured and Indian peoples
—The occupational distribution of the working population—The consequences of the
growth of manufacturing industry.

6 THE GROWTH OF LEGAL RIGIDITY IN
THE LABOUR MARKET [PART ONE]
THE UNDERLYING FACTORS   110

The broad framework—The marriage between trade unionism and the traditional prejudice—The mining industry and the Colour Bar—The Pact Government and the consequences.

7 THE GROWTH OF LEGAL RIGIDITY IN
THE LABOUR MARKET [PART TWO]
THE CONTENT OF LEGISLATION   128

Early laws regulating labour conditions—The training of artisans—Regulation of industrial employment.

8 THE GROWTH OF LEGAL RIGIDITY IN
THE LABOUR MARKET [PART THREE]
THE CONTENT OF LEGISLATION
(continued)   158

The General Regulation of Employment: The Mines and Works Act—The Factories, Machinery and Building Work Act—The Pass laws—Controls on the movement of Africans and attempts at labour mobilization—The Native Reserves—The movement to the towns and the Natives (Urban Areas) Act—The effect of the Natives (Urban Areas) Act on the labour market—Other legislation—The implications of occupational apartheid.

9 THE CONTEMPORARY SCENE   179

The advent of apartheid—The impact of war—The post-war expansion—The effect on the labour market—African migration and the rural areas—Interim apartheid.

10 THE TRIUMPH OF THE TRADITIONAL
PREJUDICE   196

Introduction

THIS STUDY IS AN ATTEMPT to provide a general view of the structure and stratification of the contemporary industrial labour market in South Africa, and to explain the pattern it has assumed by isolating some of the more important forces which have influenced its development since the discovery of diamonds in the 1870's, when South African industrial history may fairly be said to have begun.

What I have tried to do, within the compass of this work, is to indicate the factors and influences which by accident or design have moulded the industrial labour market into its present shape, and I make no claim to have written a complete account of the role played by labour in the development of industrialism in the Union. Such a work would have required very detailed historical research and study, and also a different line of approach from the one I have adopted.

It may be helpful to visualize a 'map' of the labour market in the same way as we look at the map of a town. Most modern cities are the result of a certain amount of deliberate planning superimposed on a haphazard design originally dictated by economic and social forces of various kinds: geographical situation probably determined the initial site, and the subsequent disposition of streets, buildings and open spaces was the result of a multitude of individual and corporate decisions, themselves motivated by ideas and intentions of many different natures. An over-all plan for urban development has become fashionable only in fairly recent years, but today, in most large towns, new development is subject to the requirements of town-planning regulations.

If the analogy may be permitted, the evolution of the South African industrial labour market may be described in similar terms. Originally, the pattern of agriculture and simple trade was disturbed by the discovery of diamonds in the Kimberley area, and the impetus given to industrial development was greatly strengthened by the commencement of large-scale gold-mining operations on the Rand some years later. Mining thus provided the momentum for what Professor Rostow has called the 'take-off' of the economy: it was the initiator of the transition from a completely agricultural to a substantially industrialized society. Subsequently, the growth of secondary and tertiary industries assisted the process of transformation, until South Africa reached the stage it is in today, where much of the economy is highly industrialized, and where over 70 per cent of the white population live in towns and have no direct connexion with the land.

The emergence of an industrial, urban labour force began in Kimberley, as the result of the geographical location of diamonds; from there it spread to the Witwatersrand and gradually, as manufacturing industry, transport, trade, and other services developed, it became numerically greater, more widespread, and much more highly diversified.

The composition of the labour market has been dictated mainly by the existence of the various racial groups who were settled in the territories which became the Union of South Africa, supplemented by immigration, both spontaneous and contrived, from neighbouring territories and from overseas. The levels of productivity, stability, and skill which have been achieved are similarly due in part to the individual qualities and initiative of the people themselves, partly to the conditions and opportunities created by private and public bodies, and partly to custom and statute operating in the socio-economic sphere. From the beginning, vertical mobility, i.e. progress up the job scale, has been subject to what is popularly known as the 'colour bar', although this is probably an over-simplification in that it suggests one rigid barrier, whereas in truth there are many barriers, some more rigid than others and not all operating simultaneously.

So if we look at our 'map' of the South African labour market today, it is seen to be of considerable size, with a fair amount of diversification. We also see that it is racially stratified to a marked degree, and increasingly subject to over-all planning, and what may be termed 'traffic directives'. Indeed, one of the features which would stand out on such a map would be the number of roads or avenues which are, by law, restricted to certain racial groups, and also the large proportion of culs-de-sac, which impede the progress of the non-European sections of the population, whether they be African, Indian or Coloured.

In some ways the best approach to this study might have been—to borrow a term from the vocabulary of the film industry—by way of flash-backs. In other words, a description of the state of the industrial labour market in South Africa today would be unfolded, with a series of interpolations tracing the evolution of the various features which are remarkable and of interest. This treatment, however, would have suffered from the defect of lack of continuity and the reader might be left, as the cinema-goer often is left, not quite sure where the story began or ended. For this reason I have preferred to adopt a predominantly, though not strictly chronological approach, starting with the beginnings of industrialization in the last quarter of the nineteenth century and continuing with its development through the twentieth century up to the present day. It should be emphasized that this method of approach can only be termed quasi-historical, as only those elements or influences which have had a lasting effect on the make-up and regulation of the labour force have been included and dealt with in any detail. Thus, the temporary introduction of Chinese labour and the Poor White problem, both of which—and particularly the latter—would merit exhaustive analysis and discussion in a full-scale historical study of the role of labour in South African economic development, are in this book considered only in so far as they explain and illuminate the map of the labour market which we can draw today.

It is hoped that the general interest felt at the present time about everything concerning South Africa will justify this small excursion into an aspect of the organization of the economy which deserves more attention than it generally receives, and may help to place it in better perspective.

The Country, its Peoples and its Beginnings

THE SOUTH AFRICAN DILEMMA

THE UNION OF SOUTH AFRICA came into being only half a century ago with the political union in 1910 of the Cape Colony, Natal, and the two former Boer Republics—the Transvaal and the Orange Free State. The former German colony of South-West Africa became a mandate of the Union after the First World War and is today an integral part of the country, although its exact legal status remains the subject of international controversy. Surrounded or partly surrounded by the Union are the High Commission Territories of Basutoland, Bechuanaland, and Swaziland, which are the responsibility of the United Kingdom.

These facts are generally known, as is the date 1652 which marks the first white settlement in South Africa. From that day to this, throughout the intervening centuries, events in the subcontinent have excited interest and stirred imagination in Europe, the United States, and more latterly in the whole world. Among the most dramatic of these events was the three-year struggle at the beginning of the present century between the two Boer Republics and Great Britain. The very nature of the war aroused concern everywhere: on the one side stood Britain, at the pinnacle of her Victorian power, in command of a rich and powerful Empire; on the other side were two weak and largely backward territories. The wider problems of a multi-racial society were largely overlooked in the drama of the conflict between Britain and the Boer Republics, and they continued to be overlooked in the years following the war which were characterized by a period of reconstruction and attempted reconciliation, leading to Union. Throughout the twentieth century, there has, in fact, been a gradual sacrifice of the broad humanitarian ideas of the liberal Cape Colony

1

to the more rigid, racially prejudiced attitudes of the former Republics.

It is always easy to express wisdom after the event, particularly when more than half a century has elapsed, and it serves little purpose now to suggest that the colour problem might have been less intractable today had the statesmen and politicians of that time shown more prescience of the future and had a wider vista of understanding. Whether the Anglo-Boer War could have been avoided is a question for historians and political theorists, as is the verdict on the post-war policies put into effect by Lord Milner. Likewise, little can now be gained by conducting post-mortems on the Act of Union, except as part of a realistic appraisal of the needs of the present, in contrast to the past, and using this knowledge for the effective solution of contemporary problems. The world today is vastly different from the world at the beginning of the century, and one of the most important changes, by which South Africa is only one of many countries to be vitally affected, is the fact that non-white races can no longer be regarded as the mere, inarticulate pawns of imperialist expansion and domination. The very meaning of the word 'colonialism' has become debased, and none can safely afford to ignore the aspirations of the non-white peoples, nor, for that matter, overlook their significance, both actual and potential, in all spheres of power politics, particularly in the United Nations and its many specialized agencies, and in the intrigues of the cold war.

It is interesting to mark another change which has come about in South Africa itself: we find today a passionate rejection on the part of those in authority of the world's concern with South Africa's problems—a striking contrast in attitude to the burning eagerness for world intervention shown by the Boer leaders sixty years ago.

Today, of course, it is the so-called colour problem which forms the subject-matter of world comment and criticism, and which pervades and indeed dominates all important issues in South Africa—political, economic, cultural, and social. The dilemma is present in every aspect of southern African life: how can a settled community be evolved in which all races can live in harmony, and grow rich in an atmosphere free from sectional discrimination and from the fear of subjugation and the debasement of western civilization.

The population of South Africa today is estimated at slightly below 16 million (approximately 3 million whites, 11 million Africans, 1½ million Coloureds and ½ million Indians). It is thus 21 per cent white and 79 per cent non-white. Political power rests exclusively with the whites, who are divided into Afrikaans- and English-speaking roughly in the proportions of 60 : 40. The members of the white group are justly proud of the part they have played in developing the country and transforming it into a modern industrial state, with a consequent raising of the standard of living of all sections of the population, yet they are becoming slowly more aware that these achievements, considerable though they are, will not alone suffice to maintain their superior status. On the other hand, there is no doubt that more and more of the non-whites are realizing the indispensable contribution which they make to the life of the country and are rapidly becoming increasingly resentful of the inferior status to which they are relegated, simply on the ground of the colour of their skins.

The underlying fear of the subordination of the white group to the non-white majority, and the debasement of the civilized, western way of life, has resulted in an attitude of mind among many whites, expressed most clearly by official policy over the last ten years, which is unable or unwilling to visualize the organization of South African society as an integrated whole, but prefers to think in terms of separate development, racial segregation and the preservation of white rule. This racial, group approach to the South African dilemma, which, of course, underlies the evolution and maintenance of the colour bar in industry, can be at least partly explained by the nature of the circumstances which accompanied the development of South African society.

On the one hand, the knowledge that the Europeans were responsible for introducing to the primitive African the norms of western civilization, and more recently the benefits of advanced technology, encouraged the evolution of a racial egocentricism which tacitly refuses to acknowledge that the indigenous inhabitants, however primitive they may have been in the beginning, may now be capable of becoming part of the new dynamic society which has ousted their primitive institutions, of contributing towards its development, of appreciating its value, and of enjoying its eventual fruits.

On the other hand, group bias is encouraged by the fear that close or undue association with members of what were, and in many cases still are, backward societies could bring about a lowering of the standards to which inhabitants of civilized societies of the western type are accustomed. The fact that today the competitive situation between the white and black groups is internal—in contrast to the external competition between the dynamic society and the primitive, static societies which characterized the eighteenth and nineteenth centuries and which gave rise to a series of violent clashes—does not seem to have wholly allayed white fears. The Kaffir Wars and other struggles between the white and black races left deep scars which persisted long after conflict gave way to co-operation in the technological function, and the illusion of the 'primitive savage' cuts sharply across the realities of the emerging urban, industrial worker, particularly as the advance of the African has been uneven, rather than regular. The bringing of the races together in industrial employment thus gave strength to white feeling that primitivism had been admitted to their ranks and might constitute a threat to the advanced society which they had created.

It may well be that to the outsider, who does not feel the white South African's pride, or fears, the problem appears comparatively simple and its solution not impossible. Yet in spite of the obsessiveness of colour prejudice, and the uncompromising nature of government policy in recent years, there is no doubt that a growing number of white South Africans are giving the problem more realistic consideration than was the case in the past. However, official policy is committed to the Nationalist Party's programme of apartheid, which has as its theoretical basis the belief that white survival can only be ensured through reducing the contact between the various races to the barest minimum. It is not easy to devise a rational basis for the concept of apartheid, for while to some it is seen as leading to the eventual division of South Africa, into white and non-white sectors, there are many of its supporters who prefer to think of it as ensuring the 'traditional' way of life and in economic terms as the best means of ensuring that no black man shall be allowed to occupy a job wanted by a white man. In essence, this is the basis of the economic colour bar.

As a political concept apartheid must be regarded as part of an historical pattern, but its upholders have tended to shift their justification of it to suit changing situations. With the spread of industrialization it has become increasingly difficult to maintain a separation of the races; in fact it is justifiable to argue that the needs of the advanced economy cut sharply across the illusion of 'separation'. Furthermore the growth of the economy has lessened rather than intensified the threat of white debasement in the economic sphere. Unable to challenge the reality of inter-racial co-operation in the economic sphere and the evident fruits of such co-operation, it has become necessary to shift the emphasis of the ideal of apartheid to loftier moral planes, and it is now seen as the only means of saving 'white civilization' even if this should result in the shelving of economic advantage.

Thus, historically the non-white 'threat' started as an external danger, as manifested in the Kaffir Wars, became internal with the fear of white debasement through the use of cheap non-white labour, and is now once again being made external. Official policy, guided by these motives, is actually against the continuance of industrial development if it results in the evolution of a truly multi-racial community, embracing an emerging sophisticated non-white population.

The situation has become fraught with a series of dangerous paradoxes and foremost among these is that created by the policy which insists upon the desirability of re-creating disintegrating tribalism in primitive societies alongside the advanced economy. When the stage is reached of legislating for the permanent retention of primitivism, the paradox of apartheid becomes most blatant. On the one hand the exponents of the community approach to South Africa's problems are accused of threatening and undermining white civilization, while on the other hand the emerging African is condemned for his aspirations and advised to re-embrace tribalism as the surest means of protecting him from the corruption of this same civilization. It becomes virtually impossible to comprehend a policy which refuses non-whites a proper place in society on the ground that they are not qualified for it, while at the same time denying them worth-while opportunities to qualify. It is perhaps this somewhat crude paradox which is causing whites of all shades of opinion to re-examine their own attitudes and look for more equitable solutions.

The present study is, of course, concerned with the problem in the industrial sphere. While the full significance of occupational colour differentiation first began to emerge with the expansion of mining after 1870, and showed itself especially with the later development of secondary industry, many of the underlying attitudes were already formed long before the end of the nineteenth century. It should be borne in mind that at that time the cultural gulf between the whites and the non-whites, particularly the Africans, was very real, while in the case of the Coloured and Indian peoples the stigma of slavery and indenture died hard. In order to give some perspective to the developments which followed the growth of an advanced economy in South Africa, it is necessary to examine very briefly some of the features of early South African society.

HISTORICAL BACKGROUND PRIOR TO 1870

The coming of the European to South Africa was not so much design as the result of the opportunities of geography. It had been the aim of all adventurer explorers from the Middle Ages onwards to discover a sea route to the East and open up a new and safer means of conducting the lucrative Eastern trade in spices and rare silks than by the long, arduous and dangerous land route of the Middle East. The discovery of the West Indies, and for that matter of the Americas as a whole, had been a by-product of this quest, and the Cape of Good Hope was no exception. Africa was the unknown continent and was to remain so until the second half of the nineteenth century. Vast deserts separated the Mediterranean coast-line from the unknown south and on the whole the coast of Africa was forbidding and uninviting. Although legend held that the Phoenicians had sailed their frail craft down the coast of Africa and round its southern shores, few believed that in this direction lay the answer to the quest for an easy route to the East.

It was the Portuguese, at the height of their maritime and commercial supremacy, who eventually turned legend into fact by sailing past what they named the Cape of Storms and reaching India by way of the Indian Ocean. Later, the Dutch and the English followed suit, but few ventured beyond a momentary stay at the Cape itself. However, in 1652, the Dutch East India Company first made use of the possibilities of the Cape of Storms, by then known as the Cape of Good Hope, as a provisioning point and strategic base, and from then onwards the southern part of the African continent was brought within the orbit of European life.

The Dutch were not interested in founding a colony, and the officials who were sent to establish the base were instructed to avoid giving the impression to any indigenous inhabitants they encountered that they had come with the object of colonizing. Nevertheless, from the beginning, the force of circumstances militated against the achievement of these aims and the avoidance of contact between whites and the indigenous Bushmen and Hottentots proved impossible in practice. Thus from the very earliest days, the race problem in South Africa revealed a divergence between what was considered desirable and what was to prove possible.

In spite of the efforts of the Company, and later of the Dutch authorities, to contain the area of white settlement within the effective jurisdiction of the Cape Peninsula, its range was consistently extended and contact with the indigenous inhabitants became greater with the widening of the moving frontier.

By the time the British finally took over the Cape in 1806, South African society had begun to assume many of its contemporary forms. Among most whites there had already developed the illusion of a 'white' country and a refusal to admit to the reality of multi-racialism. Henceforth South African history was to be characterized by the schisms of race. Even the whites were no longer a homogeneous group, for while the French Huguenot settlers of 1688 were to be completely absorbed by Boer culture and language, the British settlers retained their identity and it was the Boer who felt the need to preserve language and heritage against the new-comers. As far as the non-whites were concerned, they found they were unwanted in the new society except for the labour they could provide and when physical frontiers between white and non-white disappeared, the artificial barriers of the colour bar were gradually erected to take their place.

The primitive Bushmen, who with the Hottentots had roamed around what is now the western Cape, proved unable to resist the advance of white settlement and by 1870 they had virtually disappeared. The Hottentots as nomadic pastoralists had not taken kindly to white settlement which threatened their coastal grazing-lands and denied them safety from the marauding Bushmen. Yet by 1800 the frontier had spread to the Fish River, with the Hottentots reduced in numbers and effectiveness through smallpox and white man's liquor. By this stage, however, in the eastern Cape contact had been firmly made with the Bantu tribes, who for several centuries had been making their way through Africa in a south-easterly direction.

The whites had begun to evolve distinct characteristics moulded by the nature of the country and the new society. In the settled areas in and around Cape Town the institution of slavery enabled them to enjoy an existence free from the burden of manual work. Even though slavery at the Cape manifested few of the excesses which characterized it elsewhere, it played a significant part in moulding the attitudes of white South Africans to manual labour and in fostering colour prejudice. The uncivilized heathen non-whites were looked upon as inferior and it was natural that slavery should have reinforced this attitude.

The first slaves had been introduced soon after the arrival of van Riebeeck and his party in 1652. The founder of the settlement had lost no time in asking for slaves to be sent to the Cape —his first request was sent to the Company within six weeks of his arrival—and it is interesting to note that he also advocated the importation of Chinese labourers.

Within a hundred years of van Riebeeck's arrival, the institution of slavery had made an important impact on the whole way of life at the Cape, where the majority of the slaves were concentrated. Further east, existence on the frontier was vastly different: the leisurely, settled plantation existence gave way to a simple, rough way of life which was to mould a race of men, self-reliant, hardy, and resentful of attempts to govern them. It was largely from this type of pioneer that the trekkers of 1836 were drawn.

The nature of the Bantu tribes encountered by the frontiersmen reinforced ideas of racial superiority, and the bitter conflicts with the black people in the eastern Cape served to intensify dislike of British policy which aimed at the gradual assimilation of the races into a common society. From this resentment sprang the idea of the trek, and the famous Retief manifesto which became the guiding light of the Boer people. The bloody wars between Boer and Bantu in the Orange Free State and Natal which followed the trek provided the legends on which young Afrikanerdom was reared. It is common practice today for exponents of apartheid to compare the 'struggle for western civilization' with the exploits of the Voortrekkers against the Bantu. The interior of southern Africa was thus opened up by people firmly convinced of colour inferiority. There was little scope for the ideas of J. J. Rousseau, or for those of the later missionaries who taught brotherly love and equality before God. Nevertheless, where servants were concerned, the attitude of the Boers was strict and paternal rather than harshly domineering.

After 1806 the British were content to remain in the coastal areas: the settlers of 1820 were placed on the eastern frontier and after the annexation of Natal to the Crown in 1843, that territory gradually became anglicized. With the spread of the white frontier, the various Bantu tribes constituting the African population were progressively contained in those parts of the country which came to be known as the Native Reserves. The so-called 'Native Reserves' are today grouped as follows: (1) the Ciskei; (2) the Transkei; (3) the British Bechuanaland Reserves; (4) the Natal Reserves; (5) Zululand; (6) the Transvaal Reserves; (7) the Orange Free State Reserves.

THE COLOURED PEOPLE

Slavery was abolished in 1834 and the Hottentots gradually merged with the former slaves to form the Coloured population. The majority of the slaves had come from the East (the Moslem religion has been retained to this day by the Cape Malays who in many respects form a distinct subgroup in the Coloured community). Miscegenation between whites and slaves added to the Coloured population which later was further increased by racial mingling with the Bantu. The majority of the Coloured people worked on the farms or as domestic servants, but many were skilled craftsmen—a tradition which has been maintained through the years.

THE INDIAN POPULATION

The coming of the Indian to South Africa is closely linked with the development of sugar-cane cultivation in Natal in the first half of the nineteenth century. The Zulu proved unwilling to leave the Reserves to work on the plantations and, in spite of attempts to force him to do so, white planters continued to experience a shortage of labourers. Indentured labour had proved a satisfactory substitute for slavery for sugar-planters in Mauritius and elsewhere, and it was only a matter of time before Natal followed suit.

Negotiations began in 1856 for the importation of Indian coolies but it was not until 1859 that the Indian Government finally agreed to an experimental importation. The Indians were brought to Natal at the expense of the authorities and indentured for three years. Employers paid wages of 10s. a month, plus food and lodging, increasing to 12s. in the third year. They had, in addition, to repay the expenses of transporting the Indians.

The first Indians arrived towards the end of 1860 and by 1865 there were well over 6,000 at work. The indentured Indians were mainly low-caste Hindus, but these were soon augmented by the arrival of wealthier and more cultured traders, largely Moslem. As a group, the Indians were to play a significant role in the economic development of Natal, not only in the sugar industry but in coal-mining, agriculture and trade generally. The importation of indentured workers was stopped in 1911, while Act No. 22 of 1913 (the Immigration Legislation Act) gave the Minister of the Interior wide powers to prohibit the entry into the country of persons deemed undesirable and to restrict their internal movement. As will be seen, the restrictions placed on Indians have widened considerably since that date.

THE PRE-INDUSTRIAL SOCIETY

By 1870, political boundaries were being finally drawn; the Republics of the Transvaal and the Orange Free State were in being, while the Cape was to be granted responsible government under the British Crown in 1872. Natal was moving in the same direction, and was granted the same status in 1893.

In the economic sphere, agriculture was the mainstay of the whole country: in the Cape, wool had superseded wine as the chief export, and in Natal the sugar industry was becoming predominant. The diamond discoveries of 1869 were to have immediate consequences. They came at a time when agriculture was in the throes of a recession and when the Cape stood to lose much as a result of the opening of the Suez Canal. Yet these immediate, windfall advantages were to be far surpassed by the long-term benefits. With the discovery of diamonds came South Africa's first industrial society and, with it, the problem of the industrial colour bar.

The Age of Diamonds

THE BEGINNING OF INDUSTRIALISM

THE DIAMOND DISCOVERIES were to alter the face of South Africa and begin a process of change which would bring within the orbit of world-wide industrial civilization a poor and largely primitive subcontinent. The discovery of diamonds meant, in the long run, that the existing paternal economy would give way to an industrial economy, in which relationships in the labour market would substantially alter. In place of the personal contact which existed between master and servant under the conditions of agriculture, there was to be a more remote and competitive relationship in the new mining and industrial economy. Contact between master and servant was not always to be direct: while the white man remained in the dominant position, his functions were gradually split into those of employer and employee overseer, while the black man's position, as a basic labourer, was one in which contact with the white employer was largely through the white overseer. Yet there was to remain a stubborn refusal to abandon the harsh outmoded attitudes of the past and come to terms with reality. To understand these changes, it is necessary to look at the history of the development of the diamond diggings.

THE IMPACT OF THE DISCOVERIES

The actual story of the discovery of diamonds has been told and retold and has now an almost legendary quality: identification of the first stone, found on the banks of the Orange River, by the trader O'Reilly in 1866; the finding of the 'Star of Africa' in 1867; the opening of the alluvial diggings on the Vaal near Klipdrift and finally the discovery of the dry diggings in Dutoitspan in 1870.

The economic implications of these discoveries were, of course, far-reaching and went beyond the sphere of the labour market. The economy as a whole was given a new lease of life; suddenly there were created new and lucrative outlets for the products of agriculture, while trade generally enjoyed an unprecedented boom. Furthermore, the releasing of new wealth resulted in the speeding up of transport; railway construction was given great stimulus. The splendid isolation which had been enjoyed both by white and non-white was now drawing to an end; they found themselves caught up in the intricate mechanism of a universal industrial society. South Africa, by virtue of her promised mineral resources, could no longer isolate herself. There consequently began a process of townward migration which was to continue until this day and which placed strains on all sectors of the economy, creating problems of adaptability which in turn led to tensions and maladjustments in the urban and rural labour markets. The whole process of change which began in the 1870's led first to the emergence and then, eventually, to the disappearance of the Poor White problem and to the creation of a population of poor blacks who belonged neither wholly to industrial society nor to the changing tribal society of their origins.

MIGRATION TO THE DIAMOND-FIELDS

The newly opened diamond-fields acted as a magnet to fortune-hunters from all over the world, in addition to those local inhabitants, both white and black, who were soon caught up in the diamond fever. The motley collection of would-be diggers who converged on the diamond-fields was made up of men of all nationalities, age, and social class.[1] Some were already well-to-do, seeking to supplement their fortunes, and bringing with them much-needed capital, while there was also a fair quota of disreputable camp-followers. Throughout South Africa people threw up their occupations to go in search of the eternal diamond.[2] Boer farmers forsook their farms and trekked to the diggings, complete with their wives, families, and possessions. Many of these farmers were to constitute the beginning of the large army of impoverished debris-washers whose circumstances were, in some ways, not unlike those of the later Poor Whites. In their simple naïveté and with their lack of

[1] For descriptions of the period see C. A. Payton, *The Diamond Diggings*, 1872; F. Boyle, *To the Cape for Diamonds*, 1873; Dr. J. W. Matthew, *Incwadi Yami—or 20 years personal experience in South Africa*; J. Angove, *In the early days*, 1910.
[2] See 'Among the Diamonds', in *Cape Monthly Magazine* (Feb. 1871, 2nd Series, vol. 2, p. 125).

formal training, not a few fell easy prey to the ruthless society which was to characterize the diamond-fields in the early days. The inability of many of the Boers to cope with the more wily immigrants was to reduce them to poverty and to the role of white overseers of black labour.

While it is possible to explain the attraction of white diggers to the diamond-fields in terms of the eternal lure of wealth, it is not easy to isolate the motives for the immigration of the black diggers; nor is it a simple matter to weigh the importance of any particular motive in point of time. From the moment diamonds were discovered, the scene changed with remarkable rapidity and consequently measurement of any sort is difficult. Unlike the Europeans, few of the primitive Africans had any sense of the exchange market. From early accounts it is quite clear that the greater number who presented themselves at the diggings were primitive in the extreme with few wants in the European sense. Payton gives us an interesting description of the appearance and make-up of the average African digger during the early days on the diggings:

> A Kaffir's notions of dress are primitive in the extreme; his only garment the ancient mutya or loin cloth, with perchance huge plumes of gaudy feathers adorning his woolly head, and a necklace of tiger claws, shells, or beads; knowing probably no language but his own, or at the best but a few words of Boer Dutch. . . .[3]

In spite of their apparent lack of need to satisfy wants in the European sense, Africans soon flocked to the diggings in small bands, sometimes from hundreds of miles away, and often enduring untold privations *en route*. There was certainly, in the early stages at any rate, little need for systematic recruiting of African labour, though during temporary shortages of labour enterprising recruiters would send runners to bring back workers, with results not always satisfactory to the latter.[4] The early mining methods meant that mining was spread out among individual white diggers employing at the most two or

---

[3] C. A. Payton, op. cit., p. 137.

[4] See Report of Native Labour Department, 1876, in Griqualand West *Government Gazette*, No. 51 of 20 Oct. 1877. H. M. Robertson writes: 'contractors also sometimes took advantage of the Natives' simplicity, and defrauded them, or absconded, leaving them stranded and without passes. This led to a certain distrust of recruitment for the diamond fields, which often recoiled upon the innocent.' ('150 years of Economic contact between Black and White', *South African Journal of Economics*, Part 2, vol. 3, no. 1, March 1935, p. 9.)

three Africans, and the wages paid varied at around 10*s*. a week. Some employers provided their African workers with the material necessary for making crude shelters, but as few of the Europeans in any case occupied more than tents, accommodation was not as a rule provided.

While there is no accurate assessment of the numbers employed during the early stages, we can get a useful impression of the labour market from the writings of contemporary authors. For instance, the German, Ernst von Weber, who arrived early on the diggings and wrote one of the best accounts of those days, estimated that during the years 1871-5, there had been an emigration of about '300,000 savages coming particularly from the furthest districts of the north, from the lands of the Matabele and the Zulus, from the lands of the Limpopo and so representing a travel of foot of several months duration'.[5] Based on the assumption that the workers usually stayed three months, during which time they could earn enough money to acquire a musket, his estimate gives an average of about 20,000 working on the fields at any given moment. It is not easy to establish accurate figures of the number of Africans employed, largely on account of high turnover; in a census taken in June 1877 the male adult urban population was given as follows:

	Kimberley	Dutoitspan	Bultfontein	Barkly
Europeans	3,908	461	423	112
Others	5,519	867	1,481	82
Totals:	Europeans: 4,904, Others: 7,949.			

If, however, one allows for the fact that at the time to which the census refers not only were the alluvial fields losing their attraction, but there was also a minor slump taking place, then von Weber's figures are not necessarily exaggerated.

Von Weber was of the decided opinion that the principal motive for black migration to the diggings was to earn the price of a rifle, and the African who 'after three months' work had acquired this longed-for treasure, asked for nothing more from European civilization and headed back by the quickest path to his Native kraal'. The same author estimated that during the four years 1871-5, some 300,000 rifles had been distributed among various tribes 'living north and east of

⁵ Ernst von Weber, *Vier Jahre in Afrika*, 1878, vol. 2, p. 443 et seq.

Griqualand and particularly to the Basutos, Zulus, Batlapins, Mashonas and Matabeles'.[6]

This analysis of motives for early migration to the diggings is borne out by other writers of the time. Boyle, for example, tells us that he had seen a sight

which was calculated to startle one. . . . This was a sale of rifles at the store of Messrs. Reid. Those who bought were Corannas and Kaffirs. The street appeared to be possessed by a Negro army. Round the shop was a crowd of hundreds pressing in. From its open door a stream of armed men struggled out ceaselessly.[7]

J. P. Taylor gives a similar account:

At knock-off time our Kaffirs used to pass down streets of tented shops owned by white traders and presided over by yelling black salesmen, whirling guns above their heads. These they discharged in the air, crying: 'Reka Reka, Mona Mtsheka.' A deafening din. A sight never to be forgotten. The small store-keepers used, in those days, to bring up wagon-loads of antiquated muzzle-loading rifles for sale to the Kaffirs, who frequently were met along the road proceeding to their homes armed to the teeth.[8]

Some enterprising shopkeepers even went so far as to allow Africans to pay by instalments. Angove writes:

When at last he had selected the gun he intended buying, the boy gave the shopkeeper as much money as he could off the price, as earnest-money. The gun was then labelled and put away in a corner of the shop. Each succeeding Saturday afternoon the boy would repair to the shop, and after feasting his eyes on it, the weapon would be replaced. When the time of his departure came from the fields, the Kafir went to get his gun, and after paying the balance of the purchase-price due on it, with much joy claimed it as his very own, as a child would a glittering toy.[9]

This sale of guns was nothing more than the time-honoured lucrative trade in what is today popularly termed 'surplus military equipment'. To read into it any deeper motive is questionable.

On the question of banning the sale of guns, J. B. Currey had the following to say, having calculated that 200,000 guns costing 'at least two million sterling' had been sold to Africans on the diamond-fields.

[6] Ibid., p. 444.
[7] F. Boyle, op. cit., p. 158.
[8] J. P. Taylor, *A Pioneer looks back*, 1939, p. 42.
[9] J. Angove, op. cit., p. 61. See also S. P. Engelbrecht, *President Thomas Francois Burgers*, 1946, Eng. ed., p. 139; F. Boyle, op. cit., p. 159.

Suppose this amount had been carried away in coin by the Natives —a practice which, I may state, is obtaining rapidly amongst them— what then? Would not the Griqualand and other traders have followed them, and supplied them in their own homes with the commodities they wanted, as long as they paid for them in ready money? and such trade conducted in the wilds of the interior where the Native might be tempted to plunder, even if the white man were certain not to defraud, might be more dangerous than legitimate business, under the eye of the policeman, in an English colony.

If the Natives are to be allowed to earn money they must either be allowed to buy guns openly or they will be supplied with them clandestinely, for ready money attracts trade as surely as the pole does the needle. They must be allowed to earn money, for we cannot do without them. Labour must be had, and even the most consistent opponents of the black man have not as yet proposed to substitute for him anything obtainable by importation, from English peasants to Chinese coolies. We have the Native, and we must make the best of him.[10]

Africans coming to the diggings were soon, however, to acquire the urge to satisfy other wants, particularly European-style clothes, which became increasingly a symbol of civilization to them. Least desirable among the range of new wants was the rapid addiction to European liquor and particularly to cheap local brandy popularly called 'Cape smoke'. There were, in addition, signs of the beginning of the spirit of adventure and the idea of a challenge of manhood which were to draw many Africans to the mines and which were to become part of African custom.

THE CHARACTER OF THE EARLY DIGGINGS

Nevertheless, the primitive simplicity of the average African digger, in contrast even to the most backward European, combined with the fact that few remained for long enough to become truly accustomed to their new surroundings, made easy their relegation to the role of hard labourers in the indus-trial sphere. In a sense this was naturally assisted by the fact that, in the early stages, the simple nature of the diggings permitted the labour market to operate along the then familiar lines of the paternal economy. New-comers were soon to take their cue from existing attitudes; it is interesting to find the English journalist Payton reflecting, after a short sojourn, views which were to become familiar in the South African scene.

[10] J. B. Currey in *Journal of the Society of Arts*, vol. 24, 1876, p. 379.

'He [the Kaffir] arrives on the fields as raw material, fit for any amount of hard work, and requiring the treatment of a big child, with no petting or spoiling, but plenty of scolding and occasional castigation if he is disobedient or lazy.'[11]

While, of course, many diggers brought African servants with them to do the hard work, others engaged labourers on the spot. Not all were thus fortunate, however, and many did their own digging. Meanwhile, the intensely competitive nature of the new society, with bankruptcies the rule rather than the exception,[12] hastened the breakdown of mining individualism and rapidly gave rise to two distinct classes of society—those with capital, and who thus had the ability to exploit the need for concentration, and those who relied on the capitalists for a livelihood. There was thus emerging a white industrial worker who was to become the main opponent of the African in the labour market. Unskilled and untutored, the bulk of these whites were to become overseers of black labour, though initially at wage-rates not much higher than those received by the supervised. In a letter of 1 May 1872, von Weber gives us a good idea of the developing pattern:

The white overseer of my claim workers, an Afrikander, i.e. a Dutchman born in Africa, received £5 stg. per month salary, 5% commission on all diamond finds and free lodging, which cost me £5 to £6 stg. per month, as meat was consumed thrice daily and a considerable quantity of sugar, coffee, tea, bread, etc., were also used up. Apart from him I had, from time to time, two or three white workers with a weekly wage of 10 to 15 shillings besides free board, and from 5 to 12 Kaffirs, who originally had a weekly wage of 8 shillings per man as well as board; but as the influx of Kaffirs does not keep pace with the growing demand for labour, and as no Kaffir will stay in service if someone else offers him a shilling a week more, wages rise from month to month. On the whole, the digging of my quarter claim requires for wages and the feeding of my people, for fodder for my mules and for the up-keep of my equipment some £100 per month.[13]

The African did not always enjoy favourable treatment,

[11] C. A. Payton, op. cit., p. 138.
[12] For a discussion of the financial state of the diggings see C. W. de Kiewiet, *Imperial Factor in South Africa*, 1937, p. 49. 'At the close of 1874 the diamond fields were on the verge of collapse . . . it was a population that had to face the difficulties of falling diamond prices, the high cost of living, increased taxation, collapsing and unworkable claims, and the inroads of speculators and the mining companies.'
[13] Von Weber, op. cit., p. 124. See also S. T. van der Horst, *Native Labour in South Africa*, 1942, p. 79.

especially during the rule of the 'Diggers' Committees' prior to the annexation of the territory of Griqualand West to the Crown by Sir Henry Barkly on 27 October 1871, and the liberal official British policies which followed this annexation were not well received by the whites. Theal, the historian, who lived on the fields in 1871, aptly reflects the prevailing white attitudes:

Under the Free State administration the difference between civilised and uncivilised men had been recognised, and the latter were subjected to certain restraints. . . . They were prohibited from roaming about after nine o'clock in the evening, they were not allowed to buy or sell diamonds, they were not permitted to purchase intoxicating liquor without an order in writing from their employers. . . . Now all this was changed. The naked barbarian had exactly the same rights as the most refined European, and had no more restraint upon his actions. He at once yielded to the temptation of strong drink, stole diamonds which he was now able to sell, and created disturbances. . . . He became insolent, worked as much or as little as he chose. . . .[14]

The African began and continued to suffer under distinct disadvantages. It was not only the bewildering pattern of the new society, in which everything, including languages, were new to him, but his background was that of a primitive authoritarian society in which the will of the individual counted for little and in which life mattered even less. The physical hardships endured at the diggings were probably small compared with the privations suffered in getting there, while these probably compared not unfavourably with daily life in the subsistence economy. Angove comments: 'The Kafirs from their homes beyond the Transvaal were often in a most deplorable condition when they reached the Fields, and in many instances they were almost unable to walk, from poverty, their only covering being, perhaps, that of an old sheepskin.'[15] Even if we allow for a tolerance of the physical environment, however, we cannot accept this in itself as accounting for the disparity between white and non-white wages, nor can we hold the influences of supply and demand solely responsible. By 1886, African wages varied between 7s. 6d. to 8s. 6d. with food and 12s. 6d. to 15s. without food, whereas European wages were from £4 to £8 per week.

[14] G. Theal, *History of South Africa since 1795*, vol. 5, 1908, p. 266. For the history of the annexation see de Kiewiet, op. cit., and also E. Walker, *History of South Africa*, 1st ed., 1928, p. 345 et seq.
[15] J. Angove, op. cit., p. 69.

Overseers received £4 to £5 and mechanics £6 to £8.[16] Probably of far greater importance is the fact that the Europeans enjoyed initial advantages while their relative stability gave them greater opportunities for organization. Thus when the need for reducing costs arose it became usual to think in terms of African labour—a feature which was to characterize the early history of gold-mining. The development of these patterns was to accompany the reorganization of the diamond-mining industry into larger units.

THE IMPACT OF AMALGAMATION UPON THE LABOUR MARKET

There were two important factors which militated in favour of the merging of individual mines—the need for more scientific mining methods requiring concentration of capital and the need for closer control of diamond output. At the early alluvial diggings, the sifting of sand from the diamonds was relatively uncomplicated compared with the problems which were to arise in extracting diamonds from the deep-set blue ground of the New Rush.

During the early years, the practice was for diggers to pay the owner of the land a small diggers' 'right fee'. This practice was continued after the purchase of the various diamond-bearing farms by land companies; the fee was then about 10s. for each claim, which invariably measured about 30 feet square. The size of the claims and the fact that few, if any, of the diggers ever held more than one claim, meant that the diggings were soon turned into a 'jumble of holes, pits, and burrows'.[17] The control of the position was handled democratically through elected 'Diggers' Committees' and transgressors were expelled from the diggings. The same procedure was applied to general 'law breakers' (see 'Rules of the Diamond Diggers Mutual Protection Association, 1870', in the Diamond Commission Report of 1882). There were in any case limits placed on the number of claims which could be held by any individual: initially the limit was two, but Ordinance 10 of 1874 (clause 18) allowed the holding of up to ten claims by persons, firms or *joint stock companies*. The complete abolition of restrictions was effected by Ordinance 12 of 26 November 1876.

[16] S. T. van der Horst, op. cit., p. 81.
[17] Gardner Williams, *The Diamond Mines of South Africa*, 1902, p. 196.

2

At the Colesberg Koppie (Kimberley Mine) an attempt was made to introduce some control of the diggings by preserving roadways in order to ensure access to all parts of the surface of the mine. Gardner Williams gives a good description of the results:

A great many more claims had been granted to license-holders before the survey, for there had been no accurate measurement of the kopje, and there was a consequent overlapping and conflict of locations and spreading of claims beyond the limits of the diamond-bearing ground. In the settlement of contests the claims were split up by concessions, bargains, and sales, until there were not less than 1,600 separate holdings of claims and fractional parts running as small as 1/16, or about 7 square yards. A lucky claim-holder would sell off parts of his claim or the whole at high prices; for bidders were ready to pay large premiums beyond the license fee of 10*s*. exacted from every working owner, whether his claim was full size or a paring. The competition for a share in the riches of the ground was only less keen at De Beers, and there was a like subdivision of claims there, and not infrequently at Dutoitspan and Bultfontein.[18]

It became increasingly clear as diggers dug deeper into the ground that the simple unscientific methods they were using would not enable them to continue mining to any great depth. The very nature of the ground, with its comparatively loose soil, meant that there was the constant risk that the roadways, which were repeatedly being narrowed, would crumble and collapse into the claims below. Few had the financial resources to acquire the equipment and 'know-how' necessary for authentic mining operations.

These difficulties meant that many diggers began to lose heart and either sold their claims at low prices or left them altogether. It was then that small companies, aided by Ordinance 12 of 1876 which abolished restrictions on claim-holdings, began to acquire blocks of claims and thus set the scene for the reduction of the number of individual claims to a group of several mining companies.

By 1880 the number of claims in the Kimberley Mine had been reduced to 398¾, Old De Beers 609, Dutoitspan 1,453, and Bultfontein 1,003.[19] The process was hastened by the fact that overproduction and indiscriminate illicit diamond buying

[18] Ibid., p. 197.
[19] Report of Sub-Committee relative to the commercial aspect of the Diamond Mining Industry (Cape Diamond Mining Company, 1882).

was causing the market for diamonds to fall. The first true mining companies appeared in the latter part of 1879 and the early part of 1880, while the final elimination of the individual digger was assured by the slump of the middle 80's. In the *Economist* of 10 March 1888, it was noted that

1883-4 was a period of limited production and falling prices with intense competition between producing companies, especially in the Kimberley Mine. The effect was that Kimberley Central Company which had been making large profits 1880-3 (dividends rose from 10% to 30%) paid nothing 1884-5 and only 5% at the close of 1886. De Beers had not done well earlier but kept up its dividend through the depression—average of $8\frac{1}{2}$% 1884. Most of the other companies earned nothing and some practically suspended operations.

In contrast to those fortunate diggers who were able to sell their claims for a fair price to the syndicates, there were many less fortunate who were ruined by the caving-in of the roadways into their diggings. Few of them could afford the loss of time and considerable outlay required to clear the rubble and make their claims workable again.

The gradual consolidation of the claims meant that the age of the individual digger with his two or three African assistants disappeared, and more and more white diggers either left the diggings completely, perhaps to try their luck in the Transvaal goldfields, or became employees of the syndicates, who alone had the resources needed for advanced mining.

To be a miner in the early days did not require any unduly exacting qualifications—even as late as 1880, good character was the main criterion—but with the development of more scientific methods of mining and particularly with the opening of underground workings in 1885, it became increasingly necessary to import professional miners and other skilled men. There was thus introduced in the labour market a new element which, through scarcity value, was to play an important part in enlarging the disparity between white and non-white wage-levels. The fact that from the earliest beginnings these skilled miners, who came mostly from England (and particularly from Cornwall), were white, meant that it was not difficult to continue the old divisions on colour grounds, and as the chief threat of competition, and consequently of the elimination of scarcity value followed by wage-reductions, came from the non-white element, it was natural that the vested white group would tend to resist black encroachments at all cost. In essence, therefore, everything was in favour of keeping the non-white 'out' by adopting a rigid 'closed shop' principle based upon colour. Not that there was any need to resort to concrete measures during the years before 1900 because of the disadvantages under which the non-whites suffered.

The fact that the mining companies were prepared to accept these divisions cannot be explained satisfactorily in terms of economic advantage alone, but rather on the ground that (as was to be the case throughout the later history of mining) they had little or no choice because of the collective strength of the white miners. The non-whites from the very beginning lacked all the effective weapons of collective bargaining; made up of men from a wide variety of tribes, often acutely antagonistic towards each other, they lacked a sense of unity, while their constant turnover meant a lack of continuity. But perhaps most important of all was their complete lack of education and training, which inevitably meant an absence of effective leadership. These factors, combined with existing customary prejudices—which found expression in the attitude of regarding all non-whites as largely uncivilized and uncivilizable—and the original manner of mining in the diamond areas, meant that it was convenient for the newly formed syndicates to adopt *in toto* the framework of the labour market as it existed.

By the time the final amalgamation took place, with the formation of the De Beers Consolidated Mines, Limited,[20] in March 1888, the labour market was beginning to take on permanent features of rigid division, and the illicit diamond buying question and the growing army of debris-washers were to assist in the evolution of these rigidities.

The pattern which was to emerge was that of the Europeans showing every sign of preparedness to use their collective strength to ensure their exclusive supremacy in the labour market. Gradually the concept of trade unionism, and, for that

[20] For an account of the negotiations which preceded the amalgamation see Annual Reports of De Beers Diamond Mining Company and De Beers Consolidated Mines, Limited, and also Sir Lewis Michell, *The Life of the Rt. Hon. Cecil John Rhodes*, 1910, 2 vols. After the formation of De Beers Consolidated, there remained a number of independent companies, but the diamond-mining industry now centred on the activities of De Beers.

matter, of socialism, became accepted in the minds of European artisans as the means of maintaining their own position against non-white inroads.

The idea of the labour market being split into two sections might in theory present employers with a situation in which, in the course of negotiations with employees, they could, advantageously, play one section off against the other. In practice, however, it did not always work out as simply or conveniently as this; the rigidity of the labour market, in fact, created a variety of complications which were to be far from satisfactory to the average industrial or mining employer.

The exclusive attitude on the part of white labour, which had its basis in the paternal economy, its origin in the diamond-mining industry and its development in the gold-mining economy was to become an important factor in the political and economic life of the country. What began in industry as essentially a move by skilled trade unionists to protect themselves from being ousted by less skilled workers, gradually spread to all occupational planes; whereas race was initially coincidental, with the non-white not being regarded as worth consideration, the advance of industrialism and non-white emergence made the purely 'colour' factor of far greater importance in determining rigidity in the labour market.

ILLICIT DIAMOND BUYING

From the earliest times, the problem of diamond stealing occupied the attention of diamond diggers, initially at the alluvial diggings and later at the dry diggings. Hans Sauer, brother of J. W. Sauer, the liberal Cape politician, writes of the fields in 1883:

Adventurers of the worst types of all races abounded, having come to the fields for the express purpose of taking a hand in the illicit diamond buying business, a remunerative calling which was then rampant. It was estimated by the diamond mining companies that at least three million pounds' worth of diamonds were stolen every year by their employees and sold by them to the illicit diamond buyers.[21]

At first the main consequence of stealing was the hardship it caused those diggers who were robbed of their diamonds, but,

[21] Hans Sauer, *Ex Africa*, 1937, p. 43.

as the industry grew, the implications became of far wider importance, and it became particularly imperative to prevent stealing when the need arose for a greater control of diamond production in order to stabilize the market. To achieve this it was essential to devise ways and means for the effective control of the flow of diamonds, thus ensuring that the diamond market was not deflated by an excessive supply of under-market-price illicit diamonds.

Illicit diamond buying indirectly played a major role in the moulding of the labour market, and was partly responsible for the creation of the closed compound system, which was to become a permanent feature in the lives of African mine-workers. It also afforded the first opportunity for showing how much more effectively white miners were able to organize themselves in resistance to the policies of the mining companies; the African being forced to accept whatever arrangements were designed for him.

The tendency to think of every African as a potential I.D.B. agent only helped to harden white prejudice towards non-whites, exacerbated the existing colour consciousness and prepared the way for a firm acceptance of the need for permanent barriers between the races. While there was undoubtedly some cause for resentment there was also a failure to face the facts. The primitive African knew little of the moral codes of the new society and was thus an easy dupe to the wiles of dishonest whites.

From the outset, unscrupulous persons used a variety of ways to corrupt Africans by persuading them to steal diamonds from their employers. Angove vividly describes the activities of some less reputable 'Kafir eating house' proprietors, who provided free meals on the understanding that those enjoying such hospitality would leave as often as possible 'a diamond or diamonds in the pannikin in which the soup was served'. Workers were thus tempted to spend their time on their master's claims constantly on the look-out for 'soup' diamonds.[22] The new-comers to the fields usually arrived in a half-starved condition and thus fell an easy prey to these wily approaches. Furthermore, they soon succumbed to the temptations of liquor and would go to great lengths to steal diamonds in order to

[22] J. Angove, op. cit., p. 67.

obtain a supply of alcoholic beverage. In the early days, and in the absence of proper authority, the diggers often resorted to the lynch law to deal with suspected diamond thieves.

Diamond stealing was given a boost by the system known as 'kopje-walloping' by which some diggers, instead of having fixed offices, wandered around the diggings buying from all and sundry and not always from the legitimate diggers. Angove writes:

In the early Seventies there was a class of diamond buyers known as 'Kopje-wallopers'—that is to say, having taken out a licence for the purpose, they were allowed to go where they pleased and buy diamonds whenever opportunity offered, and no one could prevent them doing so, as they had complied with the law, and were protected by their licences. It may be easily understood that a law which enabled individuals to do business in that manner was like placing a premium on I.D.B. The Kopje-walloper bought diamonds from those who had any and cared to sell to him, and he was not concerned whether he bought from either black or white, or whether the diamonds had been stolen or come by in an honest manner; his business was to buy. It was not unusual to see that class of diamond-buyer bargaining for diamonds in all sorts of out-of-the-way places, or standing on the margin of the mine, where he accosted everyone coming from or going to the claim.[23]

The system of kopje-walloping was discontinued in 1876, as a result of a government proclamation disallowing the 'purchase of diamonds in places other than the offices of licensed bankers or diamond dealers', while Act No. 48 of 1882, known as the Diamond Trade Act, attempted to regulate the trade more rigidly in Griqualand West. Severe penalties were introduced for illicit diamond buying, and the police were given wide powers of arrest, while searching of mine employees was permitted. The problem was, however, that while the trade was thus regulated in Griqualand West, illicit buyers were free to move about in other parts of the country without fear of hindrance or arrest. The *Economist*, for example, wrote on 18 October 1884, commenting on the Act, that

the illicit traffic has not been suppressed, it has simply been transferred to other districts, which do not come under the Act. Thus, for instance, at a recent meeting of the Cape Town Chamber of Commerce, it was stated that there were about 20 runners who habitually travelled between that town and Kimberley, bringing back with

[23] Ibid., p. 64.

them stolen diamonds obtained from people working in the mines, and it is roughly estimated that the value of diamonds stolen and disposed of in this way amounts to about a million sterling a year.

In order to close this gap, the Act was eventually, in 1885, extended to embrace the entire Cape Colony.

The problem remained, however, of the ease with which diamond stealers could transfer their diamonds across the borders of the Boer republics, which did not look upon diamond stealing and smuggling with the same disfavour as the other territories. It was clear that some other more effective means of control would have to be devised if illicit diamonds were not to continue as a major factor in upsetting the stability of the already precarious diamond market, and it was decided that the best possible way of reducing diamond thefts would be to concentrate control on the sources rather than on the main disposal points farther away from the mines.

During the early stages at the diggings, in an attempt to control stealing, the Diamond Diggers' Committee had restricted the holding of claims to Europeans, but this restriction was removed after the annexation of the territory in 1871. After the removal of restrictions on Africans holding claims, feelings among the white diggers ran high, and lawlessness broke out, with the diggers demanding a return to the old state of affairs; soon near anarchy reigned—with arson and acts of violence becoming prevalent. Finally, following a round table conference in July 1872, the authorities agreed to the white diggers' demands 'that no Kaffir or other coloured person be entitled to hold a licence to search for diamonds' and 'that no Kaffir or other coloured person shall be entitled to hold a licence to buy, sell or otherwise deal in diamonds'. In an effort, however, to meet some of the further complaints of white diggers, a proclamation was issued which principally regulated relations between employer and employee, but, incidentally, placed some control over diamond stealing; among other things, it permitted the searching of servants without warrant; any diamonds found in their possession were assumed to belong to the employer.

Searching in earnest did not, however, commence until 1883. All employees, both white and black, leaving the mines or their floors were subjected to a search to uncover any secreted diamonds, and they were also required to wear special clothes while on the job. The mine area itself was carefully fenced and the only exit was via a search-house.

The original Ordinance permitting searching had been passed in 1880,[24] amid opposition from Europeans, but was left in abeyance until 1883, when J. X. Merriman, who at that time held office in the Cape Government, visited the fields. He expressed himself in favour of searching, in spite of the indications of white opposition, suggesting that 'they [the Europeans] will soon see the reasonableness of the searching law and the protection which it will afford to the honest men against any who may be dishonest'.[25]

As a result, searching began at all the mines in March 1883; at the Dutoitspan and Bultfontein Mines arrangements for carrying out this system rested with small committees; in each case an inspector and registrar of the mines, and a claim-holder selected by the government.

The enforcement of searching was, however, strongly resented by the Europeans, and finally, in October, the overseers and mechanics who had by this time formed themselves into associations, went on strike, on the ground that the 'stripping' called for was 'offensive and unnecessary'. After a three-day stoppage of work, some agreement was reached to the effect that there would be no enforcement of the system of a change of clothes in searching houses, on entering or leaving the floors of the mines. While this agitation was going on, there appears to be little doubt that the searching system was having some effect, especially among the African workers. In a letter in the *Daily Independent*, dated 10 July 1883, a correspondent wrote that he had been told by a storekeeper that Kaffir workers were avoiding the mines owing to 'the searching system being carried out too strictly there and that they [the Africans] could make nothing but their net pay'. The agreement to refrain from compelling Europeans to remove their clothes brought about a period of relative quiet, until, however, the responsibility of guarding the mines was taken over by the Detective Department in January 1884.[26]

[24] Ordinance No. 11, 1880.
[25] Leading article in *The Diamond Fields Advertiser*, 12 April 1884.
[26] See the Reports of the Inspectors of Diamond Mines in the late Province of Griqualand West, 1883. (G. 30/84.)

A storm blew up shortly afterwards over an instruction by the chief of the Detective Department that men had to remove their boots and open their mouths as part of the searching system. This was regarded as the 'thin end of the wedge' and a mass meeting of employees was immediately called by the Mechanics and Artisans Protection Association to consider the matter. It is of particular interest to note that the chairman described the move as 'calculated in my opinion, to bring us one step further down to the degradation to which only Kaffirs will submit and which only a man with no self-respect would do'. The meeting itself was interesting in that it clearly revealed the evolution of an attitude now familiar in the labour market. The white employees, while regarding themselves as working men at variance with their employers, considered themselves to be of a distinctly higher class than the black workers. One speaker, for example, stressed that he cared little how severe the law against diamond stealing was so long as there was no stripping of *white men*. There was also the constant warning that they (the white men) would use the franchise to achieve their aims. One speaker stated that 'a working man would not be intimidated, as he feared some had been in the last election'. The fact that Europeans were able to use the ballot box as a coercive weapon placed them in a much more effective position than the African. This was to become of increasing importance in determining the position of white and non-white in the labour market.[27]

An almost prophetic warning was voiced by Mr. Schreiner, elder brother of the Cape politician, W. P. Schreiner, when, although deprecating the searching system being applied to white men, he warned against thinking in terms of colour, rather than in terms of class. In fact, he suggested that, on the diamond-mines, there were two classes—one which could be trusted and the other which apparently could not. He felt that it would be wrong to think solely in terms of the upper class consisting of white men only, as many of this trustworthy class were men 'with colour in them'. He felt that the searching of Africans could be pursued because they did not feel the humiliation of the whites; while, furthermore, they had, in any case, apparently submitted to the searching from the very earliest beginnings.[28]

[27] Report in *The Diamond Fields Advertiser*, 12 April 1884.
[28] Ibid.

Here, perhaps, Mr Schreiner had correctly analysed the situation, in which, somehow, colour had become mixed up in the hurly-burly of collective bargaining. The danger arises in thinking that, in fact, it was colour which lent strength to the dominant class—in this case the trustworthy class—rather than the reverse case, of the dominant class lending strength to the colour superiority concept.

The fact that the dominant stratum in our society is white can lead, by way of bad logic, to the acceptance of the belief that this dominance stems necessarily and wholly from white superiority. This may have been, and probably was, largely the case at the time under discussion, but with the passing of years there arose the danger of accepting a colour basis rather than a class basis for society.[29] Within any class structure, for society to survive, and for the dominant section to remain virile and responsible, there must be some degree of fluidity through the infusion of new blood. Some must rise while others fall. This is as true of the labour market as of society as a whole. In fact, in a predominantly wealth-conscious society, in which display is the foremost arbiter of position, the level one occupies within the economy becomes all-important. Clearly within the labour market itself, the prerequisites of success are basically aptitude, opportunity, and training, and given a free market the individual will find his own position in accordance with these prerequisites. Immediately some external factor is introduced, the natural pattern of the market is upset; this factor may take the forms of family connexions and nepotism, wealth, or influence, to mention only a few of those most commonly encountered. But while such factors may upset the smooth working of the economy, they do not necessarily totally prevent fluidity nor are they always wholly harmful in effect. The introduction of colour as the external factor can, however, lead to far greater stagnation, in that it immediately introduces rigidities which may be impossible to overcome, and may, in fact, eventually bring about a weakening of the dominant class through its very inelasticity. While leadership rested with the whites through their advantage of education and training and as providers of

[29] See I. D. MacCrone, *Race Attitudes in South Africa*, 1937, for an examination of the underlying causes of race prejudices, and R. F. Hoernlé, *South African Native Policy and the Liberal Spirit*, 1945, for a stimulating discussion of the nature of South African society.

capital, this should not have been sufficient justification for excluding worthy non-whites from fulfilling their aspirations, from playing a role in the economy compatible with their abilities, and from being rewarded accordingly.

The class-conscious approach of Kimberley miners is perhaps best illustrated by the remark of the chairman of a meeting of overseers, which followed shortly after the artisans' meeting described above. Referring to the question of stripping, and to the allegation that workers in other countries were subjected to a similar proceeding, he said:

We know very well that some of the dockyard labourers in England have to be stripped, and I will tell you how. These labourers are collected from the scum of the town and only work at the docks when they can get nothing else to do. Now, those men who are searched in England are a low class, but I maintain that we are not a low class here (applause). There is not a respectable man who would work at these dockyards, if he could get anything else to do. But are we to be classed with such men? I say, NO![30]

It is clear, therefore, that from the outset, skilled workers were considering themselves as being of a superior class in society, and so entitled to privileges denied to those whom they regarded as being inferior. The fact which is borne out by the statement quoted above, that the bulk of the workers in the lower strata were non-white, is purely coincidental, but nevertheless that they were black only tended to strengthen the acceptance of ideas of non-white inferiority. Therefore, what originated largely from class-conscious superiorities was soon, with the assistance of traditional local prejudice, to harden into colour-conscious superiority.

At this meeting of overseers, it was decided that they would take strike action if the mines persisted with the requirement that workers strip, remove their shoes and open their mouths for inspection. In fact, on 24 April 1884, the European employees of four mines struck work. The strike went off peacefully, but on the 29th 'a body of some 300 strikers, with a crowd of Cape Boys and Kaffirs numbering 1,000 to 1,500' converged upon the Victoria Diamond Mining Company, threatening to destroy its property.

A clash with the police ensued, which resulted in the loss of

[30] Report in *The Diamond Fields Advertiser*, 25 April 1884.

about six lives.[31] The fact that the rioters called upon Africans
for backing in what was purely a European quarrel, and that
the Africans joined in, is an interesting phenomenon, which
was not to be unique in the history of South African labour
relations. Commenting on this, the *Port Elizabeth Telegraph*
wrote:

> It is difficult to see what possible interest the Black man can
> have in thus assisting to promote disorder. The White employees,
> with whom they are associating in disorder, have never, in any way,
> helped them (i.e. the Africans) to assert their rights in the matter
> of searching.[32]

After the strike incident, the stripping of Europeans was
gradually discontinued.

THE COMPOUND SYSTEM

Almost contemporaneously with the searching experiment,
the idea was spreading of housing workers on mine property;
by reducing their contact with the outside world as far as
possible, it was also hoped to minimize the traffic in illegal
diamonds. This approach to the housing of mine-workers was
to lead to the 'compound system' for African labour, which in
turn was to have an important impact upon the organization of
the labour market and economic life in general in South Africa.
It set the pattern for the gold-mining industry, being inseparable
from the use of migratory labour. From the earliest beginnings
in Kimberley and elsewhere on the diamond-fields, the problem
of housing was acute, both for Europeans and non-Europeans.
As the vast majority of Africans arrived at the fields without
their families, and as few, in any case, showed any desire to
settle permanently, the easy solution to the housing problem
was to provide barrack-room type accommodation, under
conditions similar to that provided for the armed forces. The
illicit diamond buying question encouraged the policy of
housing workers in barracks, although it was not the original
nor the only factor working to this end.

Compounds for African workers existed almost as early as
the formation of the mining companies, in place of individual
diggers, and the idea of using them in order to reduce diamond

[31] Reports of the Inspectors of Diamond Mines, etc., 1884. (G. 28/85.)
[32] Quoted in *The Diamond Fields Advertiser*, 10 May 1884.

stealing was conceived in the early 1880's. The Inspector of Mines, in his report of 1882, went into some detail recommending the setting up of accommodation for all employees, separate from the town and provided by the mines. It is interesting to note that his recommendations for separate housing embraced all races, and were not exclusive to Africans. In fact, in later reports, we read of his recommending the building of special cantonments for European overseers. While the system was not carried out to the letter, it is clear that by 1883 African workers were being housed in some form of partially closed compound; being allowed out either once a week, on Sundays, or, in exceptional circumstances, during the week. Although the reduced movement had some effect in countering the traffic in stolen diamonds, it was not an unqualified success, as obviously any dishonest worker could still find ways and means of conveying the stolen diamonds to the outside world. Furthermore, the partially closed compound system entailed employing a large body of overseers, searchers, and guards.

It was not until 1885 that the diamond-mining industry turned to the now familiar system of the closed compound, but by the end of the 80's all the mining companies had adopted the practice. Under this system, workers were not permitted to leave the confines of the mining-area throughout the period of their contract—being taken from their compounds to the mining-areas by way of tunnels or closed pathways. All purchases had to be made within the mine compound. The *Daily Independent* of 28 April 1885 made the following comments:

To the Central Company belongs the honour of leading the van and adopting a scheme which, if thoroughly carried out, cannot fail to effect a momentous change for the better in our social conditions in many ways. Its object is to cut off all means of communication with the outside world, which has hitherto afforded the stable mining labourer so many facilities for disposing of his employer's property. He will henceforth never be outside the pale of his employer's authority. He will sleep and feed in the new and comfortable quarters provided for him and his fellows: he will march to his daily work in the mine and return in the evening to the place from whence he came; all his wants will be attended to by his employer; he will be able (still in the seclusion of his compound) to purchase the gaudy Manchester and Brummagen goods in which the Kaffir soul delighteth: his pap will be provided for him out of the weekly wage or he will have the option of purchasing it himself; but in any case, it will have to be cooked and eaten in the enclosure north of the North Circular Road, which might aptly be termed 'The Central Hotel'. A medical attendant and a dispensary are among the luxuries for which he has now to thank his employers, together with other means for leading a cleanly and wholesome life to which he has all along been a stranger.

While, of course, the closed-compound system, which cut workers off from any contact with the outside world during their period of employment, was evolved to meet the specific need of reducing diamond stealing, it had other indirect results, notably in combating the growth of alcoholic addiction among the workers. This had been a major problem in the area and existed even after the prohibition of the sale of liquor to Africans. During the initial stages of the partially closed compound system, the workers could still obtain supplies of liquor during those periods in which they were allowed out, but after the closing of the compounds the supply of liquor, other than African beers, was totally prohibited.

Commenting on the compound system, the Inspector of Mines made the following references to drunkenness:

One material and important result of the compound system is that on Mondays the muster-roll of capable Kaffirs is nearly, if not quite, complete, whereas previously a company could not reckon on more than one-half or one-third of their Kaffirs turning up every Monday morning in a sufficiently sober state to work. In fact, Mondays and part of Tuesdays were before usually considered as lost and partly lost days, owing to the consistently inebriated condition of the Kaffir servants on those days.[33]

One of the strange phenomena of the diamond-fields has been that, in spite of the closed compound and the rigorous methods which were used to determine at the end of contracts whether workers had swallowed diamonds, the De Beers Consolidated Company has hardly ever had to recruit labour. It has always enjoyed a fairly stable labour force; the majority of employees regularly return to the Company after periods of leave. One of the determining factors has certainly been the high standard of accommodation and amenities which were provided, even at a time when general standards of African urban housing were extremely poor. Various other explanations have been

[33] Reports of the Inspectors of Diamond Mines, etc., 1885. (G. 40/86).

advanced, though in the absence of detailed scientific study their validity must be considered cautiously, and no claim of absolute reliability can be put forward in their favour.

In the first place, the system of paying bonuses, sometimes substantial in amount, to discoverers of diamonds would appeal to the gambling instinct and must have proved a major attraction. Secondly, the fact that the general wage-level on the diamond-mines has always been higher than elsewhere must have exercised some draw. In the third place, the very nature of the closed compound has not proved entirely unattractive. It has been suggested that some of the younger workers, particularly, felt more secure by being secluded from temptation and thus being able to save more money, for they were removed from the corrupting influences of cheap liquor and prostitutes. Finally, the diamond-mines have always paid their workers an all-inclusive money wage. This form of payment usually proves more attractive to Africans than a wage which includes the provision of some amenity or service, such as free accommodation, meals, etc., for they can then prepare their meals as they wish and spend or save their wages as they choose.

In some ways the ideal type of labour under the prevailing circumstances was convict labour. Convicts in the Kimberley area had, in the past, been used for brickmaking, and as early as 1883 attempts were made to utilize African convicts in some of the diamond-mines. By 1885, the Inspector of Mines was able to report that the experiment had turned out successfully. He pointed out that some 200 prisoners were being regularly employed by one diamond-mine.[34]

The use of these prisoners had the result of ensuring a regular supply of labour, facilitated the searching system and enabled the companies to enforce a closed compound system. The use of indentured labour on the mines continued until March 1932, and, as will be seen, the South African Labour Party actually put forward a concrete proposal to the State Mining Commission considering the nationalization of mines in 1917 which recommended the use of convict labour by the State both on surface and underground work. Evidence showed that this form of labour was both cheaper and more hard-

[34] Reports of the Inspectors of Diamond Mines, etc., 1884 and 1885. (G. 28/85 and G. 40/86.)

working. There may have been some foundation for this assertion, for in the Second Annual Report for the year 1890, the General Manager of De Beers commented that the average cost of convicts was about £28 a year, and that this was small when one considered that a long-term convict was accustomed to hard work and could do 'double the amount of work that an ordinary free boy will do who receives 18s. to 20s. per week'.

THE RESULTING PATTERN

While Kimberley saw the emergence of the white mining artisan class, there were also signs of the beginnings of the industrial Poor White problem: that is to say, the existence of persons of European descent who were urbanized, but ill-equipped to play a useful and satisfactory role in the labour market without falling to a level on a par with black labourers. In a sense, poverty and unemployment among the whites arose from the amalgamation of the mining companies in 1888. One of the underlying reasons for amalgamation had of course been the need to control the diamond market and reduce output in order to maintain prices at a satisfactorily profitable level. This meant that some of the fields had to be closed down and, as a result, the miners and diggers were put out of work. The impact of the reduction of mining operations would not have been as great initially if it had not been for the large influx of would-be fortune-hunters, who came to Kimberley with the express purpose of finding diamonds, which had been missed by the earlier diggers.

Debris washing had, by the end of the 70's and early 80's, become a major and, in some cases, an exceedingly lucrative business. The debris heaps which had been piled up around the mines by the early diggers, in their haste to find diamonds, contained a great deal of yellow ground, which often secreted diamonds. With the advent of ripple washing-machines, it was possible to free the diamonds from their casings of yellow ground, especially as this ground had become softened as a result of long exposure to atmospheric conditions. Angove writes:

It was at the end of 1874 that debris-washing began. The idea caught on rapidly; there was a great demand for the ripple washing-machines. Carpenters, in consequence, began lucrative and thriving

3

businesses in making them, and had as many orders for machines as they could execute at seven pounds ten each. An industrious man could make and deliver two or three machines a day.[35]

The work was undertaken by both men and women and attracted a fair number of new 'diggers' to the fields.

Once the amalgamations were complete and the mines were able to deal more realistically with the problem of illicit diamond buying, the question of allowing the debris-washers free access to mine property, in order to raid the discarded heaps, became closely linked with the problem of security, and it became almost imperative for mining companies to restrict access to the diggings. This restriction initially took the form of complete prohibition of debris-washing, which led to a prolonged struggle between the debris-washers and the mining companies. The question was thrashed out in a series of court cases which concerned the right of the companies arbitrarily and unilaterally to close the diggings to the debris-washers. The main contention of the latter was that the prohibition of debris-washing had resulted in widespread unemployment among the people of Kimberley. There is ample evidence to show that this was, to a large extent, true, though it must be borne in mind that there would have undoubtedly been far greater unemployment had amalgamation not taken place, and had the diamond market been allowed to collapse as a result of unrestricted supply.

The companies later agreed to allow a certain number of deserving inhabitants the right to wash debris, and this in itself gave rise to interesting developments for it was soon alleged, and perhaps not without some justification, that the debris-washing right had been allocated to persons who were often not in any way distressed. The practice was for such moneyed persons to employ assistants, both black and white, to do the actual washing. In some cases, the more generous among them allowed the washers employed on their claims a fairly substantial percentage of the value of the diamonds found. In the majority of cases, however, such generosity was not encountered; it became customary to pay the washers a fixed wage, often not much above that paid to Africans, and, in time, a significant number of the local white inhabitants were dependent upon

[35] J. Angove, op. cit., p. 103 et seq. See also M.F., *Life on the Diamond Fields* (circulated privately), and Morton, *South African Diamond Fields and the Journey to the Mines*, 1875, 1877.

this form of employment for their livelihood. The fact that many of these people were totally untutored for any work which required even a modicum of training foreshadowed the Poor White problem which was to grow in importance and dominated the whole labour market until the late 1930's. Accompanying this was the development of the idea, as yet in its infancy, that white people could not be permitted to fall to the level of the African or undertake 'Kaffir-work'.

The early diamond days also laid the foundations of a wage-structure in South Africa, which was to become a permanent feature of the economy. It is patently clear that there existed in Kimberley by the end of the nineteenth century a tremendous disparity between the lowest European artisan wage and the highest African labouring wage, but the existence of this very inequality has often led people to fail to realize and appreciate that the labouring wages paid in South Africa were in fact higher than those paid to contemporary counterparts in western Europe. The abnormality existed, therefore, not in regard to labourers' wages, but as far as the artisan wage-scales were concerned. The reasons for the establishment of this abnormality, as already shown earlier in this chapter, lay in the questions of supply and demand, coupled with organizational powers and occupational stability.

In the course of time, however, whereas the lower, though not abnormally low, labouring African wage-rate was to remain fairly static, the high European rate was to become very much higher, and gradually the situation arose where Europeans were able to enjoy a standard of living equivalent to that of their counterparts in North America, while the non-European labouring classes were to remain at a standard comparable to that obtaining in much of eastern and south-western Europe. The fact of the matter was, of course, that as the South African economy was, and to a great extent still is, relatively poor and, taken as a whole, more comparable with the latter-mentioned countries than with North America, the establishment and maintenance of one section of the working population at an unduly high level of remuneration could only be achieved by a system which kept particularly low the monetary rewards paid to the other, and larger, section.

The Impact
of Gold

DISCOVERIES

THE BELIEF BASED BOTH ON FACT and fable that there was gold to be found somewhere in the African interior led to expeditions being organized for its discovery from almost the moment that the first white men set foot on southern African soil. Initial failure did not deter men from believing in eventual success; in the minds of all explorers of the unknown interior there usually lurked a faint hope of discovering the hidden treasures of Monomotapa.[1]

In spite of these seemingly fanciful hopes, men little knew that hidden in the barren area now called the Witwatersrand there were, in fact, rich gold ores which, when discovered, would transform the face of the southern continent and rudely disturb the quiet, almost lazy, tempo of the lives of the settled Voortrekkers, bringing them once again in conflict with the Imperial Factor from which they had sought so hard to free themselves.

The old workings of Mashonaland had been rediscovered by the travellers Hartley, Mauch, and Baines, but in spite of the attractive accounts which they had given of their discoveries, little real interest was shown in them.[2] Perhaps the main cause was the superior attraction of the diamond-fields. Theal writes of Tati in 1868:

At this time more than a hundred European diggers were at work, and two or three times that number of blacks were employed by them. Gold was obtained, and some specimens of quartz reef were

[1] As early as 1660, van Riebeeck sent out a fruitless expedition of thirteen members, under the leadership of Jan Danckeit, to search for the legendary state of Monomotapa: See G. Theal, *History of South Africa under the administration of the Dutch East India Company, 1652/1795*, 1897, vol. 1, p. 109. Theal writes that in 1791 'It was currently reported and believed that the English traveller Paterson had discovered rich (gold) ore' in the 'desert region north of the Orange River', op. cit., vol. 2, p. 233.

[2] See Thomas Baines, *The Goldfields of South-Eastern Africa*, 1877; 'From the Tati to Natal'. 'At the Tati Goldfields' in the *Cape Monthly Magazine*, vol. IV, 1872; Carl Mauch, *To Ophir direct or the South African Goldfields*, 1868. Mauch reported having found gold at Tati in December 1867, which caused some influx of gold-seekers.

found to be very rich; but on the whole, experience proved that mining there would not pay, and after a short time most of the diggers dispersed.[3]

Furthermore, the journey into the interior was fraught with considerable difficulties and hardly worth the trouble at a time when Kimberley offered such promising prospects. For example, the journey from Pietermaritzburg to Tati, some 829 miles, took three months by ox-wagon. Added to which, the Transvaal authorities, ever sensitive to the dangers of British intervention, were in no mood to encourage an influx of foreigners, which was certain to follow any large-scale mining. Dr. S. P. Engelbrecht comments on President Burgers's mixed feelings on the Lydenburg discoveries as follows:

Then for a while it looked as if the Lydenburg Gold Fields would be a disappointment. Burgers was certainly not overcome with grief at the prospect. On 9th July, 1873, he wrote to his wife . . . that he was pleased that the gold fields were not apparently coming up to expectation, 'as otherwise Sir Henry Barkly will jump these like he did with the Diamond Fields'.[4]

Gold meant alien immigrants coming to upset the quiet tempo of an isolation which, though drab and meagre, enjoyed freedom from the Imperial Factor and its obduracy in refusing to accept what to the descendants of the trekkers were the obvious facts of racial superiorities. Gold, therefore, meant interference and calls for franchise rights from non-Boers, not to speak of the need for a more highly organized administration, which would threaten the quiet, leisurely government of hitherto. Above all, it was possible that gold would spell the end of the freedom which had been sought by those who had trekked from the Cape Colony in the 30's.

The first impetus to gold-mining in southern Africa had come in 1873 with the discovery of the Lydenburg alluvial goldfields, which, as in the case of Griqualand West, drew a fairly large and motley collection of prospectors and fortune-hunters from all over South Africa and elsewhere.[5] Many

---

[3] G. Theal, *History of South Africa, The Republics and Native Territories 1854-1872*, 1900, pp. 232-3.

[4] S. P. Engelbrecht, *President Thomas Francois Burgers—a Biography* (Eng. translation), 1946, pp. 81-2.

[5] Among the host of works concerning the early Transvaal diggings, one of the most interesting is the pamphlet by the Rev. Gerald Herring—*The Pilgrim Diggers of the Seventies—a short history of the origin of Pilgrims Rest (1873-1881)*. See also T. Reunert, *Diamonds and Gold in South Africa*, 1883, p. 83.

came from the Australian and Californian fields, hoping that
their superior knowledge would give them some advantage.
As early as 1868 various prospecting companies were being
organized to search for gold, and from Australia 'a party of
experienced miners arrived at Natal, expecting to find gold-
digging an established industry'.[6] Later many of these 'foreign'
diggers moved to Kimberley.

Finally, the wild dreams of generations of gold-seekers
reached fruition when the Struben brothers discovered gold on
the Witwatersrand in 1884, and the main reef deposits in 1886.

THE PROBLEMS OF MINING

While these deposits were to prove the richest in the world,
their very nature precluded the chances of individual diggers
making large fortunes in a short space of time.[7] In Kimberley
it was possible, in the early stages at any rate, to employ one or
two Africans and instruct them to find diamonds; the only
real problem was to prevent them from stealing their finds.
Even in the early eastern Transvaal alluvial diggings there were
none of the easily found, rich nuggets common in Australia or
California, while a great deal more hard work and complicated
processing was called for than was necessary on the diamond-
fields. On the Rand, the low gold content of the ores, in relation
to a predetermined price for gold, meant that to mine profitably
it was essential to keep the cost of recovery as low as possible.

The low-grade ores required expensive, advanced and
complicated technology to extract payable gold from the
otherwise barren rock, and there could therefore be no question
of individual mining operations of the early diamond-diggings
variety. What was required was capital in substantial amounts
combined with advanced 'know how'—both technical and
entrepreneurial. The capital required, which could be raised by
forming joint stock companies, was already available to a great
extent from the wealth which had been accumulated in
Kimberley. The early years of the goldfields were actually
characterized by a speculative boom which started in 1888 and

---

[6] G. Theal, op. cit. p. 232.

[7] See Donald Wood Gilbert, 'The Economic Effects of the Gold Discoveries
Upon South Africa, 1886-1910', in the *Quarterly Journal of Economics*, vol. 47,
no. 4, Aug. 1933, p. 555; for a more technical discussion, Hatch and Chalmers,
The Gold Mines of the Rand, 1895.

lasted until 1889, as a result of which a great deal of money was lost. Technical 'know how' could be bought at a price, while there was a rich store of entrepreneurial knowledge to be found among the more successful of the Kimberley pioneers, who were themselves only too willing to be drawn into the new enterprise. Men like Rhodes and Beit were soon on the scene: they were well known, had good overseas connexions, and were thus able to induce British and Continental investors to take an active part in the exploitation of the Rand from the earliest stages. Rhodes and Rudd formed the 'Gold Fields of South Africa, Limited' in 1887.[8]

In contrast to the situation at Kimberley, fuel presented no problem for there were rich coal deposits close at hand. Coal had been discovered in December 1887 at Boksburg, in the near neighbourhood of the goldfields and soon several collieries (Brakpan, Springs, Olifants River, etc.) were operating.

The main problem, therefore, was not how the fields could be opened up or where the finance necessary for their exploitation could be found, but whether the raw materials and labour needed to work them could be obtained at a cost sufficiently low to enable them to yield a profit. Professor Frankel makes an interesting calculation of the net return to capital on the Rand from 1887 to 1932: by counter-balancing high yields against low yields, he arrives at the average figure of 4·1 per cent.[9]

Johannesburg and its environs were not attractive, as at this stage it was no more than a mining-camp, and in the absence of rail transport, it was some six weeks' journey from the coast, which meant it was relatively inaccessible. On the other hand, conditions in Europe and elsewhere were relatively prosperous, so that in order to attract suitable miners and artisans from abroad it was necessary to set a high standard of wages to compensate for these factors. The high cost of living was another factor which had to be taken into account. It was chiefly the result of transport costs and these, of course, also affected the supply price of capital goods to the mines, consequently

[8] See S. H. Frankel, *Capital Investment in Africa—its course and effects*, 1938, pp. 79-80.

[9] See S. H. Frankel, op. cit., p. 90; also article by the same author in *The Economic Journal*, March 1935, 'Return to Capital invested in the Witwatersrand Gold Mining Industry, 1887-1932'.

further narrowing the profit margin. There was originally no transport other than oxen—the nearest railway link being Kimberley, some 300 miles away. The cost of transporting goods from the coast to Johannesburg in 1889 was £30 a ton, although after the railway links were completed in the early 90's, it dropped to between £6 and £9 a ton.

Further factors which tended to inflate costs were the unduly high Transvaal customs tariff, and the practice of the Transvaal Government to grant concessions for the monopoly of importation and manufacture of various essentials for the mining industry, notably dynamite and cement. In 1895, for example, dynamite cost 87s. a case in Johannesburg against 21s. in Germany, while cement costing 5s. 6d. a cask in Europe cost 44s. in the Transvaal. This state of affairs lasted until after the British administration took over in 1900.[10]

THE DETERMINING FACTORS IN THE LABOUR MARKET

Many of the permanent features of the South African labour market were conceived and nurtured in the development of the gold-mining industry—the institution of the recruiting system; the encouragement and permanent establishment of the migratory system; the struggle for power between different groups of workers, the outcome of which was to be the colour bar in industry.

To some extent, the unemployment which resulted from the contraction of mining activities in Kimberley following the amalgamations helped the recruitment of labour for the gold-mines, but the right men were not always forthcoming. Indeed, some of the people who went to the Transvaal from Kimberley were of an undesirable type and included a number of agitators. The new fields also provided a useful hide-out for diamond smugglers.

Suitable labour was, therefore, hard to come by and, as in the case of Kimberley, the European artisan was placed in a position of advantage vis-à-vis the unskilled African worker. In a

[10] See report of Mining Industry Commission, 1908; evidence before the Industrial Commission of Enquiry, 1897, particularly that of H. F. E. Pistorious, p. 284. For accounts of the corruption and mal-administration of the issue of these concessions, see. J. P. Fitz Patrick, *The Transvaal from within*, 1899; D. M. Wilson, *Behind the Scenes in the Transvaal*, 1901. (A full account of the history of the concessions can be found in the report etc. of the Transvaal Concessions Commission of 19 April 1901 (C. 623/5).)

situation where the need for low costs was paramount, and in which labour constituted the major item in the cost structure, the European skilled worker, by virtue of his scarcity value, was able to divert the attention of economy-conscious mine-owners to the African. It has been estimated that in the 90's African wages amounted to between 40 per cent and 45 per cent of the total mining costs, whereas the wages of white labour accounted for between 20 per cent and 25 per cent and explosives for between 12 per cent and 20 per cent. At this time (1894) about 40,000 Africans were employed at an average wage of 61s. a month, while the cost of feeding was in the region of 10s. per month. Europeans employed numbered approximately 5,400 and their average wage was about £21 per month.[11]

Once again, as in Kimberley, the stage was set for an unequal struggle for paramountcy in the labour market, with conflicting groups competing for the lion's share of what could only, of necessity, be a limited reward. Presiding over the scene were to be the mine-owners, ever mindful that it would be necessary to maintain a reasonably attractive level of profits if investors were to continue to take a healthy part in the development of the industry, while outside the struggle were to stand the authorities: first the Transvaal Government, then the British administration, followed by the Government of the Crown Colony, and finally, the Union Government: though not always as strictly impartial observers.

The three determining factors which moulded the permanent pattern of the labour market in the gold-mining industry were the relative strength of the European, as opposed to the relative weakness of the African, the importance of keeping costs at the lowest possible level, and the firmly established official colour prejudice. The fact that the mining companies were unable to reduce effectively the cost of supply of other factors of production ensured the reliance of the industry upon cheap African labour. Furthermore, the climate of opinion in the Transvaal was not unfavourable for the development of rigidities in the labour market based on colour, for whereas in the Cape the force of authority was weighted in favour of a more liberal approach to the indigenous inhabitants, the Transvaal was founded

---

[11] Hatch and Chalmers, op. cit., p. 260; see also Chamber of Mines Annual Report for 1894.

firmly upon principles of racial inequality. The Voortrekkers, in leaving the Cape Colony, had clearly stated their attitude in this respect, in the famous Retief manifesto, while the Transvaal's *Grondwet* (constitution) totally excluded the black man from any participation in the government of the country, and relegated him to a subservient position. Therefore, whereas the structure of the labour market in Kimberley was being moulded chiefly by the force and strength of white labour, in the Transvaal the whites were also able to draw support from official quarters. Furthermore, the attitude of the authorities in the Transvaal could hardly be described as having at any time been favourable to the mining companies, even though the revenue from the goldfields had saved the Republic from certain bankruptcy.[12]

THE PROBLEMS OF LABOUR

Faced with the fixed price of gold and the consequent need to minimize costs, it was natural that the mine companies should, from the first, have turned their attention to the problem of assuring a steady supply of basic labour, at the lowest possible outlay. The only possible source of supply of this type of labour was, of course, the African section of the population and there were several factors at work during the 80's and 90's which influenced the conditions of supply and demand with regard to African workers. In the first place, the huge demand of the goldfields for labour came at a time when there were other competing demands; secondly, the African had not reached the stage where his material wants were sufficient to induce him to enter the exchange economy readily and willingly, and, thirdly, the Rand soon earned a bad reputation among Africans as a place of employment.

(a) Competing demands for Labour

At Kimberley and elsewhere on the diamond-fields, there remained a steady demand for African labour, and many Africans, especially those from the Cape, chose to seek employment in these areas. Furthermore, the opening up of the diamond diggings had initiated a boom in the general economic

[12] See D. H. Wilson, op. cit., p. 40, and J. P. Fitz Patrick, op. cit., p. 71, where he gives an interesting table showing the finances of the country from 1871 to 1899.

life of the Colony, which was given added impetus by the
discoveries of gold on the Witwatersrand. There followed a spate
of railway construction, accompanied by a general stimulus to
farming. A healthy competition for all grades of labour was
engendered which naturally encouraged an upward movement
in wage-rates, and although the rise in the wages of non-whites
was not spectacular, it was sufficient to worry mine-owners who
were concerned not only because of the cost factor, but also
because they feared that higher wages would reduce the supply
of African workers, on account of the limited range of their
wants. In the 80's and 90's, few Africans could be described as
being more than slightly acquainted with the exchange economy.
Even fewer knew what to do with their money earnings, and
there was thus a tendency, as they earned more, to work for
shorter periods.[13] In the absence of compulsion, the process of
transition from the narrowly based indigenous subsistence
economy to one based upon a more advanced system of monetary exchange is slow, particularly where it was, and still is, the
case that the people concerned were not wholly forsaking the
one environment for the other. From the earliest times, in South
Africa, the exchange economy has constituted a supplement to
the subsistence economy rather than a substitute. This has been
due partly to the peculiar requirements of the mining industry
and partly to the pressures exerted by white opinion, which, in
spite of economic considerations, showed itself from the first to
be against the total absorption of the African into urban
society. With the growth of constructive and secondary industry,
as opposed to purely extractive industry, this problem was to
develop into one of the most crucial affecting the labour market.

(b) The Impulses behind the African Labourer

The African, limited in his range of wants by his primitive
environment, had few positive impulses to earn or to accumulate
a medium of exchange or store of value in the form of money.[14]
He had none of those wants which have become associated with
western civilization, for although the original primitive tribal

[13] See Annual Report of the Chamber of Mines, 1892. For a detailed discussion of the problem of African wages in gold-mines, see S. T. van der Horst,
Native Labour in South Africa, 1942, pp. 128-36.

[14] See evidence before Transvaal Labour Commission, Johannesburg, 1904
(Cd. 1897), particularly the evidence of Mr. Ian Grant of the Chamber of Mines,
p. 479, and others, pp. 338 and 508.

economy had undergone some modification as a result of contact with Europeans, the main edifice remained: dealings with traders, for example, were largely conducted through the medium of barter, while contact with the Boer trekkers had offered little opportunity for the broadening of wants for theirs was only a simple, rural society.[15] In fact, if the accounts of some travellers are to be believed, many farmers in the Transvaal during the early period of the Republic had come close to losing all understanding of the meaning of money. The institution of the so-called Transvaal 'labour tax', by which Africans had either to do free labour for the State or on the farms where they dwelt, bears this out. Agar Hamilton writes:

The labour tax is not very difficult to understand. . . . Money was scarce, even among the whites—nearly 30 years later on the regime of President Burgers was to break down over the absence of a money economy—and the natives had no conception of its use.[16]

Indeed, when one considers the distances involved and the hazards of a journey from one place to another, it is small wonder that the Boer settlers, in their isolation, should have almost lost contact with the exchange mechanism of a regulated and organized economy.[17]

By virtue of the circumstances surrounding the process, the widening of the range of African wants was, of course, slow and gradual, while their acquisition of a technique of economizing in order to make the best use of available means was even slower. Among the inhabitants of a subsistence economy, improvidence is usually the rule rather than the exception, which does not necessarily imply any inherent shortcoming on their part, for the very nature of the system—the absence of markets, competition, profits, etc.—means that production is undertaken for direct consumption and there is little incentive to improve methods of farming. The concept of 'waiting', to produce or to consume, which is the vital element in the advanced exchange economy, is unknown in simple subsistence economies.

In such circumstances, where no endogenous motivations

[15] See C. W. de Kiewiet, *A History of South Africa*, 1942, p. 120 et seq.
[16] J. Agar Hamilton, *The Native Policy of the Voortrekkers*, 1928, p. 199. See also D. M. Wilson, op. cit., p. 18.
[17] See de Kiewiet, op. cit., ch. V, 'The Witwatersrand and the Boer War', for a lively discussion of the question.

exist which would induce people to forsake the subsistence economy and seek paid employment in the labour market, it may become necessary to introduce exogenous stimulants, either direct or indirect. Poll-tax, direction of labour, and the enforcement of pass-carrying, are all compulsive agents, though of different relative force. The poll-tax, for instance, creates a monetary commitment which the African has to acquire funds to discharge, while, on the other hand, passes and permits and the direction of labour have no monetary relevance, but introduce direct control of movement within the labour market. The need for such compulsive agents has often been interpreted as evidence of the inherent laziness of Africans, but it seems more reasonable to assume that for a people accustomed to a subsistence economy, the support of life does not require continuous and disciplined work. F. Spearpoint, referring to his experience as compound manager at the Roan Antelope Copper Mine in Northern Rhodesia, writes:

It was difficult to get a Native to engage for work, and once he did so, it was equally difficult to keep him. The mine hooter, in their minds, was instituted purely for the purpose of warning the Europeans to get up and come to work, and they never thought to associate it with themselves. In the villages, when they arose in the morning, that was because it suited them and after performing what they considered enough work for the day, the remainder of their time was filled in by resting or having a yarn with some other villager. . . .[18]

Nevertheless, the primitive African did migrate in large numbers to the European environment in search of employment, and this phenomenon must be explained by the existence of a desire to satisfy certain known and basic (or static) wants. Having acquired the means to satisfy them, the African was ready to return home, as illustrated by the purchase of guns in Kimberley, described in the previous chapter. It is also true that to this day the urge to acquire cattle, either as a symbol of status or for payment in *lobolo* (bride purchase) transactions, is a strong factor in inducing Africans to sell their labour. In the course of their sojourn on the mines or elsewhere, however, many Africans acquired the taste for other goods and services (for instance, European-style clothes, liquor, sewing-machines,

[18] F. Spearpoint, 'The African Native and the Rhodesian coppermines', in the *Royal African Society Journal* supplement, vol. 36, no. 144, July 1937.

etc.) which were only obtainable in exchange for a money payment. These additional wants would originally act as delaying factors in the realization of the initial list of wants and could be termed unpremeditated, supplementary wants which did not primarily influence the African's decision to enter the exchange economy as a seller of labour. In time, however, they became an accepted part of the orbit of primary wants; for instance a man may (as was often the case) become addicted to liquor, and then regard his selling of labour almost wholly in terms of acquiring it. Both at Kimberley and on the Rand the liquor problem did, in fact, become acute, and a great deal of thought was given to ways and means of combating it.[19]

The individual may, in addition, be influenced by the need to satisfy yet a third category of wants, which might more accurately be termed 'quasi-wants'. This is a common occurrence in more advanced communities where people may be forced to use part of their income on expenditure which they would prefer not to incur, which does not yield satisfaction, and which, on occasions, may not have been allowed for in their original assessment of wants. Examples are taxes, fines, and levies of all kinds. Thus the Africans' basic orbit of wants was artificially extended by the creation of such quasi-wants, in particular the poll-tax, which became an important factor in inducing them to leave the rural areas in order to work in the European environment.

Once a community has progressed to a point where such compulsive measures are no longer needed, they should, of course, be abolished and, if necessary, replaced by a normal progressive income tax. With the widening of African wants, and the consequent increase in their reliance on monetary earnings, the burden of the fixed universal poll-tax, which is still levied on Africans in South Africa, becomes severely regressive.

The process of change and adaptation to a new way of life or strange environment is apt to be slow even where there has been a severance of the link with the place of origin. In the case of southern Africa, the contact which the average tribal African had with western civilization was intermittent and, in some cases, too brief to have caused more than a superficial impres-

[19] See evidence of Mr. C. S. Goldmann before the Industrial Commission of Inquiry, 1897 (pp. 113-14).

sion. The fact that the family was left behind in the Reserves meant that only the male breadwinner came into contact with the advanced way of life. Such superficial advancement as took place, therefore, was limited to him and on his return home it was more than likely that he would revert entirely to his family's way of life, without making any impression on it. The contact which the average worker established with urban life was in any case limited by his work environment: the compound system reduced his direct contact with the rest of urban society. Furthermore, as long as his tribal home remained intact, there was little incentive for a widening of wants to include goods associated with women and the home—with the notable exception of blankets, pots, and, later, the sewing-machine. The nature of tribal society tended to discourage any accumulation or concentration of goods—such goods as were taken back to the villages were distributed and lost in the general pattern of life. This does not imply that the tribal way of life was left entirely unaffected. Writing in 1924, Dr. Edgar Brookes noted: 'the cheap tin mug bought from the neighbouring trader has replaced the artistically worked clay pot. The cheap imported knife has killed the Native smelting industry.'[20]

In Kimberley, in the early stages, the urge to acquire guns was sufficient to make adequate numbers of Africans available on the fields. In addition, of course, there was the growing factor of rural impoverishment, in that the subsistence economy periodically showed itself unable to maintain its peoples above starvation point, and thus the need arose to subsidize the rural home by earning money in exchange for labour in European agriculture and industry. In the absence of a readily accessible exchange economy, life in the primitive society will be precarious, and, in times of severe crop failures, the only prospect may be slow starvation. The advent of an advanced economy of the European variety in southern Africa acted as an insurance against this eventuality, and thus created a bolster against adversity. On the other hand, the spread of European land occupation led to a gradual contraction of the permissible area of African cultivation and pasture, which in turn led, in the

[20] E. H. Brookes, 'The Economic Aspects of the Native Problem', paper read at the South African Association for the Advancement of Science, Cape Town, 1924.

absence of effective knowledge of land utilization, to a further
set of difficulties, culminating in the twentieth century in some
of the most pressing economic problems of the time, which were
not only important as far as the Africans were concerned, but
were also significant in bringing about a townward migration of
whites and thus creating the so-called Poor White problem,
which is examined in the next chapter.

The gradual broadening of the orbit of African wants—the
desire to own manufactured cooking utensils, clothing, and, of
course, in time the desire to possess a watch, bicycle, and
sewing-machine—proved too slow for the vast labour requirements of the Witwatersrand mines; where in 1886 there were
only 1,500 Africans working on the mines, by 1894 the number
had surpassed 40,000, while in 1899, it had reached 96,000.[21]

It is, of course, highly improbable that the average African
who contemplated leaving the rural areas to work in the
European economy would have been able to measure up
effectively the relative advantages of the different money wages
paid in various employment centres. The difficult nature of
communications meant that the labour market in South Africa
tended to be very imperfect. For the average African the journey
to and from the minefields had to be undertaken on foot, and it
entailed, in most cases, several weeks *en route*. Furthermore,
there was no means of quickly passing messages from one
centre to another. On the other hand, in particular centres such
as the Rand, until agreement was reached among the mine-
owners for wage-fixation, conditions approximated towards
equilibrium of supply and demand, and as the supply of
workers usually lagged behind demand, there tended to be
sharp competition for labour among the mine-managers,
resulting in wage-rates being driven above what was regarded
as a desirable maximum. Lionel Phillips comments:

In those days, more so even than now, a native worked to secure
a definite sum of money. The higher his wages the shorter his stay,
and the keen competition which this system created resulted in the
most productive mines getting an undue proportion of labour
because of their ability to outbid their poorer neighbours. The

[21] See C. S. Goldmann, *South African Mines; their position, results and
developments; together with an account of Diamonds, Land, Finance, etc.*, 1895-6,
vol. 1, p. 16, and the Chamber of Mines Annual Reports for 1894 and 1899.

ill-effect of this was double-edged. It tended to restrict expansion and it militated against the efficiency of the labourer.[22]

Nevertheless, the tendency towards a relatively high wage-rate on the Rand was not always sufficient to induce additional Africans to come to the area. This can probably be explained by the fact that the African as a 'target' worker sought to sell his labour in order to satisfy a particular want or a limited range of wants. As he had no real desire to remain indefinitely away from home, the time which he was prepared to work in the industrial environment was largely dictated by the time it took him to realize his wants. Other things being equal, the Witwatersrand, therefore, proved attractive in that the high wage-rates meant that it took less working time to satisfy a given set of wants, but the conditions *en route* meant that there was always the danger of losing the money or purchases through molestation or robbery. It was, therefore, often thought preferable to work in Kimberley or elsewhere; for instance, on railway construction. The importance of this factor became clear in the period following the reduction of African wages from 45*s*. to 30*s*. a week on the gold-mines in 1897, for by this time there was beginning to develop some understanding of the meaning of money, but it is also likely that Africans were influenced by rumour and labour touts.

(c) *The Unpopularity of the Rand*

The interference and molestation to which Africans travelling to and from the Rand were subjected proved a constant worry to the mining companies, and this was certainly a major factor in increasing the difficulties of labour supply to the mines. It had early become evident that the individual mining companies would be better placed to deal with problems of mutual concern if they had some medium of collective action, which could provide services of a co-operative nature. To meet this and other needs, the first Chamber of Mines was formed in 1887; in 1889 it became the Witwatersrand Chamber of Mines; in 1897 it was renamed the Chamber of Mines of the South African Republic, in 1902 the Transvaal Chamber of Mines, and in 1954 it assumed its present title of the Transvaal and

[22] L. Phillips, *Transvaal Problems*, 1903, p. 39; see also Chamber of Mines **Annual Report** for 1889, p. 10.

Orange Free State Chamber of Mines. The Chamber itself has no power of control over individual members and exists primarily to provide them with certain co-operative services. The growth of the group system has tended to lessen its import-ance in some respects, though today the welfare, training, and social services it provides for members are considerable.

One of the earliest problems faced by the Chamber was the question of molestation of African labour, but in spite of constant representations to the Transvaal Government these irregularities continued until the British administration took over the Transvaal in 1900. Suggestions made by the Chamber of Mines for the effective provision of shelters and protection for Africans were ignored by the authorities or passed over by polite but ineffective acknowledgements.[23]

There can be no doubt that the accounts given by returning Africans at their kraals of the privations endured *en route*, and even on the mines, together with the fact that many never returned to tell any tale, must have had a strong influence in preventing others from undertaking similar journeys. The trip to the mines must have, by comparison, made a journey in Europe in the Dark Ages appear almost safe. The workers had to face robbery by extortion from farmers *en route*, the unscru-pulous wiles of labour touts, and molestation from bogus police. Highway robbery of Africans returning from the mines became a lucrative occupation; even the legitimate authorities were not always immune from the temptation to extort from the Africans, while some farmers found a convenient means of supplementing their labour supply by forcing Africans who wished to pass through their farms to give labour (often for periods as long as nine months) in return for the required transit authority. In its third annual report for 1891, the Chamber of Mines noted that 'police officers in the employ either of the Government or of the N.Z.A. Railway Company were stationed on the Komati and Krokodil Valleys turning back Natives who were coming to work on the mines and compelling them to work on the railways'.

The pass system which was in operation in one form or

[23] See the Chamber of Mines reports for 1891-7. D. M. Wilson, op. cit., gives an interesting account of how Kruger dealt with complaints from 'Uitlanders'—p. 62 et seq.

another from the earliest days of the republics, opened up the way for other abuses: soon there were reports circulating that police were removing passes from Africans and either destroying them and later 'selling' the workers to labour touts, or extorting fees from the workers in return for the confiscated passes.

Abuse of authority was not confined to the Transvaal: in the Free State where it was customary to fumigate the workers passing through the area against the possible spread of disease, irregularities in the application of health measures were such that they prompted Sir James Sivewright to send the following message to Bloemfontein:

Transkeian Natives complain bitterly of being jostled, thrashed, and, in the course of fumigation, even robbed of their hard-earned wages by police in charge of fumigating station between Transvaal and Free State. They say they are detained unduly long in the fumigating room, and many brought in fainting state. . . .[24]

Thus the workers often arrived on the fields in no fit state to embark upon any strenuous work; many died from sheer exhaustion, and others were unable to acclimatize themselves to their new surroundings. It is perhaps small wonder that service on the Johannesburg mines was, in time, to be regarded by many as proof of manhood.

(d) Methods of Procuring Workers

With the slow acquisition of wants and the consequent absence of wage-earning incentives, an obvious alternative was to institute a system of recruitment, either direct or indirect. The desire for adventure, which was to play an important part in African custom, was not sufficient in itself to overcome the shortage of labour, and, furthermore, the lack of security of travel made it essential that there should be some organized control of the movement of workers from their homes to the mines. It was also becoming clear that the mines would have to go farther afield than South Africa to ensure adequate labour.

Obviously the extremes of slavery and convict labour were out of the question but the mining companies, not without justification, contended that it would be impossible to embark upon systematic recruiting at some expense to themselves without certain guarantees, particularly regarding the tenure of

[24] Quoted in the Chamber of Mines Annual Report for 1896, p. 171.

service of African workers. They could point to the inadequacy of the then existing Masters and Servants laws, which were harshly applied with little regard to servants' interests. They suggested a revision of the pass laws, which would not only meet their own requirements, but which would afford the African workers a greater measure of security of movement in the Transvaal. The history of the Chamber's efforts to secure amendment of the pass laws in order to facilitate recruitment of workers provides a classic example of the way in which the Transvaal was administered at the time, and the almost insuperable difficulties which had to be faced by the companies.[25]

Although some efforts had been made to recruit labour from the Cape, the experiment had not proved a great success, for the labour position in the Cape was by no means easy, as was borne out by the 1890 Select Committee, and by evidence before the Cape Labour Commission of 1893.

NEW SOURCES OF LABOUR

It thus became evident that local supplies of labour were inadequate to meet the rising demands of the mining industry and that other sources would have to be explored: the obvious choice was Portuguese East Africa, where there existed a large untapped reservoir of African labour. Such recruiting, however, presented problems in negotiation, which could best be tackled in concert rather than by the mining companies acting individually. In any event, the Portuguese were reluctant to allow unrestricted recruitment without some measure of control, both from the point of view of African welfare and in order to facilitate the collection of recruiting fees.

The Chamber itself provided the machinery for negotiation with the Transvaal and the Portuguese authorities, but something further was needed to handle the actual recruitment. To this end, the Native Labour Supply Association was founded in 1896; later to become the Witwatersrand Native Labour Association in 1900.[26] The decision to seek labour requirements outside of those territories which were in 1910 to become the Union of South Africa was significant for a number of reasons.

[25] See Chamber of Mines Annual Reports for 1893, p. 4; 1894, p. 4; 1895, p. 13.
[26] See Chamber of Mines Annual Reports for 1900 and 1901. For a discussion of the work of the Association, see their report for 1906, Appendix 1, pp. 4-8.

Firstly, it was eventually to mean that the indigenous inhabitants of a greater part of central and southern Africa were to become participants in the mining and industrial development of South Africa. Secondly, the dependence of South African mining and industry upon this type of labour made the problems of urbanization and stabilization even more difficult, and tended to make permanent the system by which workers left their homes alone to do spells of work in the confines of the mine compound, returning to their families at the end of their contracts. Thirdly, it encouraged the interdependency of the Union and other central and southern African territories, which in turn was to give rise to some pressing political, economic and social problems.

The search for labour to operate the mines did not, however, end in Africa, and before long the Chamber of Mines was reporting in its annual statements offers of labour from all over the world.

Offers came from as far afield as Hungary, on the one hand, and the West Indies, on the other. The majority were turned down on the grounds that the work of recruitment was too great and likely to prove uneconomical, but in the case of white workers, the objection was one of principle. It was feared that a wholesale introduction of white labourers—from southern Europe particularly—would upset the traditional pattern of life within the country (a fear which was again to manifest itself seventy years later). Furthermore, the mining companies had little hope of Europeans being long content with the low wages which the African miners were content to take.[27] Comparisons showing that the wages paid to labourers in Europe were in fact lower than those paid to Africans were in substance correct, but failed to take into consideration, on the one hand, the high cost of living on the Rand, and, on the other hand, and perhaps more important, the prevailing climate of opinion. The Africans' standards were admittedly lower, while the migratory system, initially at any rate, reduced the need for a money wage: the African regarding his wage as a supplement to rather than a substitute for his rural income.

There was, furthermore, little doubt that European labourers

[27] See Report of the Transvaal Indigency Commission, 1906-8 (T.G. 13-08). Part 2, ch. 2, p. 34.

would have soon learnt the benefits of concerted action, in
order to improve their position alongside that of the skilled
workers.

Some early exponents of a white labour policy sought to
draw strength from the example of California and Australia;
once again failing to consider the circumstances in South
Africa.

The question of using white unskilled labour was raised again
after the conclusion of the Anglo-Boer War, when the reopened
mines experienced an acute shortage of unskilled labour
resulting partly from the fact that African workers had returned
to their homes during the war, partly from a feeling of dissatis-
faction over the lowering of wages in 1896, and partly because
of fears of harsh treatment in the Transvaal. In addition to the
treatment which had been meted out to workers by the Transvaal authorities, conditions on the mines were far from
satisfactory, both in the compounds and underground. There
was also a high death-rate resulting from workers being under-
nourished or unacclimatized. The British army of occupation
had, furthermore, created wider opportunities for African
labour in addition to the new demands created by the
reconstruction programmes.

It was clearly essential that in order to facilitate general
recovery, the gold-mines had to begin operations as soon as
possible. In 1902, a Committee of Consulting Engineers
reported to the Chamber of Mines that far less progress had
been made in resuming operations than was anticipated, owing
to the shortage of African labour (the labour strength being
42,218 in June 1902 compared with the estimated requirement
of 97,800). This they attributed to four causes:

1. The continuance of the guerrilla war until June 1901.
2. The reduced schedule of African wages.
3. The large amounts earned by a considerable number of
   Africans during the war.
4. Abundant harvests.[28]

Nevertheless, the Executive Committee decided 'that under
present conditions, and the present cost of living, the use of
unskilled European labour is economically impossible', while

[28] Report of Special Committee of Transvaal Chamber of Mines, in Chamber
of Mines Annual Report for 1902, p. 55.

they were 'opposed to the introduction of unskilled Europeans at such wages as would not admit of their existence as *civilised* members of the community'.[29] Later, the Chamber, in modified terms, expressed itself against the importation of white labour 'at wages which would not admit of their living at a standard of comfort to which they had been accustomed in Europe'.[30]

Either way, there was thus a tacit acceptance of a standard below which Europeans could not be permitted to fall. Furthermore, given this 'civilized' standard of living, it was clear that without a radical change in the basis of South African society, the mines would not be able to operate without a reservoir of cheap non-white labour, to whom the standard was not applicable. Even if one accepts the contention that Hungarians or Italians could have been supplied at rates at par or even below the prevailing African rates (excluding costs of transportation), the overriding problem of 'civilized' standards remained.

Faced, therefore, on the one hand with the difficulty of inducing the indigenous non-whites to undertake paid labour and, on the other, with customary white prejudices about 'Kaffir' work, it was not surprising that the authorities should begin to think in terms of foreign non-white labour. The Indians had proved a great asset in developing the Natal sugar industry and in the coal-mines, but their importation to the Rand was out of the question owing to objections on the part of the Secretary of State for India, in regard to restrictions imposed upon Asiatics in the Transvaal. It was thus decided to send a representative to the Far East, California, British Columbia and Malaya, to investigate the possibilities and merits of importing other non-white labour. He later reported favourably on the advantages of indentured Chinese. The introduction of Chinese labour was permitted by an Ordinance (No. 17 of 1904) to regulate the introduction into the Transvaal of unskilled non-European labourers, entitled the 'Labour Importation Ordinance, 1904'. It was passed on 10 February; on 18 June, 1,055 coolies arrived in Durban, and by the end of the year 20,918 were employed on the mines.

Meanwhile, there was a growing agitation for the use of local

[29] Report of Executive Committee of Transvaal Chamber of Mines, Chamber of Mines Annual Report for 1903, p. 30.
[30] Chamber of Mines Annual Report for 1903, p. 153.

white labour on the mines. Coming at a time when the number of land-dispossessed whites was growing, due especially to the aftermath of the war, the idea was not unpopular, and when linked with the suggestion that it was undesirable for the white community to depend upon black labour, it had a distinct appeal to sentiment. Led by F. H. Cresswell, the Manager at Village Main Reef Mine, the movement put forward the contention that the mines could be run far more efficiently on an all-white basis, as fewer supervisors would be needed and only a quarter of the labouring strength required than when Africans were used.[31]

The attitude of Cresswell and his supporters, although it was to become part of a political movement, and help convert traditional prejudices into a national frame of mind which was much later to dominate South African society, hardly came to terms with reality; above all, it overlooked the deep-rooted aversion of every white to doing manual labour, which, as will be seen in the next chapter, was to become a major obstacle in overcoming the so-called Poor White problem. In any event, one may question whether the root of the trouble did not stem from the conception of the African population in terms of a separate entity, rather than as an inseparable part of the body economic, which could play a healthy role in industrial development, and enjoy a share of the fruits of their labours.

It was, in a sense, unfortunate for South Africa that the very nature of the gold-mining industry made for an acceptance of a pattern both unsuitable and unnecessary for the wider industrial economy which was to develop. Nevertheless, without the gold-mining industry, the country as a whole would have long remained a relatively poor agricultural community, while an acceptance of the Cresswell scheme, even if practical, would have postponed the emergence of the African and prolonged his backwardness.

[31] See Margaret Cresswell, *An epoch of the political history of South Africa in the life of Frederic Hugh Page Cresswell*, undated; also F. H. P. Cresswell, *The Chinese Labour Question from within—facts, criticisms and suggestions, etc.*, 1905. Cresswell joined the South African Labour Party in 1910 and became its leader shortly afterwards. He was elected to Parliament in the same year and was Minister of Defence and Labour in the 1924 Hertzog-Cresswell Pact Government and remained a member of the Union Parliament until 1938. He died in 1948 in his 82nd year. During his career he was an avowed protagonist of the rights of white labour in the face of non-white competition, and a strong supporter of Hertzog's segregationist principles and policies.

Cheap African labour enabled an otherwise possibly non-productive entity to become the fountain-head of industrial advancement in South Africa.[32]   The fact that the rigidities which have been created in the industrial labour market have prevented many non-whites from being able to enjoy a reward commensurate with their abilities cannot be blamed wholly on the gold-mining industry without which the fruits of indus-trialization, which have facilitated the development of all sections of the population, would not have been enjoyed.

Although Lord Milner and even Chamberlain understood the underlying feelings of men like Cresswell, they were soon expressing doubts as to the efficacy of an 'all-white policy' for the mines.[33]   Milner himself could not, of course, be described as having been 'liberal' in his attitude towards non-Europeans. He approached the question of using white labour for the mines not as one who saw it as a threat to the African, but rather as one who saw it in terms of a threat to European standards. Speaking to a deputation from the White League, he said:

Our welfare depends upon increasing the quantity of our white population, but not at the expense of its quality. We do not want a white proletariat in this country. The position of the whites among the vastly more numerous black population requires that even their lowest ranks should be able to maintain a standard of living far above that of the poorest section of the population of a purely white country. But, without making them hewers of wood and drawers of water, there are scores and scores of employments in which white men could be honourably and profitably employed, if we could at once succeed in multiplying our industries and in reducing the cost of living. . . . However you look at the matter, you always come back to the same root principle—the urgency of that development which alone can make this a white man's country in the only sense in which South Africa can become one, and that is, not a country full of poor whites, but one in which a largely increased white population can live in decency and comfort. That development requires capital; we have got the capital, but it also requires a large amount of rough labour. And that labour cannot, to any great extent, be white, if only because, pending development and the subsequent reduction in the cost of living, white labour is much too dear.[34]

On the other hand, he failed to see the importation of

[32] S. H. Frankel, *Capital Investment in Africa*, 1938, p. 75 et seq.
[33] Cecil Headlam (ed.), *The Milner Papers* (South Africa), 1933, vol. 2, 1899-1905, p. 457.
[34] Cd. 1895, 1903, pp. 36-44.

indentured workers (as opposed to settlers) as being an ultimate threat to the country as a whole. Writing to Bishop Hamilton Baynes in 1904, he said:

. . . To say that Chinese labour is a *substitution for white labour* is, quite simply, a lie. . . . Without a sub-stratum of coloured labour, white labour cannot exist here, and when the very rich mines are worked out, the whole country will return to its primitive barrenness.[35]

Milner's attitude was, in a sense, a key to understanding the 'Chinese labour' question, which now with the passing of time can perhaps be viewed in truer perspective, although even after a half century there is the tempting 'red herring' of introducing a discussion on the wisdom of bringing a further racial element into an already multi-racial society. A true appreciation of the problem requires an understanding of the underlying motives; the attitudes of white workers, and, above all, the use to which the Liberal Party and others in Britain put the question.

Nor can one ignore the wider issues at stake involving the clash of Boer interests with those of the mining companies. One commentator, John Strachey, describes it as the conflict of:

two distinct layers of imperialism in South Africa. There was an in-rushing tide of British mining and land-speculating imperialism, determined to exploit 'Kaffir' labour in the new and incomparably more profitable way of gold- and diamond-mining instead of in farming. But in possession was a previous layer of somewhat home-spun Boer imperialism, content to exploit African labour on a relatively small scale upon its farms. . . . both sides were Europeans intent upon the exploitation of the labour of far more primitive societies, either in agriculture or in the extraction of raw materials, such as gold and diamonds, for their own benefit. Thus all the generous view of the British 'pro-Boers' of the turn of the century must to-day seem a little beside the point.[36]

While one may perhaps question whether, in fact, no benefits accrued to the African—as implied by Strachey—he does expose the roots of the situation in which the interests of the emerging races were to become relatively unimportant in the struggle for sectional white hegemony. It is clear today that during the Anglo-Boer War, and particularly during the immediate post-war years, liberals and other humanitarians in Britain were inclined to lose sight of the wider race problems in their

[35] *The Milner Papers*, op. cit., p. 488.
[36] John Strachey, *The end of Empire*, 1959, p. 93.

vigorous defence of Boer interests. The consequences of their attitudes were to be of permanent importance in succeeding years.

The Chinese labour question provides an interesting insight into this sort of confusion. On the one hand, there existed vigorous opposition to the attempts to introduce Chinese coolies into the Transvaal, while on the other hand, there remained a strong defence of Boer interests leading to the granting of responsible government to the Transvaal by the British Liberal Government in 1907. Milner and the mining companies were accused of resorting to Chinese slavery, but little real attention was paid to the fact that the opposing Boer faction were themselves believers in a far more rigid approach towards non-whites.

While the avoidance of these wider issues was to be of far-reaching significance, it is nevertheless important to consider the Chinese labour question itself and its immediate consequences for the development of political opinion.

In the first place, could the mining industry have been reinstated as swiftly without Chinese labour? All the available evidence suggests the contrary.[37]

In the second place, there is no doubt that white labour would have proved uneconomical, even if sufficient could have been found to do 'Kaffir-work'. In 1904, the government mining engineer reported that the employment of white unskilled labourers had proved unsatisfactory as they largely 'cannot be relied upon to work for a continuous length of time', while 'the majority take to this employment as a stop-gap, and cannot, or will not, do the necessary amount of steady work to successfully compete with coloured labour'.[38]

Accepting the need for alien non-white labour, there remain the charges that South Africa was to be saddled with a further 'undesirable' racial element, and of 'Chinese slavery'.

There is little evidence to show that anyone had the intention of allowing the indentured Chinese to settle in the country.[39] Allegations of lawlessness among the Chinese labourers tended

[37] The Transvaal Labour Commission considered the question of the labour shortage in some detail and found the demand for African labour greatly exceeded the supply, see above, p. 57, see also L. Phillips, op. cit., p. 38.
[38] Annual Report of the Government Mining Engineer for the year ended 30 June 1904.
[39] The Milner Papers, op. cit., p. 476.

to be exaggerated by opponents of the scheme; an examination of the records of some of the mines during the period shows that while there was a fair proportion of opium addicts among the workers, crimes of violence were probably no greater than among the indigenous Africans. Workers convicted of any crimes were, in any event, returned post-haste to China.

The arrival of the first Chinese labourers in 1904 proved most opportune for the pro-Boer Opposition in Britain. The cry of 'Chinese slavery' proved itself a remarkably potent election slogan; and the Liberals, soon realizing its value among a British electorate conscious of humanitarianism, lost no opportunity of embellishing the question with all the drama they could devise, and with no sparing of 'politician's licence'. J. E. Wrench writes:

There have been few more discreditable episodes in British political life than the 'Chinese Slavery' Election in January, 1906. Liberal pro-Boers even went to the extent of suggesting that if this iniquitous Government had its way, the importation of Chinese 'slaves' to the slate quarries of Wales would be the nation's next step on the downward path. Perhaps, as was pointed out by Mr. Amery at the time, the best excuse that can be made is the one given in Swift's essay on Arbuthnot's 'Act of political lying': 'It happens very often that there are no other means left to the good people of England to pull down a ministry and government they are weary of but by exercising this their undoubted right: that abundance of political lying is a sure sign of true English liberty.'[40]

There followed, of course, the landslide election victory of the Liberal Party in Britain and pressure was successfully brought to bear to end the use of Chinese labour on the mines. In 1907, the Transvaal repealed the 1904 Labour Importation Ordinance and the Chinese were returned at the end of their contracts. In all, 63,453 had been imported, reaching a maximum of 57,828 in 1907. The following table shows the strength percentage of Chinese to other workers on the mines for the period 1904-9:

YEAR	WHITES	COLOURED	CHINESE
1904	13·6	76·8	9·6
1905	10·9	63·7	25·4
1906	10·3	74·3	15·4
1907	9·6	63·3	27·1
1908	9·7	79·2	11·1
1909	10·8	86·0	3·2

[40] J. E. Wrench, *Alfred, Lord Milner—the Man of No Illusions*, 1958, p. 259.

The last Chinese labourers left the country at an opportune moment for the mining industry, when a recession was developing in other activities, so that soon the mines were able to find all the labour they needed.[41]

This stormy episode in mining history was additionally important in that it had set the course for F. H. Cresswell and his friends: henceforward there was to be a new element in the labour market—the white labour political protectionists who were to play no small part in evolving the legal colour bar.

Furthermore a precedent had been created which was not without significance in bringing about the conditions necessary for a more rigid application of the colour bar in the mining industry. Ordinance No. 17 of 1907 (Transvaal), 'to regulate the introduction into the Transvaal of unskilled non-European labourers', sought to prevent Europeans from possibly being supplanted by the Chinese by stipulating in section 9(a) 'that so long as the labourer [defined in section 1 as 'a male person belonging to a non-European race other than one of the races indigenous to Africa south of 12 degrees north of the Equator'] remains in this colony he shall be employed only on unskilled labour in the exploitation of minerals within the Witwatersrand district and *in particular shall not be employed in any of the trades and occupations specified in schedule* 1 . . . except for unskilled labour therein' (my italics). Schedule 1 listed some fifty-five trades and other categories of mine-work usually done by Europeans.

[41] See S. T. van der Horst, op. cit., p. 172.

The Spread
of Industrialization

THE DIVERSIFICATION
OF THE ECONOMY AND
THE WHITE COMMUNITY

THE AGENTS OF CHANGE

SOUTH AFRICA'S industrialization is distinguished by certain characteristics of its own, although in many respects it can be compared with the process of industrialization which took place in other countries. The United Kingdom, for instance, underwent a similar transformation from a relatively self-contained agricultural community to a highly industrialized country, closely linked with the world economy through international trade, and the accompanying problems of adjustment, rural impoverishment, and even racial clash have been echoed in South African experience. The immigration of Irish peasants to England aroused feelings only too familiar in South Africa: the Irish were looked down upon, often exploited, and regarded as 'an example of a less civilized population spreading themselves as a kind of substratum beneath a more civilized community'.[1] Yet if there is a familiar ring, the similarities soon end and merge, in the South African setting, into a concert of problems unique not only in their individuality but also in their combination. Underlying the changes which took place in the economy were feelings of inter-white jealousy and racial prejudice, the poverty of many whites and the poverty and backwardness of practically all non-whites. The basic problems which industrialization and urbanization bring in their wake, which are complex enough in any environment, were rendered even more intractable in view of the features peculiar to the South African scene.

[1] J. L. and Barbara Hammond, *The Bleak Age*, Pelican ed., p. 37.

By the time secondary industry had begun to develop on an appreciable scale, certain patterns were clearly discernible in the labour market. As was shown in the last chapter, the gold-mining industry had become firmly based upon a substratum of cheap, non-white migratory labour, and the colour line between skilled and unskilled work was soon to be made permanent. There were, of course, no skilled Africans and, until the development of apprenticeship schemes, relatively few opportunities for local people to become skilled, while there was some logic in the contention that as the gold-mines were a wasting asset, the conditions prevailing were transient and could therefore be regarded as exceptional.[2] Nevertheless, there was every encouragement to regard the pattern of the mining industry as a model for the economy as a whole.

Although the development of mining on a large scale initiated the beginnings of a new era of economic life in South Africa, the process of transformation was not abrupt and for over half a century after the discovery of diamonds the country remained predominantly agricultural and relatively poor. But the process of development was continuous, if slow, for, once the momentum of industrialization had started, the growth and diversification of economic activity were inevitable. In other words, from a situation where agricultural production was undertaken to satisfy wants more or less directly, the country passed into a stage where industrial ventures, using capital and roundabout means of production, were commenced. Thus, the mines were worked in order to sell diamonds and gold and make a profit for their owners: this involved the purchase of raw materials and equipment, and the payment of wages to workers, of interest on borrowed capital, of taxes to the State, of dividends to shareholders in limited liability companies, and so on. Much of this expenditure would, in the normal course of events, be spent again, some of it within South African territory, and so new consumption patterns were established and imports and eventually local production were stimulated. Transport and other services also developed to meet the needs of the expanding economy and themselves gave further impetus to the process.

Gold and diamonds thus provided the magnets necessary to

[2] See Report of Economic Commission, 1914 (U.G. 12/14), p. 32, para. 4, and p. 151, para. 273.

attract the agents of economic change: investment capital, entrepreneurship and skilled labour—vital factors of production which were not available locally and without which the resources of the country could not be developed. Nevertheless, although investment in mining had a 'multiplier' effect throughout the economy, there were many factors which hindered the progress of full-scale industrialization. In the days of the Transvaal Republic, official policies were a constant stumbling-block, while later, after Union, official policy was not always aware of the true needs of the economy and reflected the prevalent 'group' approach.

The labour market itself came to contain a large number of displaced white workers, driven from the land by poverty and resentful of their reduction to what they considered an inferior status: to a great extent, their rehabilitation became the main object of official action, and the maintenance of civilized labour standards meant a very high level of wages for whites which, when combined with the relatively low productivity of all South African workers, meant that the Union's industrial potential was internationally uncompetitive. Tariff protection thus became an added essential and was, together with the effects of the two world wars of the present century, to play a decisive role in the development of South African industries. In the Report of the Commission of Enquiry into policy relating to the protection of industries it is categorically stated that 'it has been the consistent policy of the South African Government since 1925, that any branch of industry that can be established on a sound economic basis with a reasonable measure of protection should be granted tariff assistance'.[3]

Finally, the position of the non-white, and particularly the African, in the labour market was of vital importance. Here rural poverty also played a dominant role in driving Africans to the mines and later to the towns to seek work, but from the beginning, the migratory system was in operation: having completed a spell of employment, the African returned to his home in the Reserves.

THE DEVELOPMENT OF SECONDARY INDUSTRY

In point of time it is possible to divide the development of secondary industry in South Africa into four main periods:

[3] U.G. 36/58, p. 11, para. 74.

first, the growth of servicing industries to the mines; secondly, the expansion of manufacturing industry as a consequence of the closing of traditional sources of supply of imports following the outbreak of the First World War; thirdly, the further expansion resulting from the stimulus given by the adoption of policies of tariff protection after 1925, and finally, the rapid development which followed the Second World War and the imposition of import control in the post-war period. It is also important to remember that developments in the mining field have continued up to the present day, and although the growth of secondary industry has meant a relative decline in the importance of gold in the over-all balance of payments, the opening up of the Far West Rand and Free State goldfields in recent years, and the exploitation of uranium, have been of great significance in maintaining the momentum of expansion.

Some idea of the growth of manufacturing industry is obtained from figures given in the annual census of industrial establishments showing the growth in numbers employed over the past twenty-five years. In 1933-4, a total of 229,502 workers were employed in private manufacturing industry: 102,232 whites and 127,270 non-whites. Ten years later, in 1943-4, the total number employed had doubled, being 451,176, of whom 154,790 were whites and 296,386 non-whites. Another ten years brings us to the latest figures available; those for 1953-4. In that year the total number employed had almost doubled again, being 854,295, of which 267,138 were whites and 587,157 non-whites.

Prior to the discovery of diamonds and gold, such manufacturing industries as existed were largely concentrated at the coast, but they were of little significance, consisting in the main of undertakings concerned with the processing of consumer goods. As late as 1911, manufacturing contributed only 7 per cent to the estimated National Income, by 1927, the proportion had risen to almost 14 per cent, in 1937-8 to nearly 18 per cent and in 1956-7 to 23·4 per cent. In contrast the contribution of mining industry fell from 20·3 per cent in 1917-18 to 18·6 per cent in 1927-8, and 13·5 per cent in 1956-7. Agriculture also showed a similar decline in importance from 21·6 per cent in 1917-18 to 18·2 per cent in 1927-8 and 14·3 per cent in 1956-7. The volume and value of output of each of these sectors have, of course, increased considerably; the changing percentage contributions to national income are given here to emphasize the growing importance of secondary industry in the economy as a whole.

Industrial development became concentrated in four major centres which, in order of importance, are the southern Transvaal region, the western Cape, the Durban–Pinetown area, and the Port Elizabeth–Uitenhage area. It is not necessary in this study to detail minutely the individual industries which have become established in the Union during the present century, but nevertheless mention should be made of the important iron and steel industry in the Transvaal (established in 1928); engineering both in the Transvaal and, to a lesser extent, in the Port Elizabeth area; the chemical and rubber industry in Durban; industries connected with the preparation and processing of food and drink, particularly in the western Cape; motor assembly and leather goods in the Port Elizabeth area, and textiles, clothing, footwear, and printing in Durban, the Transvaal, and the Cape. This list is, of course, not exhaustive; it simply serves to give some idea of the diversity of secondary industry in South Africa today.

The southern Transvaal area is still the economic heart of South Africa and in 1953-4 this area contributed about 48 per cent of the total value of the Union's private net manufacturing output. In the same year, the western Cape contributed 15 per cent, Durban–Pinetown about 12 per cent, and Port Elizabeth–Uitenhage about 7 per cent.

Alongside the structural changes in the economy which accompanied industrial growth, a marked change in population distribution took place, with a shift of population from the rural to the urban areas from 1911 onwards, as far as whites were concerned, and from 1921 onwards for non-whites. Not only did the 'pulls' of industrialism contribute to this townward flow, but there were, in addition, the significant 'pushes' generated by rural impoverishment.

The extent of these changes can be gauged from population returns collected at successive censuses. Population returns for 1911, 1921, 1936, 1946 and 1951 showed an over-all increase in the numbers of all sections of the population, as can be seen from the following table.

Census Year	White '000	African '000	Asiatic '000	Coloured '000
1911	1,276	4,019	152	525
1921	1,521	4,697	164	545
1936	2,003	6,596	220	769
1946	2,372	7,831	285	928
1951	2,642	8,556	367	1,103

The percentage of each group which has become urbanized during the same period shows a considerable increase. As far as the white group is concerned, it is estimated that in 1951, 2,071,000 (78·4%) were urban dwellers, compared with 1,361,000 (67·9%) in 1936, and 671,000 (52·3%) in 1911. The 1951 census shows 284,000 Asiatics (77·4% of the total Asiatic population) as urbanized compared with 157,000 (71·7%) in 1936 and 83,000 (54·8%) in 1911.

For the Coloured people the comparable figures are 713,000 (64·6%) urban-dwellers in 1951, 440,000 (56·3%) in 1936, and 255,000 (48·7%) in 1911.

The increase in urbanization of the African population over this period is particularly marked: whereas in 1911 572,000 Africans (12·7% of the total African population) were recorded as town-dwellers, in 1936 the number had risen to 1,246,000 and the percentage to 18·9 and by 1951 the number of Africans in towns was 2,290,000 or 26·8% of the total African population.

Professor Sadie has pointed out that these figures indicate the 'de facto position only as on the night of the Census'. In other words, many of the Africans who appear as urban-dwellers will have been migrant workers, residing temporarily in the towns for purposes of work. Of the total of 2,290,000 Africans shown as urbanized in the 1951 Census (two-thirds of whom were concentrated in the main industrial areas), Professor Sadie estimated that at least $1\frac{1}{2}$ million were settled in the towns. This estimate was accepted by the Tomlinson Commission and is quoted in its Report.[4]

----

[4] Summary of the Report of the Commission for Socio-Economic Development of the Bantu areas . . . (U.G. 61/55), p. 28, para. 24.

THE GROUP APPROACH

Although increasing industrialization and its accompanying urbanization brought the various races together more closely in the community, this only served to strengthen the fears already held by the white group of subjugation by the more numerous and less advanced non-whites. A study of the figures given above will show the extent to which urban populations have grown during the twentieth century, yet participation in the common economic function by no means lessened the existing prejudice.

Balanced economic growth is unlikely to take place when the factor of production, labour, is not regarded as a whole but is split into racial groups, defined rigidly by legislation with the object of protecting and bolstering the dominant white group, with scant regard for the opinions or welfare of the non-white.

A situation is created in which little or no real attempt is made to evolve a pattern of development formulated in the interests of the community as a whole. Virtually all policy approaches to South African problems have reflected the interests of the white group alone and while the non-whites participate in economic life, the fact that they are—as far as possible—confined to non-competing groups[5] means that at no time has the economy really enjoyed the full advantages which could flow from the over-all labour potential. Professor Frankel has illustrated the stultifying economic consequences of this approach in the case of the Indian community of Natal which was, from the beginning, treated as a distinct group, not integrated with any other. He writes:

This not only inhibited the evolution of a meaningful society for Indians in South Africa, but also froze the economic pattern of the sugar industry itself. The whole economic evolution of Natal was retarded by the failure to establish the Indian immigrants as a creative part of South African society.[6]

As time went on, the dominant white minority became more and more concerned with rigidly defining the role which each racial group could play in the labour market, and this tendency

[5] S. Herbert Frankel, 'Whither South Africa', *S.A. Journal of Economics*, vol. 15, No. 1, 1947, p. 33.
[6] S. Herbert Frankel, *The Economic Impact on Under-developed Societies*, 1953, Essay II, 'Some Aspects of Technical Change', p. 25.

became particularly marked during the years of South Africa's most rapid industrial expansion—that is since the end of the Second World War. In succeeding chapters we shall examine in detail the legislative structure which has been built up to make these divisions and barriers permanent, and to control mobility of all kinds. For the moment, however, we must take account of the make-up of the industrial labour force, both white and non-white, and their attitudes and circumstances; and of the pattern established in the labour market as a whole, which was largely carried over from the mining industry, but was extended by the introduction of a new range of semi-skilled jobs in manufacturing industry.

THE COMPOSITION OF THE LABOUR FORCE: WHITES

The Anglo-Boer War, which ended in 1902, left permanent scars and made difficult a union of the white races. There were, in any case, marked differences in background of the British and other settlers and the Afrikaners. For the most part, the initiators of the new industrialism came from the English-speaking section of the white population: familiarity with the urban environment enabled them to exploit investment opportunities and to take the entrepreneurial advantage. The Afrikaners, on the other hand, at that time were largely rural people, with little urge to migrate to new urban societies. The Afrikaner's longing for the country has been a recurring theme in Afrikaans literature (J. R. L. van Bruggen's poem 'Heimwee' is a good expression of this yearning), and even today it is doubtful whether many Afrikaners would prefer city to rural life if the choice were open to them, though, of course, their achievements in the world of industry, commerce, and finance have been outstanding in recent years.

In the early frontier society wealth played a relatively unimportant part. The trek Boer was similar in some respects to the African, as regards both the nature and paucity of his wants, as was, for example, reflected in his holding of livestock. The frontiersman, on the other hand, sought to acquire land, not so much as a means of obtaining wealth (i.e. value in exchange) but rather as a means of subsistence and as a source of independence.[7] The trek mentality, which had been nurtured by a

[7] See L. C. A. and C. M. Knowles, *The Economic Development of the British Overseas Empire*, 1936, vol. 3, p. 70.

distaste for authority (the Imperial Factor) and encouraged by the abundant lands provided by the moving frontier, allowed a degree of flexibility in farming which, when connected to the Roman-Dutch laws of family equality in inheritance, was to prove incapable of meeting the needs of a settled society.[8] The moving frontier, in fact, made it possible for those whites, who wished, to enjoy the pleasures of the landed estate; while through the convenience of the labour provided by, initially, the slave, then the apprenticed Hottentot, and, finally, the unsettled and detribalized 'Kaffir', it was even possible to enjoy a taste of a feudal aristocratic existence. Professor J. S. Marais comments:

. . . to do slaves' work was beneath the dignity of the sons of free burghers, and so farmers' sons shunned the inhospitable town, and the tradition grew up that there was no occupation worthy of an Afrikaner but that of landholder, except indeed one of the learned professions, to which hardly any rural colonist would aspire in the 17th and 18th centuries.[9]

There was no need to equip oneself for a trade or profession, nor was there any urge for education as an adornment of cultural living. There were in any case few facilities for such pursuits.[10]

In such circumstances, there was little need for money or for skill in managing it. The life, though bleak and often essentially mobile, suited the freedom-loving Afrikaners, for their Puritan background had shaped a race with austere tastes prizing independence above all else. There was little incentive to develop intensive farming, for until the opening up of large-scale mining, there were few outlets for any surplus produce which farmers might be fortunate enough to have. Transport was difficult and journeys to the large centres were only resorted to when necessity dictated. Even after the development of mining, the new demands for agricultural products were not sufficiently tempting to compete with 'the option money' which was offered to farmers by speculators. The consequence of

[8] See W. M. Macmillan, *Complex South Africa*, 1933, p. 81 et seq.
[9] J. S. Marais, *The Cape Coloured People*, 1939, p. 4. See also H. M. Robertson, '150 years of Economic Contact between Black and White', *S.A. Journal of Economics*, 1935, vol. 3, part II, p. 5 et seq.
[10] See de Kiewiet, *History of South Africa*, 1941, p. 184 et seq.; also A. Trollope, *South Africa*, 1878, vol. 2, p. 12 et seq.

mineral right speculation was that farmers tended to neglect the development of their land which they regarded as a speculative asset rather than as an agricultural resource.

Furthermore, the political motives for trekking reduced the desire to retain contact with the settled areas. Those wants which it was not possible to satisfy directly, such as cloth, gunpowder, etc., could be obtained from traders by barter. On the other hand, until at least the latter part of the nineteenth century, the moving frontier allowed scope for continued expansion: there was ample room for all.

The impact of industrialism upon the Afrikaner was not, therefore, so very different from its impact on the African. The moulding of Afrikanerdom had taken place in a setting completely removed from the events which were reshaping the economic life of Europe. When the Great Trek began, there was a consciousness of the political changes which were shaping the destiny of the world, but not perhaps of the even more significant realities of the Industrial Revolution. It was in this atmosphere that the Afrikaner republics were to develop and, by the odd cast of fate, that the process of industrialization was to begin in Africa.

The English, on the other hand, particularly the 1820 settlers and later the mining immigrants, if not born of an industrial society, had close links with it. Viewed in combination with the innate financial instinct of the Jew, this was sufficient to instil a reluctance on the part of the Afrikaners to enter the business sphere, for while they knew something about land, their unfamiliarity with other environments made them suspicious and fearful of falling victim to the wiles of more experienced business men.[11] The fact that it was not the wealthier element among the Afrikaners who migrated to the urban areas, but those who were forced there by impoverished circumstances, was also important,[12] for this produced a desire even among those who later succeeded in urban society, to return to the land and prove themselves as agriculturists. Success in one sphere seldom wholly compensates for failure in another. The alien feeling on the part of the Afrikaner was

[11] See E. G. Malherbe, *Education in South Africa*, p. 19; J. F. W. Grosskopf, *Rural Impoverishment and Rural Exodus*, pp. 115-16, being Parts III and I of the Report of the Carnegie Commission on the Poor White, Stellenbosch, 1932.
[12] See Report of the Transvaal Indigency Commission, 1906-8 (T.G. 13/08).

also accentuated by the fact that the language of the city was English and not Afrikaans. It is only in recent years that Afrikaans has taken its place alongside English as a commercial and industrial medium.

These factors were to be of considerable significance in the economic development of South Africa, and were to play no small part in casting the attitudes of Briton and Boer. Economic thinking was thus subject to the pressures, on the one hand, of the predominantly rural Afrikaner and, on the other, of the predominantly urban English, with the political die cast in favour of agriculture.

In the field of collective bargaining, the restrictionist attitude of the initially predominantly English-speaking skilled workers was to be reinforced by a refusal on the part of the larger section of the Afrikaner people to see any need for a modification of traditional ideas, which saw all manual work in terms of 'Kaffir work'. There were also other influences at work, for while white trade unionists saw the immersion of the non-white into industry as a threat to the privileges of white labour, some liberal-minded sentimentalists saw it as a threat to the simple tribal life of the black man. There was thus from the start a serious contradiction of approach: a refusal on the part of many whites to admit the desirability of allowing non-whites (and particularly the African) the right to participate in the growth of industrialization (even at the lowest level in the labour market) and the unwillingness of the majority of whites to undertake any form of manual work or, at least, to undertake it at a wage-rate which the African was prepared to accept. Industrialists, on the other hand, concerned with maximizing their profits, showed every indication of readiness to meet their needs where the supply was cheapest and the labour most amenable. The concept of 'civilized living' was thus difficult to reconcile with economic reality. Furthermore, agriculturists saw the growth of industry as a threat to their own supply of cheap labour.

The history of the labour market throughout the first half of the twentieth century was consequently to be marked by a growing maze of contradictory compromises, moulded on the one hand by the pressure of change, and on the other by a refusal to meet the needs of change, influenced always by the fundamental differences of approach of the two white sections of the community.

THE PROBLEM OF THE POOR WHITE[13]

(a) The underlying causes

In any society a disruption of status nearly always brings in its wake to those deposed a host of almost insoluble problems of adaptation to changed circumstances, particularly where there is no immediate change in the environment. This is as true of social as of economic life, and indeed in the modern industrial society the closely knit interdependency of the two makes the consequences of disruption of status even greater. This is particularly apparent in the story of white rural impoverishment in South Africa and in the consequent difficulties which these so-called 'Poor Whites' had to face when they forsook their rural environment for the urban areas.

The Poor White problem arose principally because of the failure of agriculture, both as a consequence of the conditions of land tenure and of the circumstances surrounding agriculture itself.

Few of the rural whites were agricultural labourers in the sense known in the older countries, nor were there many tenants at money rent. The majority were of a class which fell somewhere between employee and tenant, and came to be known as 'bywoners'. The Economic and Wage Commission of 1925 described the 'bywoner' as:

the natural product of the increase of population in a self-contained, almost patriarchal, pastoral community. He finds succour for himself from the produce he is enabled to raise with his patron's assistance on land assigned to him by his patron; while the latter secures a more or less effective use of land that he could not use effectively himself, and a number of white assistants, without whom he would be entirely dependent on Native or Coloured labour. The relation under favourable conditions is one that even today meets the needs of both parties, and the system should be reformed and developed rather than extinguished. But it is often an indeterminate relation: the 'bywoner' has security neither of tenure nor of status. The system has no power to hold him to the land when other forces are tending to drive him off the land. Unlike the peasant or occupying owner in

[13] For a full discussion of the Poor White problem see the Report of the Carnegie Commission, Stellenbosch, 1932.

other countries, and unlike the regular labourer for wages in agriculture, the 'bywoner' is attached only loosely to the soil and is steadily being drawn into the towns.[14]

The problem was, of course, intensified as a result of the changes which took place in farming after the turn of the century, when the moving frontier had come to its end and it was no longer possible to trek and find pastures new. This resulted in a transition from extensive pastoral farming to a more settled agricultural pattern and intensive stock-raising, which proved beyond the scope of many traditional farmers.

Furthermore, during the first two decades of the twentieth century, agriculture suffered several severe reverses—the Anglo-Boer War at the beginning of the century had precipitated a major crisis on the land, while there was a collapse in the prices of primary produce after the First World War. In addition, South African farming was constantly subject to such ruinous manifestations as drought, hail, floods, stock and plant diseases, and a variety of pests. The sum of all these adverse circumstances led to the driving of the precariously poised poorer agriculturists from the land.

(b) The nature of the problem

The uniqueness of the Poor White problem was not poverty, nor its dimensions, but the state of mind which accompanied it. Here were people who had enjoyed in some measure or other a 'landed' status, finding themselves in a new environment, which did not always come up to expectations,[15] and being forced through their ill-equipment to compete with persons whom the dictates of their tradition classed as inferior. To many the humiliation proved too much and it was often considered preferable to accept poor relief or even face starvation, rather than take labouring jobs or 'Kaffir work'; a fair proportion turned to the alluvial diamond diggings in the hope that a series of lucky finds would restore their 'status'.[16]

[14] Report of the Economic and Wage Commission, 1925 (U.G. 14/26), p. 106, para. 181.
[15] The Report of the Industrial Legislation Commission, 1935 (U.G. 37/35), pointed out (para. 108) that many rural whites failed to appreciate the harsh realities of town life, being drawn there by the deceptive 'glitter of urban wage rates'.
[16] See the Report of the Transvaal Indigency Commission, op. cit., para. 67, and the 2nd Interim Report of the Unemployment Commission, 1921 (U.G. 34/21), p. 4, para. 19.

The Poor Whites constituted a serious economic as well as a psychological problem; the Carnegie Commission estimated, in 1932, that about 10 per cent of the white population or 220,000 people could be regarded as 'Poor Whites'. The existence of an unemployment problem of such dimensions played an important part in preventing sophisticated non-whites from advancing in the job scale, for traditional prejudice would not allow any non-white advance in the face of white unemployment. Furthermore, the idea that no non-white was legitimately entitled to employment of any kind as long as white unemployment persisted, led to the policy of substituting white for non-white workers. Substitution was a feature largely peculiar to government employment, but to some extent private enterprises particularly the trades, were forced to follow suit as a result of the pressure of public opinion.

It was thus not difficult to see why the problem occupied the attention of commission after commission, yet in the long run, its solution rested with events rather than man's deliberate designs, largely because of the failure to treat poverty on a national rather than a sectional basis. Nevertheless, even today, the ghost of the Poor White problem hovers on the fringe of South African thought.

(c) Attempted solutions and their impact on the economy

The universality of poverty was such that its prevalence in the South African economy was not of any particular significance in comparison with elsewhere. The growing demands in most countries for a redistribution of wealth so that the poor could have more and the rich less were, however, wholly inapplicable to the South African scene. Fabulous individual fortunes had, of course, been made in mining, but the country as a whole was comparatively poor. The 1925 Economic and Wage Commission estimated the Union's national income at £186 million, with agriculture contributing £47 million, mining £37 million, and manufacturing industry £31 million. *Per capita* income was approximately £26. The solution to poverty in South Africa lay, therefore, not so much in questions of distribution or fairer shares, but rather in seeking ways and means of enlarging the national product. It was perhaps a pity that a great deal of the energies of planning were absorbed not so much in the overriding problem of economic growth, which necessitates a consideration of the problem as a whole and not in racially isolated compartments, but in the creation of artificial bolsters to Poor Whites, which had the negative aim of preventing Europeans from sinking socially and economically to a level below what may be described as the *white survival line*, i.e. the line separating what was considered to be civilized living from so-called uncivilized living.

The maintenance of 'civilized standards' was the main platform of the Nationalist-Labour Pact Government of 1924, so that a good part of official policy was directed to this end, both administratively and legislatively.

General Hertzog, the then Prime Minister, sought to define 'civilized standards' in an official circular (No. 5 of 1924): 'Civilized labour is to be considered as the labour rendered by persons whose standard of living conforms to the standard generally recognized as *tolerable from the usual European standpoint*' (my italics). The concept of civilized living was thus arbitrary and dependent upon definition. In keeping with the group approach, the tendency has been for a sliding scale of interpretation, so that the 'tolerable European standard' has tended to be raised in keeping with economic development, on the implied assumption that a gap between white and non-white should be maintained; with no direct competition at any employment level.

At the time the Economic and Wage Commission had doubts as to whether such standards could be easily assessed in monetary terms:

The pseudo-scientific estimates of the amounts on which a worker can maintain himself and a family have no absolute authority or universal validity. They are merely rationalized and systematized budgets of typical wage-earning households which, in the circumstances of the time and country in which they are made, would be regarded as just lifted above the level of want. It is impossible to define and express in figures any 'just', 'fair' or 'civilized' wage and apply it to particular disputes.[17]

The 1937 Cape Coloured Commission on the other hand had this to say:

[17] U.G. 14/26, p. 200, para. 96.

The system of determining empirically different standards of living
for sections of the population leads to anomalies and injustice and
the Commission is of the opinion that a better system is to extend
opportunities to each section of the community to improve its
economic position to the fullest extent.[18]

In any event, even isolated action based on the concept of
'civilized labour' and which aimed at the broadening of opportunities for whites could only become effective or feasible when
the Poor Whites were suitably equipped for advancement.
This meant the extension of training facilities. The failure, at
the same time, to appreciate the value of concentrating efforts
to effect simultaneous broadening of non-white opportunities,
meant the loss to the economy of the obvious advantages of
an over-all increase in productivity and effective demand.
Professor Henry Clay pointed out as early as 1930 that:

every increase in the Native's economic capacity, every extension
in his economic range, by increasing his output, increases in the
same degree his power to purchase . . . and so offers a market for
an increased output of goods in general, in which additional White
labour will find employment.[19]

(d) Changes in job stratification in the labour market and the race problem

A broadening of opportunities came, nevertheless, with the
growth of secondary industry, when the stratification of the
labour market slowly changed and allowed a more even
gradation of skill. The old rigid division between the skilled
and unskilled worker gave way to a more gradual slope and
resulted in the emergence of a new class of worker in the
labour market, who could neither be described as skilled nor as
unskilled, but rather as 'semi-skilled'.

Skilled work in this context may be described as that requiring
a measure of craftsmanship for which specialized training or
experience is essential. Unskilled work is taken to refer to tasks
requiring little or no intelligence or training—the worker being
needed solely as a source of power. It was, of course, this
'muscle and brawn' work which basically formed what was

[18] Commission of Enquiry regarding the Cape Coloured Population, 1937
(U.G. 54/37), p. 32, para. 141; see also R. F. A. Hoernlé, *South African Native
Policy and the Liberal Spirit*, 1945, p. 22 et seq.; also the Report of the Industrial
Legislation Commission, op. cit., p. 35.
[19] Report on Industrial Relations in Southern Rhodesia, 1930, paras. 122-3.

looked upon as 'Kaffir work' and considered beneath the dignity of whites. The 1908 Transvaal Indigency Commission regarded this aversion to undertake Kaffir work as being at the root of the Poor White problem. On the other hand by 1925 the Economic and Wage Commission was somewhat optimistically postulating that 'the prejudice against taking unskilled work, on the ground that it is "Kaffirs' work" . . . has diminished and is gradually disappearing'. It would seem, however, that even to this day feelings about 'Kaffir work' remain strong. In 1958, for example, an experiment which was attempted at the University of Stellenbosch, as part of a drive of character building, to encourage students to clean their own rooms and make their own beds, ended in failure due to widespread objection based on the argument that this was in fact 'Kaffir work'.[20]

The bulk of the Poor Whites were not in any way qualified to undertake skilled work, and a fair percentage were, furthermore, not fitted to undertake the training necessary to qualify, or were too old to enter into apprenticeship schemes.[21] The only alternative means of qualifying for more skilled work was to enter a particular field on the lower levels and gradually work up to more responsible positions, as was the custom in the older industrialized countries, such as the United Kingdom. This practice was, however, made extremely difficult by the aversion on the part of most Poor Whites to undertake 'Kaffir work', even if this did not entail actually working alongside Africans.

Some of the benefits of industrialism were counterbalanced by the enactment of minimum wage laws; it has been argued and quite rightly, that the industrial wage-regulating legislation had the effect of excluding many Poor Whites along with non-whites from occupations where minimum wages were sufficiently high to make it unprofitable for employers to employ them. In such circumstances it might thus be possible to justify State relief programmes but only where they were regarded as stop-gap measures and not seriously considered permanent expedients as racial bolsters. There are very real dangers to the

[20] See Report in *Die Burger* of 6 November 1958, and leading article which appeared in the same paper on 10 November 1958.
[21] See J. R. Albertyn, *The Poor White and Society*, being Part V of the Report of the Carnegie Commission on the Poor White Problem, 1932, particularly chapter 1, p. 3 et seq.

economy as a whole where important sectors become rehabilitating points with disregard of cost and based solely on the need to protect a single racial group. In 1934-5, for example, Europeans constituted 66·3 per cent of all government workers but received 91 per cent of the over-all wage-bill. Furthermore, the average European wage of £233·7 per year was £30 *more* than the average paid in industry, while that for non-whites was £47 per year and £2 *less* than the average for non-whites in industry.[22]

The policy of substituting whites for non-whites in various government departments at subsidized wages met with the following comment from the 1925 Economic and Wage Commission: 'Unless strict and continuous account of the results of such substitution is kept, however, the need for making the policy pay its own way may be overlooked, and an undue cost incurred in substituting Europeans in posts in which they cannot be as economical as Native labour.'[23] On the other hand there is also the risk that such protection will reduce the incentive of the protected to equip themselves for more useful roles in society. On this question the 1940 Industrial and Agricultural Requirements Commission commented:

The civilized labour policy in public works does not, however, contribute most effectively towards the rehabilitation of these people ('civilized' unskilled workers). . . . by providing them with a reasonable living, it keeps them employed permanently on work which is not commensurate with their innate potentialities, so that they possess little opportunity and even less incentive for self-development.

The Commission further criticized as restrictive the payment of 'unskilled' wages based on journeymen's rates of pay as a result of a generous interpretation of unskilled work.[24] As will be seen the position changed substantially following the period of rapid expansion after 1939, when it became necessary to fill many categories of jobs in the sphere of government formerly occupied by Europeans with non-whites.

The more ambitious scheme of the Labour/Nationalist Government of solving the problem by the exclusion of the non-white from the industrial sphere was even less feasible. It is difficult to envisage a situation in which the industrial and

[22] S. Herbert Frankel, *Capital Investment in Africa*, 1938, p. 137.
[23] U.G. 14/26, p. 135, para. 243.
[24] U.G. 40/41, para. 171.

agricultural sections of the population are divided strictly on race criteria, which in effect means the creation of two communities within one society—an industrial white community and a primitive, largely non-white, community based on subsistence farming. The artificial barrier of race would have meant, even with advanced agricultural methods, the arbitrary removal of an entire people from the industrial sphere, many of whom might be better suited to industry than agriculture, and many of whom were already permanently settled in the industrial sphere.

In any event, there is little evidence to suggest that with the total exclusion of the non-white from the industrial community, and in the absence of large-scale immigration of basic white labour, local Europeans could have been pursuaded to undertake manual work. During the last half-century there have been many vain pleas from politicians to their supporters to develop a consciousness of the dignity of labour, as a cornerstone of separate development. Even the most ardent separationist has not succeeded in evolving an acceptable, practical scheme. Writing as late as 1958, an Afrikaner intellectual complained that 'far too many Europeans of both language groups and members of the major political parties have grown so accustomed to seeing menial work done by non-Europeans, that they do not want to go along with it', thus creating 'a hurdle in the way of separate development of far greater weight than all foreign criticism and antagonism to official policy'.[25]

The development described above of a gradation of jobs in the sphere of manufacturing industry meant that, initially, the ill-equipped Poor Whites could be accommodated at levels above those which were regarded as only fit for the inferior races. The new categories of semi-skilled jobs, which largely involved machine-minding of one kind or another, did not call for a very high degree of intelligence and required the minimum of formal training. The very nature of these jobs thus provided a convenient means by which the Poor White could be readily absorbed into a useful occupation while, at the same time, receiving a wage approximating to the so-called civilized standard.

The majority of the non-whites were occupied in basic

[25] Prof. J. H. Coetzee writing in the *Rand Daily Mail* of 24 November 1958.

labouring jobs, and in such circumstances, the purely industrial problems which stemmed from the migratory system of African labour were not of immediate consequence. The fact that workers seldom remained in a particular job longer than eight or nine months was of less importance where the workers concerned were engaged in tasks requiring no training, and while there was an adequate reserve of manpower. From the industrial point of view, the migratory system was only to become a serious consideration once industry had developed to a point where its needs for semi-skilled, as well as for skilled workers, were such that they could not be supplied solely from the ranks of the Europeans, and where supplies of African labour were becoming relatively less abundant.

THE CHALLENGE TO INDUSTRY

It is outside the scope of this work to consider the organization of agricultural labour in South Africa, nor it is possible to undertake an analysis of the consequences of the use, by agriculturists, of their considerable political powers to influence the pattern of the labour market as a whole to suit their own requirements. Agriculture has rigidly clung to an archaic eighteenth-century paternal system, totally unsuited to the needs of a modern economy, while at the same time it has succeeded in repeatedly exempting itself from all forms of advanced industrial legislation. On the other hand, the industrial pattern has been further warped by the pressures exerted by mining interests, stemming from their need to retain the migratory system.

Today, however, with the increasing participation of Afrikaners in industrial activity, a new pressure group is being slowly moulded, embracing both English and Afrikaner, which may well become a force capable of altering the structure of the South African labour market. The fact that industry now constitutes the most important sector in the South African economy should encourage industrialists to use whatever powers are available to them to induce the country as a whole to accept the changes necessary to bring South Africa into line with other modern industrial states.

6

The Spread
of Industrialization

THE PART
PLAYED BY THE
NON-WHITE POPULATION

THE AFRICANS

(a) Introduction to the industrial society

WHEREAS THE INDUSTRIALLY uninitiated white workers shared with the industrially uninitiated Africans a similar helplessness in the new, industrial environment, they faced it in different circumstances. In both cases rural impoverishment was the underlying motive for their migration to the industrial centres (though the African was also affected by the external compulsive agents described in chapter 3), but the partly emerged African, in contrast to the white worker, could regard his earnings in the town as a subsidy to the proceeds of his rural plot, and consequently was able to exist more easily on a low money wage. The fact that the migratory system allowed the payment of lower wages to Africans than would have been possible under other circumstances, was of course an important influence working towards the permanent retention of the system, especially in the case of the gold-mining industry. In the course of time, however, the growing bankruptcy of the Reserves, and the fact that many Africans had settled permanently in the towns, meant that the low non-white wage was not supplemented from other sources and a serious socio-economic problem has resulted.

Apart from the pattern already set by the mining industry of a low non-white wage-rate, and the employment of migrant African workers, the most significant difference between the circumstances of the poor African and the poor white was the potent reality of the white vote, as opposed to the virtually complete political powerlessness of the African, who therefore had no means of bringing about changes or improvements in his conditions of employment by his own efforts.

It must also be remembered that the African coming to work in the industrial environment encounters immense problems of cultural change. In the transition from the primitive, tribal agricultural environment to the advanced industrial economy, he has to adapt himself to a new, higher way of life, with an entirely different set of spiritual and material norms from those to which he has been accustomed: old ways and old beliefs must give way to new. There is a tremendous gap to be bridged between a modern industrial society and a tribal system based upon communal land ownership and dominated by magic and superstition.[1] It may even happen that wages outstrip the growth of new wants because of a failure to appreciate and understand the use of money, which is alien to the traditions and concepts of primitive, barter economies.[2]

It is possible to formulate a pattern showing the attunement of the African to industrial society: *firstly*, there is the process of introduction, *secondly*, the process of adaptation, and *thirdly*, the process of absorption. These three phases should not be thought of as rigidly separate, for even in the individual case there will be some overlapping, while at any given time there may be a greater number of Africans in one particular stage of attunement, which will therefore be more apparent than the others. In South Africa, for instance, the process of introduction was predominant in the late nineteenth and early twentieth centuries, with the opening up of the mines, but it gradually merged into the second stage of adaptation, while the third stage, of absorption into the industrial economy, can now be said to be running parallel with the second, the first having been largely accomplished. It is to be expected that as Africans pass into the second and third stages, and become increasingly familiar with the more sophisticated society they have entered, they will not only develop new material wants and new patterns of behaviour, but that they will also widen their ambitions for

[1] See F. Rodseth, 'Natives and the Gremlins of the Mines', *Optima*, March 1956.
[2] See the 1925 Economic and Wage Commission Report, op. cit., p. 92, para. 151; also the report of the Native Economic Commission 1930-2 (U.G. 22/32), p. 3, paras. 8-15; p. 30, paras 199-208.

advancement, socially, economically and politically, and the erection of artificial barriers to progress in any of these directions is unlikely to enhance their usefulness as productive members of society.

In South Africa, the retention of the migratory system has tended to blur the separate identification of the stages of attunement, which have, in any case, been slowed up both by the existence of white prejudice towards non-whites, and by the handicaps suffered by the emerging Africans who were thrust into a strange way of life, alien to their own, and required to learn new languages and adjust themselves to a different moral code, while at the same time adapting their habits to the disciplined nature of industrial society, with its emphasis on punctuality and regular hours of work. The understandable clumsiness with which Africans have often faced these problems has served to encourage white prejudice and feelings of superiority, while their reluctance to leave their primitive environment and eagerness to return to it tend to reduce their usefulness as industrial workers. No one can give his best in a society which he feels he has been driven to enter, or in which he feels he is not wanted, other than as a provider of basic labour.

Furthermore, the maze of legal restrictions which regulate the African's life in urban areas is not conducive to the development of a sense of social and economic responsibility, or of a liking for the urban environment, quite apart from the contradiction to the requirements of an expanding economy which such restrictions represent. As will be shown in succeeding chapters, these legal barriers have, over the years, become increasingly rigid and complicated, and flexibility in the labour market has become the exception rather than the rule. While many Africans have taken advantage of such opportunities for advancement as have presented themselves, particularly to enter the teaching and other professions, the majority are forced to remain on the lowest rungs of the employment ladder, in spite of a growing shortage of labour in the middle and higher levels of employment.

(b) The subsistence economy

Throughout the foregoing chapters we have seen how the African entered the exchange economy as a seller of labour and how, like the rural Poor White, he was drawn townwards by the interaction of two forces: on the one hand the impelling force of rural poverty, and on the other the attraction of urban opportunity. True there may also have been some sense of adventure, but it would be avoiding the real issues to place too much emphasis on this aspect.

At the root of the matter lay the inability of an outmoded agricultural system to support the needs of its people in a changing environment. It would be too much to expect a primitive, pre-wheel economy even barely to satisfy the requirements of a people not only increasing in numbers but continually broadening their orbit of wants under the impact of the exchange economy. Furthermore, the needs of Bantu agricultural organization could not be met once all available land had been taken up, while the anti-progressive tribal system allowed little flexibility in the subsistence methods of agriculture practised by the Bantu. To be effective, any improvement required a change in the very basis of society. The impact of modernity has, of course, had a disintegrating effect, but the tribal subsistence economy remains at the foundations of the rural Bantu society, acting as a barrier to progress and to the efforts of hard-working officials.

All subsistence farming is in essence extensive and wasteful and that practised under the tribal organization of the Bantu is no exception.[3] In the last resort, the all-important factor is land. In the past as the population increased, new lands were sought out and as one area was exhausted it was abandoned and new areas brought into cultivation. Where others stood in the way of expansion a struggle for supremacy followed, with the weaker succumbing to the stronger. Such Malthusian checks certainly helped to relieve the pressure on the land, but life was mainly a bare existence, veering unevenly from feast to famine as nature dictated. In such circumstances, where so much rested upon chance, it is small wonder that the great mass of the people should be caught up in a mesh of taboo, superstition and fatalism.

There were other equally stultifying practices. The greater

[3] For detailed discussion of the problems of the Reserves see the various volumes of the *Keiskamahoek Rural Survey*, 1952, and the Reports of a series of Commissions, particularly that of the Tomlinson Commission (U.G. 61/55), the Native Economic Commission (U.G. 22/32), and the various apposite Reports of the Social and Economic Planning Council, especially U.G. 32/46.

part of the land was communal pasture, and cattle-holding was a cult so that the already overburdened land was forced to carry the additional weight of too much livestock. While such a system was allowed to remain it was futile to attempt to educate the people in new methods, and as there were no scientific methods of farming, the rape of the land was pursued with complete disregard for the future. It was as if time stood still in relation to human endeavour, but not in relation to the destruction of the soil. With the old lands rapidly deteriorating and with no new land becoming available the only outlet for the growing population was migration.

European farms provided a shelter for many families and labour was given in return for the right to squat. But for increasing numbers it was the towns which provided a means of 'escape'. Some migrated as family units, settling as town-dwellers and bringing up their children outside the orbit of tribalism. These were to form the nucleus of a new and developed African people—no longer backward or primitive but caught up tightly in the urban industrial machine and appreciative of its products—a people differing only in colour from the industrial workers of any large city.

It would be as unrealistic to ignore the facts of this advancement as it would be to ignore the fact of the essential primitiveness of tribalism. The urban African may be conscious of the drawbacks of town life and will often express his yearnings for his rural origin in a variety of ways but this does not mean that there are no African town-dwellers, or that all Africans are longing for a return to tribalism. The widening opportunities open to the urban African have stimulated latent aspirations and have encouraged the growth of a new *élite* with little or no contact with the backward areas and acknowledging no adherence to tribal authority. In fact they have become a distinct part of the socio-economic pattern of South Africa; while it may be possible to ignore their existence in the short run, to plan without considering them may be dangerous and in the long run even disastrous. Official policy would appear not to admit to these facts; it is perhaps apposite to quote the then Secretary for Native Affairs in this regard:

. . . many people have the wrong impression that there are two kinds of Bantu in South Africa: those who live in the Bantu reserves and those who have made their homes with the White people in the rest of the country. That is not so. All the Bantu have their permanent homes in the reserves and their entry into other areas and the urban centres is merely of a temporary nature and for economic reasons. In other words they are admitted as work-seekers, not as settlers.[4]

But for the majority the escape valve became the migratory system, through which it was possible to subsidize the rural home without having to give it up. The practice was adopted by all rural Africans both in the Reserves and on European farms, and relatively few remain untouched by the system; it has been shown that upwards of 50 per cent of the able-bodied men are away from the Reserves at any given moment.[5] The writer himself found that in Cape Town only a small percentage of the African workers in that city were stabilized.[6]

The necessity for the men to go out and seek a money wage to bring the sub-subsistence economy to a level of subsistence has been repeatedly shown;[7] improvements have not come with the passage of time, and the pressure of population has become greater. Yet while it has become increasingly imperative for the male inhabitants to earn money in order to save the rural family from starvation, the drawbacks of the migratory system merely intensify the adverse pressures. There is a vicious circle in operation reducing the already low productivity of the areas; many families are left without anyone to plough or to harvest, while desertions by male migrants may occur, although Professor Hobart Houghton is of the opinion that 'comparatively few married men *abscond* and the vast majority, even if they have been absent for a long time, return eventually to their families'.[8] As the worker himself becomes more attuned to urban society he shows less inclination for agricultural production and tends to regard the life in the Reserves as primitive. In any event the Africans have shown that they may,

[4] W. W. M. Eiselen, 'Harmonious multi-community development', *Optima*, March 1959.

[5] D. Hobart Houghton and Edith M. Walton, *The Economy of a Native Reserve*, Keiskamahoek Rural Survey, 1952, vol. 2.

[6] See G. V. Doxey, 'Fabcor', unpublished thesis, University of Cape Town, 1956.

[7] See the interesting discussion in *Present inter-relations in Central African rural and urban life*, Rhodes-Livingstone Institute, 1958, and particularly Prof. Clyde Mitchell's 'Factors motivating migration from the rural areas' (p. 12 et seq.), in which he examines and evaluates the views and findings of a number of authorities on the reasons for such migration.

[8] D. Hobart Houghton, op. cit., p. 128.

in fact, be capable of becoming far better industrial workers than farmers; they have exhibited a particular aptitude for repetitive factory work.[9]

The absence of significant attempts to overcome the problems of the Reserves could not be blamed on a lack of knowledge of the facts; economists and others were continually drawing attention to the need for development of the latent possibilities of these areas and to the part which the Reserves could play in attuning the African population to the requirements of the modern economy.[10] As early as 1930 the Native Economic Commission saw the backwardness of the Reserves as being at the root of urban poverty and saw the cure as a 'wise, courageous forward policy of development of the reserves':

The economic development of the Reserves—which postulates social and educational development . . . of the Natives in those areas —transcends in importance every other phase of the Native economic policy. It affects directly a very large proportion of the Native population. Indirectly it is at the root of the whole Native economic question. The undeveloped state of the Reserves, with the consequent pressure of the population on the land, is largely the cause of the universal Native demand for more land. It is directly one of the important causes of the steady drift to towns: the dead uniformity of life in the Reserves results in an emigration of a large number of Natives who desire to follow occupations other than primitive pastoralism and peasant farming. This includes many of the more advanced Natives. The Reserve Natives are thus continually being deprived of many of their people who, by following more advanced methods, would gradually work like a leaven throughout Reserve communities. . . .[11]

(c) The migratory system

In the beginning, at least, the migratory system was able to play some part in effecting a smooth transition from the subsistence tribal economy to that of the more advanced industrial system. By coming to the mines, or later, to the towns, for periods of work and then returning home, Africans were able to maintain an effective link with the rural areas.

[9] See the interesting discussion by S. Biesheuvel, 'The occupational abilities of Africans', *Optima*, March 1952, p. 18. In addition, among the growing volume of literature on the subject, see particularly *The African Factory Worker*, University of Natal (1950).

[10] See particularly S. Herbert Frankel, *The Economic Impact on under-developed societies*, 1952; T. Soper, 'Labour Migration and Labour Productivity', *Race Relations Journal*, vol. XXV, Nos. 3 and 4, 1958.

[11] U.G. 22/32, p. 15, paras. 96 and 85.

The 1925 Economic and Wage Commission, for example, argued in favour of a *transitional* retention of the system on the grounds that it eased the problem of adaptation and checked tendencies towards demoralization.

The low non-white wage-rate which the migratory system made possible was not the only factor which contributed towards its permanent establishment as a feature of the mining industry. In fact, there have never been clear-cut alternatives, partly because in the early days people feared the prospect of a settled African population around the mines which were, in any case, expected to be of limited life, and partly because the industry became increasingly dependent upon labour from outside the Union of South Africa, i.e. Portuguese East Africa, the High Commission territories and the tropical African countries. In such circumstances, it was difficult to encourage a permanent or semi-permanent migration of the African family unit, and in any case official policy has been consistently against the stabilization of African workers about the gold-mines.[12]

Nevertheless, criticism of the use of migrant labour and arguments in favour of the stabilization and training of African mine-workers date from early in the history of the gold-mining industry. Giving evidence before the Industrial Commission of Enquiry, in 1897, Mr. H. Jennings said:

If they [the Africans] are given facilities for making their homes in this country, and they could be induced to remain with us, I am satisfied that their efficiency could be increased two-fold, and that they could even be trained to do much higher grade work than they are now employed at.[13]

In 1914, General W. C. Gorgas, of Panama Canal fame, strongly recommended stabilization for health reasons, and because:

a Native labour force living with their families near the mine would be more stable and contented than the present force. They would be old and experienced men, and therefore more efficient and from all points of view more economical and satisfactory to the mine manager than the present force.[14]

---

[12] See S. T. van der Horst, *Native Labour in South Africa*, 1942, p. 188.

[13] Industrial Commission of Enquiry, 1897, evidence H. Jennings, pp. 218-20.

[14] Recommendations as to sanitation concerning employees of the mines on the Rand made to the Transvaal Chamber of Mines by W. C. Gorgas, Surgeon-Gen., U.S. Army; Chief Sanitary Officer, Isthmian Canal Commission, Johannesburg, 1914, pp. 13-17. See also 3rd Interim Report of the Dominions Royal Commission, 1914 (Cd. 7505), p. 16 et seq.

The acceptance of the permanency of the migratory system in the economy as a whole was influenced by additional considerations than the example of the mining industry, and the African's own disinclination to sever his ties with the Reserves. While on the one hand, the dictates of industrialism and of social conscience have always favoured a complete breakaway by the African from the indigenous economy, with resulting stabilization in the industrial sphere, white opinion as a whole has not looked with favour on large-scale African family settlement in urban areas. At first, the nature of the basic tasks performed by Africans, and the steady flow of replacements for those going back to the Reserves, meant that it was possible for employers to tolerate the migratory system, in spite of all its serious shortcomings.

The result has been that the socio-economic pattern of African life has become firmly founded upon the migratory system, with stabilization the exception rather than the rule.[15] The shortcomings of the system from the point of view of the economy, leaving out of consideration the moral and social issues involved, became more apparent after its acceptance as the pattern for the industrial labour market as a whole, for while it is possible to argue that it suited both the peculiar needs of the diamond- and gold-mining industries, and the highly organized system of labour recruitment of the Chamber of Mines,[16] it has proved itself largely inadequate to fulfil the more exacting requirements of secondary industry. It is becoming an increasingly ill-afforded expedient to permit a large part of the industrial labour force to spend the major part of its aggregate working life in the subsistence economy. Not only is there a considerable loss of productivity through this non-wage-earning existence, but a great deal of productive energy and time is dissipated in the process of moving between the two sectors of the economy. Furthermore, the system allows little scope for improving worker efficiency; the comparatively

[15] For a technical discussion of the measurement of stabilization, see J. C. Mitchell, 'Urbanisation, Detribalisation and Stabilisation in Southern Africa' in 'Social Implications of Industrialisation and Urbanisation in Africa South of the Sahara', *UNESCO*, 1956, p. 693.

[16] The bulk of African labour for the gold-mines is obtained through two recruiting organizations, the Witwatersrand Native Labour Association (which has the monopoly of recruiting in Portuguese East Africa) and the Native Recruiting Corporation. For a detailed discussion of recruitment see S. T. v. d. Horst, op. cit., p. 191 et seq.

short time which the average migrant worker spends in the industrial environment reduces the chances of his being properly trained for his job, and constitutes an important barrier to advancement, even where rigidities within the labour market do not operate too strongly. In the words of the Report of the 1948 Native Laws (Fagan) Commission:

In view of the time spent by the labourer in his journeys to and fro, the periods of idleness involved in change of work, and the inability of a labourer who moves from job to job to acquire a high standard of knowledge, skill and interest in respect of any particular work, the migratory system is wasteful and uneconomic.[17]

There is further economic waste through the loss of potential demand. As more Africans become stabilized, their purchasing power expands as a result of their greater earning capacity, and the increased aggregate demand generated in this way has a 'multiplier' effect throughout the economy. The editor of a leading non-European periodical estimated in 1959 that 60 per cent of African purchasing power is concentrated in the urban areas.[18]

It is important to bear in mind that existing legislation virtually precludes any African advancement in gold-mining, because of the colour bar arrangements of the Mines and Works Act which, as will be seen in the next chapter, largely originated in the 1918 *status quo* agreement and the 1922 revolt of white workers. Also, the bulk of the labour used on the mines is contractual, so that there is some guarantee of labour continuity. About 65 per cent of African labour on the gold-mines is recruited under contract entered into in the African's home area for a minimum period of about 270 shifts (approximately nine months). About 25 per cent is recruited through the 'assisted voluntary scheme', in terms of which the African signs an undertaking to apply for employment within thirty days. In both cases, fares are returned after 270 shifts have been worked. The remainder of the workers are voluntary, being engaged locally. The annual turnover on the mines is about 90 per cent every eighteen months, and the average period worked is about fourteen months.

[17] U.G. 28/48, p. 43, para. 8.
[18] See report of address given by Mr. T. Hopkinson, editor of *Drum*, in the *Rand Daily Mail* of 17 April 1959.

In contrast, secondary industry relies on a supply of 'free labour'. The influx control regulations (discussed below in chapter 8) do not bind workers to serve employers for any given period, and even where direction of labour is in operation, the worker can at any time leave his employment if he is intending to return to the Reserves. There is consequently little stability, with turnover at times reaching phenomenal proportions. The writer found in Cape Town that the turnover of migrant workers reached a figure of 800 per cent per annum in some cases, and few of them remained longer than three months in a single job.[19] It is obvious, therefore, that although there are more opportunities for advancement in secondary industry, with a range of semi-skilled jobs open to Africans, few are likely to reach a degree of proficiency which would qualify them to hold such jobs.

Furthermore, while on the mines the compound system met many needs, it would obviously be impossible for every industrial employer to provide his African workers with anything on the lines of the elaborate hostel, feeding and recreational facilities made available by the gold and other mining companies. In addition to the provision of adequate housing and other amenities, the continuance and extension of the migratory system to all branches of industry has brought about tremendous human problems in the absence of normal family life and in the social disintegration which accompanies the change in environment. The industrial migrant worker came into contact with a new environment, and was usually surrounded by slum conditions of living, with all the inherent temptations of urban squalor and without the stability and moral encouragement of his own family beside him. Indeed, the fact that many Africans express a preference for the migratory system probably stems from the circumstances which surround urban employment for them, and there is little incentive, or official encouragement, for them to remain permanently in the urban areas.[20]

[19] See S. T. v. d. Horst, 'A Note on Native Labour Turnover and the structure of the Labour force in the Cape Peninsula', *S.A. Journal of Economics*, December 1957, p. 275.
[20] See J. Irving, 'Factors Inimical to African Production' in *Present Interrelations in Central African rural and urban life*, Rhodes-Livingstone Institute, February 1958, p. 95.

COLOURED AND INDIAN PEOPLES

If South Africa had been peopled by only two races, the Europeans and Africans, the problem of dividing work spheres might have proved less exacting: it might even have been possible, in the early days at least, to have dealt successfully with the question of race by way of a group approach. As it is, however, there are, in addition to the Europeans and Africans, the Cape Coloured people and the Indians. As they are largely concentrated in the two provinces of the Cape and Natal (approximately 90 per cent of the Coloured people are resident in the Cape and over 80 per cent of the Indian population live in Natal) there is the temptation to regionalize their significance, particularly as they have played no major part in the development of gold-mining and are thus largely outside the orbit of South Africa's industrial heart. Nevertheless, the Indians comprise 3 per cent of the total population of the Union and the Coloured people 9·4 per cent, and their importance in the economy as a whole, particularly as agricultural workers, in the field of secondary and tertiary industry, and in domestic service of all kinds, must be recognized and no survey of the labour market in the Union would be complete without consideration of these two numerically less important racial groups.

The early history of the Coloured and Indian people in South African society has been sketched in an earlier chapter, and in this chapter the discussion will be restricted to their role in the industrialized economy and their significance as determining factors in the formation of policy relating to the labour market as a whole.

(a) The Coloured people

Until comparatively recent times, the Coloured people were regarded as an appendage to the European population: economically, therefore, and to a lesser extent politically, they have considered themselves—and have been considered—as closely linked with the European group. Official policy relating to non-whites has not always automatically included the Coloured people and until the changes brought about prior to the 1958 General Election, Coloured males in the Cape enjoyed political franchise on a qualified basis.

Prior to the establishment of industries on a considerable scale in the Cape Town area, the bulk of the Coloured people were employed in manual work and in other forms of unskilled labour of a kind which was undertaken by Africans in other provinces. Furthermore, a fair proportion of the Coloured people were involved in some way or another in agriculture, so that the problem of rural impoverishment affected the Coloured people almost as much as it did the Europeans. There was the same drift to the towns and similar problems of adjustment to urban life, with the accompanying feeling of strangeness in a new environment which characterized the rural dispossessed Poor White.[21] Initially, the drift away from the land by Europeans relieved to some extent the pressures upon the Coloured agricultural worker, but circumstances were soon to force the Coloured to follow suit. More recently, the increasing shortage of farm-workers has been met partly by mechanization and partly by employing African labour.

The problems which faced the Coloured man in the new environment differed somewhat from those encountered by the European and African; he had in the first place to face two competing groups; on the one hand, the African who was able to compete with him at a low wage and, on the other hand, the European, who was able to use the racial 'closed shop' principle to restrict the avenues of employment open to the Coloured people. It was not always possible for a Coloured person to find someone who was prepared to apprentice him, even where he had the required qualifications: exclusion was thus effected through colour bias selection, rather than by legal disqualification.

In the second place, the Coloured people's way of life approximated closely to that of the whites, and few of them originated in environmental conditions similar to those of the tribal Africans. Their home language was Afrikaans, and in some cases, English, and the only feature distinguishing them from the white group was their mixed blood. Socially, they were placed in a position of inferiority vis-à-vis the dominant white group, to which they themselves turned in a feeling of kinship. From the economic point of view, the effectiveness of the

[21] See the Report of the Commission of Enquiry on the Cape Coloured Population of the Union, 1937 (U.G. 54/37), ch. IV, p. 32 et seq.

Coloured people has been conditioned by the psychological complexes which stem from their origins, by conventional and, more recently, legal barriers to their advancement, and by the low standards of health, housing and education to which the majority of them are subject.

It is, of course, extremely difficult to define with any degree of accuracy what constitutes a Coloured person, a difficulty illustrated by recent legislation which frequently defines the European, Asiatic and African, in positive terms, and the Coloured person negatively as anyone who is not a member of the other racial groups. In some cases, definition itself is rendered superfluous because of the impossibility of identifying a person as Coloured, and many people who cannot be identified in this way have chosen to become part of the white group by 'passing' the colour line. Commenting on this practice, the 1937 Cape Coloured Commission wrote:

Due, however, to a number of social and economic disabilities affecting the Cape Coloured, and still to be discussed, which have in some respects become more severe in latter years, there is an increasing tendency for the Cape Coloured to 'pass over the line' if their appearance enables them to do so. There is ample evidence that a number of Coloured persons have already 'passed over' and been absorbed in the European population. The Cape Coloured are well aware of what is taking place. It is important, however, for the individual who attempts to 'pass over' that this fact should not be known to the European community of which he desires to become a member; so that, from the very nature of the process, Europeans generally are not aware of it to nearly the same extent as the Cape Coloured themselves, and there can be no doubt that it is taking place on a considerably larger scale than is thought to be the case by the majority of Europeans.[22]

While the social aspect of 'passing' was important, there is no doubt that the 'civilized labour' policy also had much to do with the creation of the desire to 'pass the colour line'. Although a fair proportion of Coloured people were traditionally the craftsmen of the Cape, the majority were unskilled and entry into the skilled trades, while not initially restricted by legislation as it was later on, was made more difficult by the pressure of white prejudice. Failure to achieve the minimum entry requirements—a difficult standard in view of the absence of compulsory education for Coloured children—also prevented many

[22] Ibid., pp. 30-1, para. 118.

Coloured people from becoming skilled workers, and the development of this state of affairs, in spite of official assurances that the civilized labour policy was not intended to apply to a specific race, was due not only to prejudice but also to economic circumstances. The bulk of the Coloured people lacked the economic resources necessary to equip themselves for better positions: few could afford the expense of remaining at school long enough to qualify for apprenticeship and even fewer could afford to train for one of the professions.

To this day, the Coloured people have not been able to use what limited powers they wield for their own advantage. They lack cohesion as a group, and leadership; and the fact that 'passing' enabled those who crossed the colour line to enjoy better economic circumstances, meant that many of the better-equipped among the Coloured people were lost to the group. Professor Hutt pointed out in 1938 that in addition to the economic motives for 'passing' 'there is an immense moral force urging the Coloured people to do so. They lose what must appear to them as a horrible taint. And the more sensitive of mind and spirit that they may have become, the stronger will be that urge.'[23]

Being of mixed race, and with their predilection for the dominant white group, they have not developed the elements necessary to bind them together. Furthermore, while on the one hand they have sought equality of opportunity with the white group, the majority of them, in turn, refuse to see the need for the same treatment to be given to the African population. Underlying Coloured people's attitudes there is thus a definite bias towards the group approach, manifesting itself in a refusal to regard the rest of the non-European population on terms of equality.

This acceptance of the group approach on the part of the Coloured people meant that there was generally a disposition to accept rigidities in the labour market in so far as they could be regarded as tacitly implying discrimination against the African, and their desire for protection against the African, in fact, prepared some of the ground for the implementation of the policy of apartheid.

[23] W. H. Hutt, 'Economic Aspects of the Report of the Cape Coloured Commission', *S.A. Journal of Economics*, June 1938, p. 120.

Until comparatively recently, the competition of the African with the Coloured man in the western Cape was more a fear than a reality, partly because there were ample supplies of Coloured labourers and hence no need to recruit Africans, other than as stevedores at the docks, and partly because the distance from the Reserves prevented Africans from incurring the expense entailed in risky and unfamiliar migration. With the growth of industry in the western Cape, however, employment opportunities for whites and non-whites increased, and the attraction of the relatively high wages (compared with those paid by the mining companies) offered by secondary industry and possibly, in addition, the prospect of being treated on a par with the Coloureds in a more tolerant environment, brought an ever-increasing stream of Africans into the Greater Cape Town area. Whereas in 1938-9 there were estimated to be 7,915 Africans employed in private industries in the western Cape, in 1945-6 there were 16,177, and in 1951-2, 28,534—an increase over the whole fourteen-year period of 260·5 per cent. This percentage increase was double that of the Coloured workers during the same period.

More will be said at a later stage about government policy in regard to this influx of Africans to the western Cape: for the moment it is sufficient to note its existence, as a factor affecting the position of the Coloured worker in the labour market. The development of industry in this area has meant that Coloured people, both male and female, have been drawn into employment in secondary industry in increasing numbers. The opening up of a wide range of semi-skilled jobs, to which reference has already been made, has given opportunities for advancement from the unskilled grades to numbers of Coloured people, and it is largely the gap in the unskilled labour ranks, which they left, which has been filled in recent years by the African migrant worker.

In government-controlled spheres, e.g. the public service, railways and harbours, post offices, etc., the employment of Coloured people in more responsible jobs has not until recently been allowed, owing to the white labour policy. The majority of jobs undertaken by Coloured people in these fields of employment were therefore of a labouring nature.

It must also be mentioned that many of the Coloured people

7

do not enjoy good living conditions: overcrowding, low wages, lack of education, and the effects of drink and dagga (drug) smoking, all militate against their effective competition with white workers, even in the limited spheres where this would be possible.

(b) The Indians

Over 80 per cent of the 441,000 Indians in South Africa live in Natal, chiefly in and around Durban and Pietermaritzburg, with very small concentrations around the Witwatersrand, Cape Town and Port Elizabeth. Their numerical weakness, however, has not meant that their presence in the labour market, or in the Union generally, has gone unnoticed, for while in many respects their status is not unlike that of the Cape Coloured people, to the English-speaking white Natalian the Indian question has long been a burning issue, with widespread political consequences. It is not relevant, in this context, to deal with the political aspects of the Indian question—the demands for repatriation of all Indians, their disenfranchisement, residential segregation and so on; nevertheless, attitudes towards Indian labour have obviously not been unaffected by the wider political issues.

Although they have only been in South Africa for 100 years,[24] and are markedly different from the other racial groups in their religion, language, customs, and background, a significant proportion of the Indian group have shown themselves to be the most adaptable of the non-whites. Led in the commercial sphere by a vanguard of free, immigrant traders, many have proved themselves capable of accepting the pattern of modern commercial and industrial society. In the Transvaal and the Cape, the majority of the Indian inhabitants are engaged in commerce, particularly retail trading, and in domestic service in hotels, etc. In Natal, many Indians are still engaged in agricultural pursuits (about one-fifth of the total Indian population was engaged in farming, forestry and fishing according to the 1946 census), but they have also been drawn into the orbit of manufacturing industry in increasing numbers. The 1951 Industrial Legislation Commission comments on the

[24] For a detailed and authoritative account of the Indian question see Mabel Palmer, *The History of the Indians in Natal*, being vol. X of the *Natal Regional Survey*, 1957.

'striking' increase in the proportion of urban to rural Asiatics since 1921.[25] It is possible for Indians to become apprenticed and qualify for skilled trades but they have come to play a role of particular importance as semi-skilled workers. Unlike the Coloured people, however, where the women have been accustomed to wage-earning activity, first as domestic servants and later in the factories, Indian women do not as a rule undertake paid employment, although there is evidence of a growing tendency for them to do so in recent years. On the tendency for Indians to move into industry, Professor Burrows writes that:

At least two forces have been responsible. On the one hand, there has been some development of opportunities in the better paid semi-skilled occupations. Secondly, the African has become a growing competitor in the field of unskilled manual labour, partly because of his more robust physique. Moreover, the Indian's dexterity and patience can be used to better advantage in certain types of industrial employment than in unskilled manual labour. This important fact constitutes another fundamental brick to use in planning the future of Natal.[26]

Like the Coloured people, the Indians are largely barred from advancing in government fields of employment—which includes the railways, as well as employment in government and provincial departments and in municipal service.

While their position in the labour market resembles in many respects that of the Coloured people in the Cape, it must be admitted that there exists a far stronger antipathy on the part of Europeans and Africans towards Indians than towards Coloured people. It is perhaps from the combination of background and adaptability that this antipathy has sprung. While on the one hand the European disliked the mode of living of the poorer Indian, there was an equally strong distrust and even envy of the successful Indian, whom it was felt had attained his position through unfair practices. The Asiatic Enquiry Commission, for example, listed the principal grievances and objections which were raised by witnesses in the Transvaal against Asiatic traders. These accusations, which although disclaimed by the Indian community and in general by the

[25] U.G. 62/51, p. 10, para. 64.
[26] H. R. Burrows (editor), *Indian Life and Labour in Natal*, 1943, p. 6.

Commission itself, largely indicate the typical attitude of most Europeans towards the Indian.

(1) They send their money out of the country instead of spending it where they earn it.

(2) They are a source of danger to the public health owing to their unclean habits, and require constant supervision to make them conform to sanitary and other bye-laws.

(3) They depreciate the value of property in their neighbourhood, as well as of the premises which they occupy.

(4) Their standard of living is inferior to that of Europeans.

(5) Their standard of trading and methods of business are different to those of Europeans in the following respects:—

    (a) they use inferior buildings as shop premises and pay less rent for them.

    (b) the owner of the business and his shop assistants all usually reside on the premises.

    (c) they defraud their creditors by fraudulent insolvency more frequently than Europeans.

    (d) they pay lower wages to their assistants than Europeans.

    (e) they evade the laws regulating hours of trading.

    (f) they habitually give short weight and adulterate foodstuffs.

    (g) they thus succeed in underselling European traders.

(6) They carry on businesses which should be carried on by Europeans, and close avenues of employment which should be open to Europeans.

(7) They produce nothing in the Transvaal, and do not consume the produce of the country, but import their requirements from India.

(8) They form 'rings' to keep out European competitors.

(9) Their presence has a bad influence on the Natives, who are jealous of the rights and privileges enjoyed by them, as coloured people.

(10) Their religion, language, colour, mode of thought, ideals, manners and customs are entirely different to those of Europeans; they cannot be assimilated and their presence is a menace to European supremacy.

(11) They are generally immoral and debauch the Natives by inciting them to theft, and by readily receiving the stolen property.

(12) They become too familiar with Europeans, especially females, in the conduct of their business, and thus destroy the respect of Natives for Europeans.[27]

In reply to the suggestions of malpractices, the Indians pointed out that by selling goods in small quantities and by

[7] Report of the Asiatic Enquiry Commission, 1921 (U.G. 4/21), pp. 30-1.

trading in areas which other races preferred to avoid, they provided a service to poor whites and poor Africans, particularly in the rural areas, which would not otherwise have been available.

The tendency of Indians to seek outside support from the Government of India has intensified rather than softened attitudes towards them and increased the feeling on the part of the other races that they (the Indians) are alien to South Africa. The serious riots which broke out in Durban in January 1949 showed the deep hostility which ran between Africans and Indians, even though some explanation can perhaps be found in the opinion that:

in an oppressed community tensions will be developed which cannot be discharged against the ruling class, who are too strong and would immediately punish any insubordination. They are and will be discharged through quarrels among the oppressed peoples themselves.[28]

The living conditions of many Indians approximate to those of the Cape Coloured people, and bad housing and over-crowding, lack of educational facilities, etc., all play their part in reducing the productivity of the Indian in the labour market.

Indians are also particularly affected by restrictions on movement: they have been banned from property ownership and occupation in the Free State since the days when it was a Republic, and the Asiatic Land Tenure Act of 1946—forerunner of the later Group Areas legislation—restricted their acquisition of property in Natal and the Transvaal. Their movement between provinces requires a permit issued under orders promulgated in terms of the Immigration Act of 1913. Their commercial activities as well as their places of residence and property ownership are now threatened by the Group Areas Act and associated laws which will be referred to again in a later chapter.

THE OCCUPATIONAL DISTRIBUTION OF THE WORKING POPULATION

An examination of the four racial groups which constitute the South African labour force would not be complete without some discussion of their occupational distribution in the

[28] Mabel Palmer, op. cit., p. 157. See also M. Webb and K. Kirkwood, *The Durban Riots and after*, 1949.

DISTRIBUTION OF THE ECONOMICALLY ACTIVE SECTION OF THE POPULATION*
BETWEEN THE DIFFERENT SECTORS OF THE ECONOMY

WHITES PERCENTAGES	FARMING FORESTRY FISHING	MINING	SECONDARY INDUSTRY	SERVICES	ALL SECTORS
1921	31.6	6.3	12.3	49.8	100
1936	24.5	6.3	17.9	51.3	100
1946	18.9	6.0	21.4	53.7	100
1951	14.8	6.8	26.1	53.3	100
NUMBER 1951	145,424	56,959	256,848	524,665	983,896
ASIATICS PERCENTAGES					
1921	34.9	4.3	14.1	46.7	100
1936	27.2	1.3	17.2	54.3	100
1946	17.3	0.8	24.8	57.1	100
1951	13.7	0.6	25.9	59.8	100
NUMBER 1951	12,906	543	24,484	56,537	94,470
COLOUREDS PERCENTAGES					
1921	36.5	1.3	13.5	48.7	100
1936	34.2	1.2	16.8	47.8	100
1946	27.9	0.8	22.0	49.3	100
1951	24.2	0.9	27.4	47.5	100
NUMBER 1951	97,674	3,801	110,548	191,971	403,994
AFRICANS PERCENTAGES					
1946	65.5	9.0	5.2	20.3	100
1951	62.8	8.8	7.4	21.0	100
NUMBER 1951	3,204,086 (Estimated)	450,474	377,470	1,070,749	5,102,779
TOTAL PERCENTAGES					
1946	56.2	8.0	8.7	27.1	100
1951	52.5	7.8	11.7	28.0	100
NUMBER 1946	3,518,185	499,460	541,833	1,700,227	6,259,705
1951	3,460,090	511,777	769,350	1,843,922	6,585,139

*NOTE   Europeans, Coloureds and Asiatics aged 15 years and over, and Africans aged 10 years and over are included.

SOURCES: Report of Industrial Legislation Commission (U.G. 62/51), p. 15, and unpublished 1951 census figures quoted in Report of Commission of Enquiry into policy relating to the protection of industries (U.G. 36/58), p. 2.

economy. It is interesting, in this respect, to compare (unpublished) 1951 census figures with figures taken from earlier censuses of 1921, 1936 and 1946, and the table on the previous page gives some idea of the changes which have taken place as the economy has developed and become more diversified.

It will be seen from this table that the proportion of the working population engaged in agriculture and mining has fallen, whereas in the period 1946-51, the percentage of all races employed in manufacturing industry rose from 8·7 to 11·7, and the numbers employed from 541,833 to 769,350.

Unfortunately, fuller details of the occupations of the Union's economically active population gathered at the 1951 census are not yet available, which means that the latest information on the subject, given in the 1946 census returns, is at the time of writing thirteen years old and does not reflect the tremendous surge forward in the development of the economy which characterized the late 1940's and much of the 1950's. However, the preliminary 1951 figures given in the above table show that the non-white labour force in that year constituted about four-fifths of the total. With the exception of the relatively few non-whites who have qualified for the legal, teaching, medical, entertainment, and other professions (in 1946, 9,765 Coloured men and women, 2,273 Asiatics and 33,212 Africans fell into these categories), the majority of them fall into the category of semi-skilled and unskilled workers, while skilled and salaried work remains the almost exclusive preserve of the white group.

The Report of the Department of Labour for 1956[29] gives a table classifying employees according to race and skill in certain industries and trades which were subject to wage-determinations during the period 1937-56. This table was compiled from 'data made available to the Board at the time of each investigation'[30] and therefore the figures cannot be taken as representing the exact state of affairs obtaining in the industries and trades concerned in 1956. Furthermore, wage-determinations are not made in respect of many important industries which are covered by industrial council agreements, and workers covered by determinations for unskilled labour

---

[29] U.G. 54/57, p. 27.
[30] Ibid., p. 23, para. 13.

only are not included in the table. The data shown in the table relates to workers in the commercial and distributive trades, sections of manufacturing industry and the motor industry, and so on, and the situation obtaining in these industries and trades is not an accurate picture of the situation obtaining in industry as a whole. With these qualifications, however, the information given in the table can be usefully regarded as an indication of how the labour market is divided on grounds of race and skill.

NO. OF EMPLOYEES CLASSIFIED ACCORDING TO RACE AND GRADE OF SKILL IN INDUSTRIES AND TRADES REGULATED BY WAGE-DETERMINATIONS IN THE PERIOD 1937-56

	SKILLED		SEMI-SKILLED		UNSKILLED	
	No.	% OF GRADE	No.	% OF GRADE	No.	% OF GRADE
Whites	97,115	82.7	14,025	27.7	1,200	0.8
Asiatics	6,568	5.6	5,151	10.2	5,310	3.9
Coloureds	6,512	5.5	10,242	20.2	17,226	13.2
Africans	7,287	6.2	21,202	41.9	112,636	82.1
Total	117,482	100%	50,620	100%	136,372	100%

Total: All workers: 304,474

In other words, while Europeans constituted over 80 per cent of the skilled workers, with each of the other non-white groups constituting between 5 per cent and 6 per cent of this class, in the semi-skilled category Africans constituted nearly 42 per cent of the workers, with Europeans providing 28 per cent, Coloureds 20 per cent and Asiatics 10 per cent. In the unskilled category, on the other hand, Africans made up the bulk of the labour force—over 80 per cent in percentage terms, with Coloureds as the next most important group and Indians much less significant. Europeans doing unskilled work made up less than 1 per cent of the total.

These figures not only illustrate the extent to which skilled work has remained the exclusive preserve of the white group, but also how far the development of semi-skilled jobs has enabled many non-whites to progress in the job scale away from mere unskilled, labouring tasks.

THE CONSEQUENCES OF THE GROWTH OF
     MANUFACTURING INDUSTRY

The changes which followed the spread of manufacturing industry in South Africa were characterized not only by economic change, but also by social and cultural change. The process of transformation which had been begun with the discovery of diamonds had continued with the development of gold-mining and was accelerated by the development of secondary industry; its outstanding feature was, of course, the changing emphasis of population from the rural to the urban areas. While the needs of industrialism dictated the pattern, the inadequacy of the rural areas accentuated the drift which, in the early stages, tended to be ahead of normal economic factors. The fact that urbanization took place partly through circumstances as opposed to choice, meant that from the beginning there existed an important psychological influence in the urban population which did not assist in smoothing the process of adaptation and tended to complicate the process of industrialization.

In this perhaps lies, to a significant extent, the explanation why the group approach continued to flourish in an atmosphere which by the very nature of the economic function required a high degree of co-operation among the various racial groups. That co-operation took place at all in the prevailing South African atmosphere might almost be considered an achievement; nevertheless, it has taken place and economic development has been achieved to an extent which might have been thought impossible at the turn of the century. How far the existence in the labour market of rigidities based upon colour has impaired or even warped economic development is another matter. The question as to whether, if conditions had been different, economic growth would have been more spectacular, is open. It is sufficient to stress that in spite of the racial rigidities which existed, economic growth took place to a significant degree.

The fact that the group approach owed its continuance to the consent or desire of all elements of the white population is important. While the motivations of individual underlying attitudes differed, the sum total of their final significance was the same. The mining companies saw the African as a source of cheap labour essential to the high-cost gold-mining industry, the white unions saw the non-white as a threat to their privileged position which they were anxious to have permanently entrenched, while the Afrikaners of predominantly rural origins had little desire to see the end of their patriarchal static society, but rather hoped it would be continued in their new environment. To business men generally, the continuance of a supply of cheap docile labour appeared important.

Faced with the problem of an emerging backward people, even those whites who saw in the community approach the best road for progress had fears that there might be some risk of endangering the civilization which the Europeans had brought to Africa.

In the circumstances, it was inevitable, especially if one considered the strength of the white franchise, as opposed to the near political impotence of the non-white (which made non-white opinion of little direct significance) that the great debate should have been on the best manner by which the country's economy could be allowed to develop without endangering South Africa's traditional social and political structure. The legislative rigidities, which will be considered in the chapters that follow, were born of this debate.

The Growth
of Legal Rigidity
in the Labour Market

THE UNDERLYING
FACTORS

THE BROAD FRAMEWORK

L EGISLATION AFFECTING the labour market in South Africa
falls broadly under two main headings: in the first place,
general industrial legislation relating to conditions of
work, wages, etc., and, in the second place, legislation aimed
specifically at the control of movement within the labour market.[1]
Superficially, both categories are not without precedent in other
countries; the bulk of the early industrial legislation in the
Union followed the generally accepted patterns of most
western industrial countries, though the legislation concerning
mobility within the economy can only be compared with the
various wartime expedients adopted in countries such as the
United Kingdom, and with the regulations which form part
of the pattern of controlled economies, such as the Soviet Union.

Although most of the early industrial legislation showed
little or no *de jure* recognition of race as such, the traditional
prejudice cannot be disregarded from the point of view of both
cause and effect. It is necessary, therefore, to examine the
underlying pressures which accompanied the passage of this
legislation through Parliament, to consider its consequent
effects on the various racial groups and to trace the entry of an
explicit racial bias in more recent legislation.

[1] See Guy Routh, *Industrial Relations and Race Relations*, 1953. He comments
(page 3): 'South African industrial law is a strange mixture of the ancient and
the modern. On the one side are the Masters' and Servants' laws, which have
remained as a heritage of the colonies and republics, of which the Union of
South Africa was formed: on the other side are the Industrial Conciliation,
Wage, and Factories Acts, which are, in the main, well in keeping with modern
usage.'

While the industrial legislation of the 1920's may be described as being, on the surface, at least, community-minded, it was moulded by the pressure of group interests with the underlying desire to maintain so-called 'civilized living standards'. In this regard the prevailing atmosphere of the time is all important; the Poor White problem was at its height, while white trade unionism was at the zenith of its power. The 1922 'colour-bar' strike of white miners on the Rand was still a very recent and bitter memory and all concerned were fearful of perhaps more violent outbursts. There lingered the fear that industrialists would seek to supplant white workers by introducing cheap African labour with a consequent debasement of 'civilized standards'. Furthermore, much of the discussion of the problem was dominated by the attractive red herring of segregation—ultimately it was suggested that the problem could be solved by permanently excluding the African from the industrial economy.

Fear of white 'debasement' was shared by all sections of the white community, and showed itself in the main stream of legislation which sought to entrench 'civilized standards' through minimum-wage policies. For instance, it is interesting to find the leader of the Opposition, General Smuts, basing his argument against the minimum-wage regulations envisaged by the 1924 Wage Bill on the contention that it 'was going to produce equality where there has so far been difference'.

It means this, that under this law when applied in this country, many of the industries will shut up because you will level up, you will have to level up, the wage of the black man. Look at it from another point of view. How is the white man going to be affected? We have in this country been able to pay the skilled white labourer a fairly considerable wage. Our wages paid to skilled workers in South Africa are far in excess of what are paid in any other country, except America, and we were able to do it because we paid the black man such a low wage. The Native only receiving two shillings a day, we could afford to pay 20s. to the white man and more. . . .

Supposing a black man in future is not paid 2s., but the civilized wage of 5s. because that figure seems to be the civilized wage of the Government. We have tried to get the figure from the Minister of Railways as to what he considers are the civilized rates of pay, and it seems to be 5s. per day, plus housing. That is the basis. Can we after that, continue to pay the skilled man 20s. or 25s.? Naturally that man's pay must come down. There will not be enough to go round and keep the industries going, therefore the tendency will be for black wages to go up and white wages at the top will have to move down in order to leave sufficient to go round. I say that this Bill, so far from achieving the object which is in view, will only have this effect, that it will close many industries, because you cannot, as our industries are today here in South Africa, pay the black man a wage which will be a subsistence wage for the white man and still continue to run these industries. Many of these industries will be closed, unemployment will be accentuated, great confusion and dislocation will result, and, in the end, I think we shall discard this experiment and we shall see that, forsaking the experience of the past, we have been doing the country a grave injustice, and we shall have to go back. . . .[2]

It is clear, therefore, that whereas the government supporters saw minimum-wage regulation as the means of preventing the debasement of white wages, General Smuts saw it as bringing about such a debasement. While the latter's argument completely disregards the important consequences which would flow from an over-all increase in purchasing power, there may be some grounds for an acceptance of the argument if one presupposes the total income remaining static, with a disproportionate share accruing to the European sector. In such hypothetical circumstances, any attempt to fix a minimum wage based upon 'civilized standards' would result in a redistribution of shares and it would follow that the white sector would receive less and the non-white more. The minimum wage would consequently fall somewhere between the former ratios. This, however, disregards any element of comparative productivities, so that it might equally be argued that industrialists seeking to maximize profits would, when faced with the obligation of paying a minimum wage, attempt to supplant the less efficient African by the more efficient white, which of course was what the white trade unionists sought to achieve. They had argued that in the absence of statutory minimum wages, employers found it profitable to supplant highly trained (and usually highly paid) Europeans by less efficient but cheaper non-whites.

On the surface, one might be tempted to argue that the only barrier to the non-white was his own backwardness and that once he had qualified under the somewhat uncertain definition of 'civilized standards', he would be permitted to take his place alongside the European. It may be that many of the exponents of the civilized-wage policy, particularly some trade unionists,

[2] *Hansard*, 30 March 1925, col. 1602.

were sincere in assessing the problem along these lines, while it is not unreasonable to suppose that they felt that white debasement could only be prevented by enforcing regulations which would ensure that employers would not take advantage of the willingness of non-whites to accept a wage lower than that which was considered necessary to maintain the 'civilized standard'. On the other hand, there can be no doubt that traditional prejudice did not allow any thinking which would ultimately lead to an acceptance of the non-European on a par with the European in any sphere, whether economic or social. To the upholders of the traditional way of thinking, therefore, the civilized living standard approach could possibly be regarded as the means of preventing non-white encroachment on white preserves.

There was ample evidence at the time to show that this was in fact the case and as a result of the inability of 'civilized standards' alone to withstand encroachment, subsequent developments, in which a more definite legalistic racial biased approach has become necessary to divide the white and non-white spheres of the labour market, have borne out the contention that traditional prejudice has underlined the general attitude of whites towards labour problems in South Africa.

Therefore, for as long as the bulk of the non-whites remained 'uncivilized' and the facilities for educational advance limited, there was felt to be no need to introduce direct racial discrimination in the legislation dealing with the subject. The 'backwardness' barrier would operate automatically to exclude non-whites from coming into direct competition with whites. Lack of the means to qualify was a further barrier to non-white progress, as, for instance, in the case of the Apprenticeship Acts, where, particularly among the Cape Coloured people, few could afford to allow their children to remain long enough at school to qualify for entry into the trades.

The growing problem of urban white poverty and unemployment increased the fear of the undue lowering of European standards of living; whereas in the past every effort had been made to encourage the African to enter the urban area, his presence now became increasingly suspect, and attention was directed more and more to ways and means of keeping him out, or, in the absence of this more 'desirable' alternative, of restricting as far as possible his role in the labour market to those tasks in which he would least threaten the white man.

Thus the need for a more definite recognition of the urges of traditional prejudice arose out of the circumstances of the times, particularly the demographic problems which accompanied the accelerated pace of economic growth. In recent years, it has become increasingly apparent that economic expansion calls for greater resources of skilled labour than can be met from the local white group and, in the absence of large-scale immigration, the only alternative is a softening of rigidity in the labour market by allowing some measure of non-white advance. It is perhaps a strange paradox that though industrial expansion has removed the immediate danger of white debasement through the widening of job opportunities, it has also been accompanied by a larger measure of legal rigidity than was considered necessary at the time when it was possible to conceive a greater justification for it. This may perhaps be accounted for by the misplaced anxieties which accompany newly found security, the fear of a return to insecurity and perhaps also it is an inherent part of the comfortable complacency which flows from the absence of noteworthy competition in the sphere of white preserves. Above all there remains the inability to escape from the mesh of traditional prejudice. Legislation has thus aimed at bolstering white supremacy by either curtailing the competitive advance of the non-white on the basis of keeping him in his place (which has been defined as 'any place that at any particular time the European does not think it desirable to fill'), or on the more theoretical basis of 'separate development'.

This is the gist of the latter-day philosophy behind, for example, job reservation by which non-Europeans may be permitted to occupy certain defined categories of jobs under permit until such times as these jobs may be required by whites. In other words, a relaxation of legal rigidity on occupational mobility may be permitted as long as the white worker is not threatened. This tacit admission of elasticity, even though circumscribed by reservations, is of primary importance in assessing the impact of colour prejudice upon industrial growth in the Union.

The history of labour legislation thus shows in the beginning a desire to prevent whites from falling below a *white survival line*, measured out by 'civilized standards', gradually giving way to a more negative desire to prevent non-white encroachment above what may be regarded as a *white supremacy line* dictated by traditional prejudice. The white supremacy line thus runs parallel to what are regarded as traditional white jobs, but an insufficiency of white workers at present permits flexibility, with a consequent spill-over of non-whites into the white sphere.[3] By such convenient compromise the needs of traditional prejudice and of economic growth are partly satisfied.

Furthermore, as described in the previous chapter, the development of secondary industry has meant that there has been a significant growth of new categories of so-called semi-skilled jobs requiring less skill and thus blurring the rigid division between traditional white and non-white jobs. Nevertheless the interaction of prejudice and white trade unionism has caused the labour market to become divided into a series of more or less rigid, racially defined labour compartments, with the upper compartments insufficiently filled with whites, and the lower compartments crowded with non-whites. Current legislation, however, does not aim at meeting this situation, but rather a possible situation which may arise if there is a marked fall-off in the level of economic activity. Thus whereas in the 20's and 30's legislation was aimed at meeting an existing situation, legislation of the 50's is framed to meet a conjectural situation.

In keeping with the aim of this study it is necessary to restrict consideration of legislation to its significance in bringing about racial rigidities which are reflected in the pattern of the labour market which exists in South Africa today. It would be irrelevant in this context, therefore, to consider the wider ethical implications of the disabilities under which particular race groups may suffer, except in so far as these disabilities have had a direct bearing upon the economy.

THE MARRIAGE BETWEEN TRADE UNIONISM AND THE TRADITIONAL PREJUDICE

The major part of industrial legislation, as such, had its beginnings in the 1920's during the life of the Pact Government

[3] See 'Economic Flexibility in a Plural Society' by D. Hobart Houghton, published in the *Proceedings of the Social Science Conference*, Institute for Social Research, University of Natal, 1956.

of the Nationalist and Labour Parties, whereas, of course, the Masters and Servants Laws and laws concerning movement in the labour market stem from earlier laws of the Cape Colony, Natal, and the Boer Republics.

Certainly the most important influence upon the scope of industrial legislation, in addition to white prejudice, was the collective power of white labour. Nurtured, as has been shown above, in Kimberley and on the Rand, it was perhaps to be expected that the main test of strength should have manifested itself in the mining industry, while it was an equally natural consequence that there should have been a marriage between traditional prejudice and white trade unionism in the 1924 Pact Government. It was the logical coming together of the two main groups of white protectionists. There was in any case by this stage a considerable overlapping of the two forces. Originally the mineworkers were largely men from Cornwall and the North of England and other immigrant miners concerned with maintaining their privileged position. By 1920, however, the position had altered substantially when it was estimated that some 90 per cent of the mineworkers on the Reef were Afrikaners.[4]

The genesis of these two forces has been shown above. It remains to show the immediate factors influencing their union and the consequences of it. Once again the mining industry, and particularly gold-mining, was to be in the centre of the picture. The leader of the white labour section was himself a mining man, while the fear of whites being supplanted by non-whites revealed itself earliest in the mining industry.

THE MINING INDUSTRY AND THE COLOUR BAR

In the early stages of mining in South Africa it had been possible for the white miners to maintain their position through their scarcity value. As the nature of mining altered, through increased mechanization and with the consequent development of semi-skilled jobs, the situation changed considerably, and there were now an increasing variety of jobs which could be performed by non-whites. Scarcity was thus no longer enough, and to maintain their supremacy something more was needed:

[4] See E. Gitsham and J. F. Trembath, *A First Account of Labour Organisation in South Africa*, 1926, pp. 65-9.

organization through trade unions provided part of the answer
and political pressure the other. On the relative merits of the
white and African mineworker, the 1917 State Mining Commission had this to say: 'For all practical purposes then it can be
taken that, as a labourer, one white man is equivalent to one
native. The employment of whites instead of natives on the
mines resolves itself then into a question of economics.'[5]
Some success was achieved with the enactment of the Mines and
Works Act of 1911. While ostensibly aimed at maintaining
safety in the mines, the original Act allowed the colour bar to
creep in through regulations specifying the number of white
foremen to African miners (which meant in effect the fixing of
ratios between white and black), and by regulating the issue of
blasting certificates.

There had, of course, been earlier references to 'colour' in
Transvaal mining legislation, but the 'colour bar' in the mining
industry was not finally entrenched until after the First World
War and the struggle which centred around the industry was to
have profound political consequences and open the way to a
new era of industrial legislation. The attitude of the white
miners is well reflected in the evidence given by Mr. Thomas
Matthews, then General Secretary of the South African Miners'
Union, to the 1914 Dominions Royal Commission:

... seeing that the average Kaffir is bred as a slave he has no right to
usurp our position as free men, or drive us from these mines ... I
hold that the average Kaffir should be allowed to get free, but in the
interim as he is here as a semi-slave, I have a right to fight him and
oust him. ...[6]

The same witness saw the cause of drunkenness among white
miners as flowing from white miners having to work 'for eight
hours among a crowd of dirty evil-smelling Kaffirs ... enough
to break down the moral fibre of the average man'.[7]

To the overseas trade unionist these views must appear
somewhat paradoxical, yet they provide important clues to
explaining white attitudes in South Africa as a whole, to
understanding the strange dualism of the labour section of the
white protectionists, and to appreciating the economic motives

[5] U.G. 19/17, para. 182.
[6] Royal Commission on the Natural Resources, Trade and Legislation of
certain portions of His Majesty's Dominions, Minutes of Evidence taken in the
Union of South Africa, Part II, December 1914 (Cd. 7707), para. 2048.
[7] Ibid., para. 2047.

behind the Hertzog-Cresswell Pact.[8] In this respect it would perhaps be of value to quote a further portion of the Minutes of Evidence and examination of Matthews before the Dominions Royal Commission:

Q. Then would you fight and exterminate the Kaffir?
A. No, I would drive them down to where they came from.
Q. You cannot simply say 'vanish' and they vanish. You must provide for him?
A. No, you can do the same as they did in Basutoland, send them into their own territory.
Q. So you think the policy should be to import white people and in the meantime allow the assets of our country to lie waste?
A. No, allow the Kaffir to go on the land.
Q. And drive the Boers away?
A. No, let the Kaffir go down into Natal and elsewhere and make the Dutchmen who hold the land cut it up and allow the emigrant from overseas to come here. If the land laws in this country are such that the landowners are able to hold up the land for a big rise awaiting the time that emigrants come here and take up land, you should alter them. In the *interim* we want to drive the Kaffirs out if we can—those who are here we will allow to stay here—but those who do not belong here have no right to come and settle down.
Q. You say you are a Socialist: you mean only as far as white people are concerned?
A. No, I am a Socialist as far as all the workers in the whole globe are concerned. I believe that every inhabitant of this globe shall have the opportunity to earn his livelihood, but I do not believe that a certain section shall be used as semi-slaves for the purpose of keeping others down.
Q. The Kaffir is also a worker?
A. Well, as we say, he robbed the land from the Hottentot, and he should be allowed to stay on the land. What we say is that he should not be brought here to compete with the white man on the economic conditions at present existing.[9]

Matthews's attitudes are as typical as they are irrational. The 'sovereign a day' becomes the monetary unit of 'civilized' standards and the capitalist is seen not so much as the exploiter of all workers but as a selfish force which seeks to deny the white worker his just deserts by using cheaper, non-white labour. The lot of the African becomes of secondary consideration. Matthews's argument is brought into clearer perspective

---

[8] See W. G. Ballinger, *Race and Economics in South Africa*, 1934.
[9] Royal Commission on the Natural Resources . . . etc., op. cit., paras. 2066-71.

by General Smuts's misgivings, quoted above, as to the effect
of a raising of non-white wages on the traditional 'sovereign
a day' standard of the whites.

Ultimately this dilemma boiled down to the argument that
'in the interim we want to drive the Kaffirs out if we can—those
who are here we will allow to stay here—but those who do not
belong here have no right to come here and settle down'.
Variations on this theme have dominated the economic and
social history of South Africa and have exerted a most potent
influence on industrial legislation.

How could the needs of economic progress be met while at
the same time white hegemony be maintained? If economic
development was dependent on non-white co-operation then
how could white hegemony be maintained in spite of economic
progress? The dilemma could be presented in many forms, yet
fundamentally it has become the problem of how best to maintain the traditional order of things while at the same time
allowing for increased industrialization and economic development. In spite of the theoretical dreams of generations of
separationists, the passage of years has brought the races closer
together in uneasy co-operation in the economic function with
the ultimate ideal of 'separation' becoming increasingly less
feasible yet kept alive for reasons of political expediency by the
stimulus of hope and by unwieldy legal devices.

It was convenient to lay the blame at the doorstep of:

the capitalist class [who] are quite ready to go to any extreme in
order to save a half-crown in working costs quite indifferent to what
results may follow or what effect their policy may have on the future
welfare of this country.[10]

Economic entrepreneurship whenever it concerns itself with the
broader economic view and is not solely geared to white welfare
thus becomes 'wicked' capitalism.

This strange dualism in the thinking of white labour showed
itself in another direction; a statement prepared by a committee
of the South African Labour Party recommended in 1917, to
the Commission appointed to investigate the merits of
nationalizing the mines, the employment of African convict
labour by the state on the basis of 'cost of keep', which would
have the additional 'advantage' that 'the full complement of

10 Ibid., para. 2066.

workers, always an important factor in cheap mining, would be on hand, with a surplus available at any time'.[11] While the State Mining Commission was emphatic in its rejection of the proposal, it would perhaps be interesting to contemplate what the consequences of such a move would have been.

It would appear that the economic machinery of South Africa has, over the years, become increasingly geared to the maintenance of an 'inner' privileged society for the benefit of the dominant minority and supported by the labour subsidies of the wider community. The fact that this inner privileged society has been created by the co-operation of the non-white in the common economic function is the root of the South African dilemma. With a national income *per capita* only a fraction of that of Canada, the United States and Australia, white workers in South Africa have been able to command incomes almost on a par with those received by workers in those countries. This has been made possible only by paying the non-white a far less than proportionate share of the total wage-packet. In such circumstances, the economic necessity of using the non-whites was obvious even though their participation in the industrial economy did not conform to the views of traditional prejudice. The non-whites were thus the supporters of the inner privileged society and all that went with it—a body of cheap labour creating subsidies which could be used for the benefit of the white man. The mines, the farms, the factories, all became part of the general pattern of society in which ultimately no white interest could afford to see a removal of the non-whites from the single body economic for fear of losing the subsidy provided by their labour. At best there could only be compromises and makeshifts embodied in a system of racial frontiers within the economic community.[12]

Two important commissions of the 1920's offered little hope to the idealists. The 1920 Low Grade Mines Commission went so far as to recommend, as a means of alleviating the position of the low-grade mines, that the complement of African labourers be increased and the colour bar removed, which would '. . . enable Natives to advance in efficiency and opportunity'. The emphasis was placed on training and efficiency

[11] Report of State Mining Commission 1917 (U.G. 19/17), paras. 191-3.
[12] See *Survey of British Commonwealth Affairs*, 1942, vol. 2, *Problems of Economic Policy*, 1918-1939, by W. K. Hancock, part 2, p. 43.

rather than on artificial barriers which 'may appear to be an admission of weakness and [which] undoubtedly create irritation and race hostility'.[13]

The 1922 Unemployment Commission made the following observations:

That the expansion of industry and of the field of employment and the maintenance of a high wage for skilled Europeans depend upon the supply of Native Labour is a fact which it is impossible to ignore. It is the presence of the Native workers in their relative numbers that enables the white worker, as far as the Gold Mining Industry is concerned, to obtain the wages he does. And a fact of even greater importance is that without a plentiful supply of Native labour many of the low grade mines would be forced to close down at a much earlier date than they otherwise would; which again would mean less money and less employment.[14]

Nevertheless, it was not easy to cut across time-moulded tradition reinforced by the fear of substitution. It was not the last time in the history of African mining that reorganization schemes were to be interpreted by white miners as a disguised means of supplanting them by cheaper African miners. It is sometimes overlooked that the recent problems which have stemmed from the programmes of African Advancement in the Copperbelt of Northern Rhodesia are in fact basically similar to those which led to the 1922 disturbances on the Rand.[15] In both cases there was the underlying fear that the surrender of privileges resulting from reorganization would entail an eventual undermining of the position of the white group.

On the Rand, by 1920 it had become a universally accepted practice that no non-white could work without white supervision, with a fixed ratio maintained between the races. Furthermore Cresswell and his friends, who had by this time formed the Labour Party with 'Civilized Labour' as its main platform, still firmly believed that the mines, and for that matter, all industry, could be worked without African labour. All official investigations proved otherwise. The 1917 State Mining Commission

[13] Report of the Low Grade Mines Commission (U.G. 34/20), paras. 199 and 188.
[14] Report of the Unemployment Commission, 1922 (U.G. 17/22), para. 107.
[15] Compare the Report of the Mining Industry Board, 1922 (U.G.39/22) with the Report of the Harrigan Tribunal, Lusaka, 1956. See also Julius Lewin, *The Colour Bar in the Copperbelt*, 1941.

(para. 185) found that if the government nationalized the mines it would have no alternative but 'to follow the practice obtaining on the Rand and employ native labourers'. The Commission based this conclusion on an estimate that 'the employment of white instead of native labour on the mines would have the effect of increasing the cost per ton milled by 6s. 7d.' at a time when the profits of 28 of the 57 mines were below 6s. 7d. (para. 183). There was thus a serious conflict of approach between the white miners and the mine companies who believed that it was essential that there be some relaxation of the colour bar in order to bring about a more realistic reorganization of underground working, and in the absence of an increase in the price of gold, to save the mines from a premature shut down.

The problem, however, was not capable of easy solution, for in the long run any settlement, which sought to be equitable, had to meet the needs of all sections of the population; deteriorations in white standards had to be prevented without at the same time closing the door to non-white advance.

In the first place there was the real danger which stemmed from the application of 'civilized standards' on criteria of race alone and from a disregard of the need to match the 'civilized' wage with a corresponding level of productivity. The Economic and Wage Commission warned that:

a wage rate that is enforced, whether by law, trade union action or custom, always has a selective effect on employment, largely restricting employment to those workers whose output, having regard for the price obtainable for the industry's product in the market, will cover that wage rate, rejecting all others.[16]

Thus, in order to maintain a level of full employment for all whites, at a given standard, it would be necessary to seek some means of subsidizing the marginally insufficient and uneconomic members of this group. Failing this, the inefficient white labour elements would either swell the ranks of the unemployed or compete with the African in the unskilled field—hence the persistence of the Poor White problem before the evolution of the 'civilized labour' policies. Under such circumstances the inner privileged society was only possible if subsidized by surpluses created by the low-paid non-whites, and if the non-white wage-rate remained below the white wage-rate.

[16] Report of Economic and Wage Commission, U.G. 14/26, para. 184.

Deep-rooted European prejudice constituted the second important barrier. Even if there could be a greater and more efficient use of resources and a more substantial flow of wealth, there remained the problem of overcoming the traditional prejudice which either could not admit that the non-white is capable of advance, or would not admit it because it would inevitably introduce non-white advancement and competition.

The argument that the granting to non-whites of greater opportunities would result in increased productivity and enhanced purchasing power, leading in turn to further accelerated development with a consequent over-all increase in incomes may be incontrovertible, but from the point of view of the white workers the most significant aspect of the argument was that they rightly or wrongly felt it required them to sacrifice immediate privileges for uncertain future benefits. It was not easy to reassure them that they would not be tricked out of what they considered their just deserts. They were not to be convinced by the forebodings of government commissions; how were they to know that this was not part of the grand scheme of the mine-owners who, as Matthews had suggested, were prepared to sacrifice the future welfare of the country for the sake of increased profits. In the face of such thinking it would have taken more than a team of illustrious economists to persuade the white miner otherwise.

As early as March 1920, speaking at the annual meeting of the Chamber of Mines, Sir Lionel Phillips warned:

It is no good our thinking that in future, with the strides that education is making, we can adopt a policy which might have suited the country when it was in a much more barbarous condition. . . . You cannot expect that any man who feels that he has capacity for doing more and better work should be held down by artificial restriction.

In the mining industry it was not the skilled or unskilled occupations over which the clash was to take place but rather in the intermediate categories. A good deal of the semi-skilled work on the mines, such as drill-sharpening, could be done by Africans, and—a fact which was of great importance to the industry—at a much lower wage-rate than that received by Europeans.

The problem of costs remained the most pressing question in the gold-mines. Up to the outbreak of the First World War the price of gold had remained at 84s. 11d. an ounce but immediately after the war it fluctuated between 130s. and 95s. Meanwhile costs had risen by almost 40 per cent between 1913 and 1921. In the absence of a stabilized increase in the price of gold, the only alternative means of maintaining payability was through decreasing the cost of production.

The main problem of costs lay in the field of labour and in particular in the cost of white labour. Whereas African wages had only risen 9 per cent since before the war, European wages rose by almost 60 per cent between 1913 and 1918. In the circumstances it was natural that the companies should have sought to solve their problem by reorganization. It was argued that unless this took place, twenty out of thirty-nine mines would close. Following these lines, in November 1921 the Chamber of Mines suggested to the white miners represented by the South African Industrial Federation (which had been recognized by the Chamber in 1915) three courses of action:

(1) an alteration of the contract system;
(2) reorganization of underground work;
(3) modification of the *status quo* agreement.[17]

Under the contract system, certain underground work was handed out to independent contractors and it was maintained by the Chamber of Mines that the amount paid for such work was out of all proportion to the work done. The practice of 'contracting' was as old as the industry itself, and its form varied from time to time. Originally the 'flat contract' was used, under which the price was fixed per unit of work done. The miner was supplied at an agreed rate by the company with labour, explosives, and stores, and was usually paid for work done on a monthly basis. At the time of discussion the usual practice was for the agreement to be on a 'day's pay plus contract' basis, the miner being paid a daily wage and in addition enjoying a contract on 'flat' rate. Earnings varied between £30 and £200 but were generally in the region of £100 per month. The system was open to all manner of abuse. It has, since then, undergone severe modifications and is now largely restricted to development work and specialist tasks

[17] See Annual Report of Transvaal Chamber of Mines for 1921, pp. 131-5.

such as rock-breaking.[18] It was proposed to reorganize this system together with a general rearrangement of underground work in the hope that there would follow greater efficiency all round with a consequent lowering of working costs.

The main trouble arose from attempts to modify the so-called *status quo* agreement which, together with the other proposals, was interpreted as intending the abolition of the implied colour bar which flowed from the Mining Regulations issued under the 1911 Mines and Works Act.

The *status quo* agreement of 1918 stemmed from the wartime need to prevent any disputes likely to disrupt the industry and concerned drill-sharpeners. The mineworkers had demanded that all non-whites employed as drill-sharpeners should be replaced by whites. The mine companies refused to agree to this and finally resolved that the jobs held by 'coloured' persons should continue and that there would be no substitution of one race for another. The agreement was obviously meant to meet the exigencies of the time but it came to be very widely interpreted. The companies found, for example, that they could not combine two gangs of Africans and dismiss one of the Europeans in charge; with the result that they would in practice be burdened with unnecessary and expensive labour. The agreement as interpreted by the white miners thus constituted an important barrier to achieving economies through reorganization.

In order to placate white fears, the Chamber of Mines agreed to a fixed ratio of one European to 10·5 non-Europeans but nevertheless reserved the right to carry out their schemes within the confines of this ratio. The Federation, however, replied with a demand for a ratio of one European to 3·5 non-whites, applied not only to the mining industry but to all spheres other than agriculture.[19]

The mineworkers armed themselves and went on strike calling for the protection of white workers. Nationalist Party leaders expressed tacit approval, always mindful of the value of a pact with Labour. What began as a strike of European mineworkers in February 1922 soon developed into nothing

[18] See the Report of the Mining Industry Board, 1922 (U.G. 39/22), and the earlier report of the Departmental Committee on underground mining contracts, 1917 (U.G. 38/17).
[19] Transvaal Chamber of Mines Annual Report for 1921, pp. 133-4.

less than a full-scale rebellion.[20] In all some 230 people were killed during the few weeks' fighting and in addition to this grave loss of life and the destruction of property left in the train of the strike, the ground was now thoroughly prepared for the Labour–Nationalist Government of 1924 with its emphasis upon economic policies as the salvation of the white race.

THE PACT GOVERNMENT AND THE CONSEQUENCES

In the general election of June 1924 the Nationalists won 68 seats; the South African Party 53, with Labour holding the balance of power with 18 seats. The resulting Pact Government was thus the union of the representatives of privileged white labour and the representatives of the largely poor and backward white element. It was a natural outcome that the cornerstones of the new Government's policy should have been the upholding of the 'civilized labour' concept and the entrenchment of wage rates accordingly. On the one hand, as was shown in the last chapter, the backward Poor White was to be sheltered under the 'civilized' labour policies and on the other hand white trade unionism was to be given important legislative concessions to its concepts of the 'rate for the job', which implied the determination of wages on a basis of traditional white earnings.

The Pact Government, though responsible for the bulk of the early industrial legislation in the Union, was not the originator of legislation which discriminated against various racial groups in the industrial sphere. Shortly after the 1922 Revolt, General Smuts had introduced the Apprenticeship Bill which streamlined Act No. 29 of 1918 (The Regulation of Wages, Apprentices and Improvers Act) and which was to play an important part in obstructing the advance of the non-white.

F. H. Cresswell, leader of the Labour Party, was, however, convinced that white labour could obtain the protection it needed through a rigid application of the 'rate for the job' principle. Once again we see the avowed Socialist 'closed shop' trade unionism linked with the idea of racial bolstering. Of legislation introduced by the Pact Government the Industrial Conciliation Act and the Wage Act can be regarded as a

[20] See Report of the Martial Law Enquiry Judicial Commission 1922, (U.G. 35/22).

disguised application of these ideas, but the Mines and Works Amendment Act must be looked upon as undisguisedly racially prejudiced in content. Furthermore, even though advantages have, in the past, accrued to all groups of the population from the industrial machinery created by these Acts, the limitations on advancement placed in the way of non-whites have, as will be seen in the next chapter, justified the fears of those who saw the legislation as constituting expressions of disguised racialism.

The 1920's thus saw the foundations laid for the building of a structure of laws which in the succeeding years was to undergo constant change to meet the ever-growing need for racial bolstering, while any disguising of the traditional prejudice was to become redundant through the enactment of the unashamedly discriminatory laws of the post-1948 apartheid era.

In the next chapters these early laws affecting the labour market and their successors will be considered in detail.

The Growth
of Legal Rigidity
in the Labour Market

THE CONTENT
OF LEGISLATION

EARLY LAWS REGULATING LABOUR CONDITIONS

(a) The Masters and Servants Laws

IN CONSIDERING THE industrial machinery created by statute in the Union, one cannot ignore the important influence exerted by the earlier nineteenth-century Masters and Servants laws on the framing of later legislation and in formulating attitudes towards employees, particularly non-white employees. It should be borne in mind that until 1834 the greater part of the basic labour force fell within the scope of slavery, and even if South Africa's experience in this regard was less harsh than elsewhere, the very nature of slavery was bound to foreshadow rigid attitudes of paternalism. It was in this spirit that the Voortrekkers left the Cape Colony to found new societies in which most of these paternal attitudes could be retained intact. It was a natural consequence, therefore, that the laws of the Boer Republics should have failed to admit any equality between the white and non-white races, and that there should have been a general tendency to draft and enact laws of masters and servants which appear to be unduly harsh in their provisions regarding servants.

The Masters and Servants law was first enacted in the Cape in 1841, and formed the model for all subsequent laws of this kind in the other territories and later for the Union as a whole. The Cape Masters and Servants and Apprentices Ordinance of 1856, which replaced the 1841 law, is, in fact, still in operation, with amendments, while the other provinces have very similar laws. The term 'servant' is defined as 'any person employed for hire, wages, or other remuneration, to perform any handicraft or other bodily labour in agriculture or manufacture, or in domestic service, or as a boatman, porter, or other occupation of a like nature'.

What is of particular significance is that the laws attach criminal liabilities to breaches of contract regarded by South African common law as civil wrongs. While the master is liable for withholding wages and food, his servants may be liable for a variety of offences, such as absence without permission, dereliction of duty, etc. The application of criminal actions to breaches of contract is archaic in modern society, constituting a serious barrier to the orderly settlement of disputes, and as the laws only affect unskilled labouring workers it is largely the non-white who suffers. Consequently there is an understandable tendency for non-whites to regard the Masters and Servants laws as a manifestation of racial discrimination.

(b) The Native Labour Regulation Act, No. 15 of 1911, as amended

Act No. 15 of 1911, as amended, was enacted to 'regulate the Recruiting, Employment, Accommodation and Feeding and Health conditions of Native Labour' in any mine or works and in any occupation or any area which the Minister may declare for the purposes of the Act. The Act thus embraces the entire mining industry. It provides for the licensing of recruiting agents and establishes minimum standards of accommodation, food and medical facilities and compensation for injuries.

It contains certain penal sanctions not unlike those of the Masters and Servants laws which, in addition, have the effect of attaching criminal liability to any Africans, falling within the jurisdiction of the Act, who take part in strikes. The relevant section 14(1), summarized below, stipulates that any Native labourer is guilty of an offence if he:

(a) without lawful cause deserts or absents himself from his place of employment or fails to enter upon or carry out the terms of his contract of employment; or
(b) wilfully and unlawfully does or omits to do anything which causes or is likely to cause injury to persons or property; or
(b)(bis) neglects to perform any work which it is his duty to perform or unfits himself for the proper performance of his work through

the use of dagga or other habit-forming drugs or by having become or being intoxicated during working hours; or

(b)(ter) refuses to obey any lawful command of his employer or any person lawfully placed in authority over him or uses insulting or abusive language to those in authority; or

(c) after entering into an oral or written agreement of service with a labour agent or authorised recruiting officer and accepting an advance in respect thereof, accepts another advance from another labour agent or recruiting officer in consideration of entering upon another contract of service before he has completed his term of service under the first-mentioned agreement.

Conviction for any of these offences renders him liable to 'a fine not exceeding ten pounds, or, in default of payment, to imprisonment with or without hard labour for a period not exceeding two months'.

Thus not only are penal sanctions applied to contractual obligations, but the development of normal trade union practices is seriously hampered if not wholly prevented. The 1951 Industrial Legislation Commission, describing the Act, said:

In such circumstances there is no scope for collective action for the improvement of conditions of employment and the Act consequently contains no provision for negotiation between employers and workers, or for the fixation of minimum wages. The Act is based entirely on the idea of a paternal Government looking after the interests of the people concerned.[1]

While it may, of course, be argued that the bulk of the African mine labourers, as was suggested by the Witwatersrand Mine Natives' Wages Commission, 'have not yet reached the stage of development which would enable them safely and usefully to employ Unionism as a means of promoting their advancement',[2] it is probably unrealistic to believe that the development of trade unionism among Africans can be permanently prevented, or that a stage could not be soon reached where they could benefit from healthy trade unionism. The more the spirit of trade unionism is opposed, the greater is likely to be the feeling of hostility engendered among African workers. It is in the long run far more satisfactory to allow a smooth, if gradual, evolution of collective bargaining methods, than to divert what may be healthy grievances into a hostile undercurrent of bitterness.

[1] U.G. 62/51, p. 194, para. 1445.
[2] U.G. 21/44, para. 466.

Experience on the Copperbelt of Northern Rhodesia would suggest that, given the right guidance and leadership, the African is quite capable of using the tools of collective bargaining in a responsible way.

In considering this question, however, one has to take into account that the content of the labour force of the gold-mines differs greatly from that of industry as a whole in South Africa. (The problem as it affects other occupations will be considered later.) Whereas in Northern Rhodesia there is a relatively stable and homogeneous labour force, in the Union about 65 per cent of the African gold-mineworkers come from territories outside the country, while the remainder are largely migratory and unsophisticated.

THE TRAINING OF ARTISANS

(a) The Apprenticeship Act, No. 37 of 1944, as amended

The origin of the present Apprenticeship Act is closely tied up with the question of 'civilized standards' and the Poor White problem as a whole. The widely held fear that whites would gradually be displaced by non-whites, resulting in a debasement of civilized standards, caused considerable concern about the adequacy of facilities for the training of white youths. Until 1920 there were few opportunities for organized training in the skilled trades, and it was suggested that white youths not only tended to swell the ranks of the unskilled, thus aggravating the problem of white debasement, but that they deliberately avoided entering the trades in the belief that conditions were not sufficiently attractive. The need was therefore felt for the creation of machinery which would not only regulate training facilities, but would, in turn, provide white youths with the skill necessary to enable them to raise their standards and thus avoid being swamped by non-whites.

It was in this atmosphere that Act No. 26 of 1922 was passed. The Act itself went further than setting up machinery for the regulation of the trades and control of training. By specifying minimum entry requirements, it in fact introduced a disguised discriminatory element, for few non-whites were able to reach Standard VI, which became the point of entry for most of the trades. Thus, while it may be possible, superficially, to argue that there was no racial bias and that the fixing of a minimum standard of entry ensured only that there was no debasement of artisan standards, two important points cannot be disregarded when the Apprenticeship Act is considered in relation to the colour bar in industry.

In the first place, even though there are non-whites quite capable of reaching the required standard of entry, few of them have the means to remain at school long enough to reach this qualifying point. On the other hand, and perhaps of even greater importance, is the fact that there was, and still is, a shortage of facilities for higher and primary schooling for non-whites: education for them is not compulsory, and courses necessary for qualifying as artisans open to non-whites are limited in number and location. For instance, even as late as 1959 there were only 582 Coloured boys being trained in skilled trades at a single industrial school near Cape Town. Furthermore, it has often been considered that in the case of a number of trades the entry qualification of Standard VI is unjustifiably high.

The Act has been subject to other criticisms in respect of the provisions ensuring that the standard of apprenticeship training is maintained at a sufficiently high level. Although it was re-enacted in 1944, there is still no provision made for compelling apprentices to pass any qualifying examinations, even though they may be obliged to attend classes at a recognized training establishment. As recently as 1958, for example, the Viljoen Commission had this to say about the training of skilled workers:

The deficiencies of the present system of the training of apprentices are said to be the following;

(1) the absence of aptitude testing and vocational guidance in the recruitment and selection of suitable candidates;
(2) the absence of an organised scheme of training;
(3) the absence of trade tests;
(4) the fact that, irrespective of the practical training received and his proficiency in the trade, and also of his standard of technical education, the apprentice automatically becomes an artisan on the completion of a stated period; and
(5) the fact that no incentives are provided for a talented apprentice, by being allowed for example to qualify for artisan status in a shorter period than the normal.

It would therefore not seem surprising that only a very small percentage of the apprentices are said to take any interest in their studies. *It would seem to the Commission that a system of training that*

9

is so vital to the country and subject to so many defects would need a very careful investigation and, where necessary, a very thorough over-haul, and the Commission recommends accordingly.[3]

From the point of view of the present study, the Act's signifi-cance lies in denying to a large proportion of non-whites the opportunity of entering the skilled trades and thus perpetuating the conditions of scarcity which stemmed from the early mining days when rates of pay had, of necessity, to be high enough to attract artisans from abroad. These conditions of rigidity must have a definite effect on the course of economic growth. High artisan wages mean a high cost-structure, accentuated further by inadequately assimilated training and reduced efficiency as a result of the lack of competition.

The full cumulative effects of the rigidity introduced by the Apprenticeship Act may be offset by 'circumventions': for example, permitting non-whites to do skilled work either by 'occupational passing' in the case of the Cape Coloured or by deliberate evasion of the law. In both cases quantitative measure-ment is out of the question; these inferences are based upon information gathered by the writer during several years of research in the Cape Peninsula; nevertheless the existence of such circumventions may go some way to explain why the impact of rigidity has not been as severe as might have been expected.[4]

Clearly, however, the extent of such 'devices' is limited and in most cases to the smaller establishments where control cannot be as effective as in larger concerns. They are also likely to be resorted to more frequently in the semi-skilled range of jobs, and it is most likely that standards of work performance will, as a result, be lower.

(b) The Native Building Workers Act, No. 27 of 1951, as amended

This Act provides for the training and control of skilled African building workers. While providing distinct machinery for controlling Africans in skilled jobs in the building trade, it

[3] Report of the Commission of Enquiry into policy relating to the protection of industries, 1958 (U.G. 36/58), p. 33, paras. 270-1.
[4] See G. V. Doxey, 'Racial stratification in the labour market in relation to labour turnover among non-Europeans in the Cape Peninsula', published in the *Proceedings of the Social Science Conference*, Institute for Social Research, University of Natal, 1956.

expressly removes such workers from the scope of the Apprenticeship Act (section 12) and in effect severely restricts their usefulness in the economy as a whole by defining the areas in which they can work.

For purposes of the Act, section 1(xvi) defines 'skilled work' as work performed in any of eleven very widely defined occupations and 'any other building trade or branch of such trade which the Minister may by notice in the *Gazette* declare to be skilled work'.

Section 14(1) prohibits any person in *an urban area outside of the Native areas* from employing Africans on such work. Africans may, however, do work on buildings or premises occupied and owned by themselves or their dependants, while skilled work performed upon a farm exclusively for farm purposes is likewise exempted (section 15, as amended by Act No. 60 of 1955). Furthermore, regulations promulgated under the Act permit African workers to be used in the urban areas on simple maintenance operations in respect of private property, though, presumably to protect the Cape Coloured people, the Cape Peninsula is excluded from certain of the exceptions. (*Government Gazette* 15.6.56, Government Notice No. 1061.) As reciprocity, however, other races are prohibited from operating as skilled workers in the Native areas, including urban African townships. (Section 16.)

Section 2 of the Act establishes a board known as the *Native Building Workers Advisory Board*, consisting 'of so many members, not less than seven, as the Minister of Labour may from time to time determine', which has the right to advise the Minister on (*a*) the training of learners as Native building workers and (*b*) conditions of employment.

The Minister is also empowered, after consulting with the Ministers of Bantu Administration and Development and Education, Arts and Science, to make the arrangements *he deems fit*, to provide for Africans to be trained to perform skilled work, and although the period of training may not exceed four years (section 10(1)), the Minister is empowered to determine the *maximum* number of learners to be trained during any given period (section 10(2)).

Section 13(1) empowers the Minister, after consultation with the Minister of Bantu Administration and Development, the

Wage Board established under the Wage Act, as amended, and the Advisory Board to:

make a determination prescribing minimum rates of remuneration, working hours or other conditions of employment which shall be applicable to employers and native building workers or learners or other natives employed by them on such classes of skilled work carried out in the building industry in any specified native area as may be specified in the determination.

While any determination is in operation, any other wage-regulating measures relating to skilled building work in force in the area covered by the determination are suspended (section 13(4)).

Although the Act ostensibly protects the African from competition in his own areas, its effect in the urban areas is to cut off opportunities for advancement in skilled building work by urban Africans. Furthermore, it provides an additional legal bolster to the skilled white worker in the important building industry at a time when the rapid expansion in the economy has aggravated the shortage of skilled workers of all categories. Not only is a severe limitation placed on the right of the workman to sell his labour in any part of the labour market, but there is also a serious curtailment of fluidity with consequent aggravating effects especially during periods of shortage in any particular area. As the main source of demand for building workers is likely to remain for the foreseeable future in the established urban areas, there is a real danger that this sector of the labour market will become lopsided. As will be seen below, in the Transvaal and the Orange Free State, whites, in a large variety of occupations associated with the building industry, have been given an additional bolster through the application of 'job reservation' to these areas.

REGULATION OF INDUSTRIAL EMPLOYMENT

(a) The Industrial Conciliation Act

The 1922 disturbances confirmed the need for effective machinery to deal with industrial disputes and thus prevent any repetition of violence. The Industrial Conciliation Act, No. 11 of 1924, was passed to provide for this contingency. It was redrafted in 1937 and again in 1956 (Act No. 36 of 1937 and Act No. 28 of 1956) in the light of recommendations of the 1935 and 1951 Industrial Legislation Commissions. In 1959 the Act was again amended in order to close the loopholes in the job-reservation clause contained in the 1956 legislation (Act No. 41 of 1959).

The Act applies to every undertaking, industry, trade or occupation where labour is organized, with the exception of persons employed in farming operations or in domestic service in private households, officers of Parliament, in respect of their employment as such, persons employed by the State, or any employee of any local authority, and various persons employed in educational institutions.

It establishes machinery for the regulation of conditions of work and the setting of wage-rates through the functioning of industrial councils, and for the settlement of industrial disputes by means of negotiation, conciliation or arbitration.

An industrial council is composed of representatives of registered employers' associations and of registered trade unions representing the workers in a particular industry. Each council has its own constitution, and is empowered to negotiate an agreement for the industry concerned which covers conditions of service, wage-rates, hours of work, additional benefits in the form of annual leave, bonuses, etc., and similar matters. This agreement is drawn up with the guidance of the Department of Labour and assumes the force of law when it receives Ministerial approval and is published in the *Government Gazette*. It then becomes binding on all employers and employees in the industry and area specified.

Having negotiated the agreement, the industrial council is responsible for administering and enforcing it, and for settling —or at least for attempting to settle—any disputes which may arise. If it fails in this respect, the dispute must be referred to arbitration and the Industrial Tribunal, established by the 1956 Act, may now be called upon to assume the role of arbitrator. Strikes are illegal when an industrial council agreement is in force if the matter is one covered by the agreement, and even if it is not, no strike is permitted until conciliation and/or arbitration procedures, as laid down in the Act, have been resorted to.

In practice, the system of industrial councils has worked well in sections of industry where the workers are well organized.

The importance of the Industrial Conciliation Act from the racial point of view lies partly in the definition of persons declared *not* to be employees within the meaning of the Act and who cannot therefore participate in the machinery of industrial self-government which it set up. The original Act excluded a person who fell within the scope of any Native pass laws and regulations, or the Native Labour Regulation Act, No. 15 of 1911, or any amendments thereof, or any regulations made thereunder, or by Act No. 40 of 1894 of Natal or any amendment thereof.

This in effect meant that the bulk of the Africans in the provinces other than the Cape were excluded from the scope of the Act. To meet the possibility that employers might use this as a loophole to substitute 'free' Africans for those whites who were subject to the agreement, the Act was amended in 1930 to give the industrial councils, subject to Ministerial approval, the right to extend the terms of an agreement to Africans. This practice was in fact continued in the later Acts (section 48(3)(*a*) of Act No. 28 of 1956). The exclusion, however, of Native areas under section 51(12) from the operation of the Act would in effect mean that any employer who wishes to circumvent the operation of section 48(3)(*a*) could set up his place of employment in these areas and thus be free to pay whatever wages he wished.

In the 1937 Act the definition of persons excluded from the scope of the Act remained substantially the same but was extended to include any person whose contract of service or labour was regulated by the Natives (Urban Areas) Act, No. 24 of 1923, as amended by Act No. 25 of 1930 and Act No. 46 of 1937 or any amendment of, or regulation made under, the Act.

When considering the racial bias of the Act or its effect in bringing about rigidity in the labour market, it is interesting to note that it was not the intention of the Act in excluding 'persons' to imply that any European could consequently not be excluded from the definition of employee. Thus in the case of *Bethlehem Municipality* v. *The Minister of Labour*, 1943 A.D. 75, the Appeal Court held that a European location superintendent who was appointed and licensed under the Native (Urban Areas) Act, No. 24 of 1923, was not an employee within the meaning of the

Act. The possibility of this often arising in practice, however, was rare.

However, as section 1(*c*) of Act 42 of 1946 exempted any African holding an exemption certificate issued under Proclamation No. 150 of 1934 from the relevant section (23(1)(*a*)) of the Natives (Urban Areas) Act, No. 24 of 1945, a small percentage of the African labour force in organized industries fell under the provisions of the Industrial Conciliation Act. Nevertheless in spite of this concession the bulk of the African workers were excluded from the scope of the Act.

The 1956 Act went further in excluding Africans. An employee is now defined under section 1(xii) as any person (other than a Native), while section 1(xx) defines a Native as any person who is in fact or is generally accepted as a member of any aboriginal race or tribe of Africa.

The definitions of white and Coloured persons are interesting. Under section 1(vi) a Coloured person is 'a person who is not a white person or a native', while under section 1(xliv) a white person is 'a person who in appearance, obviously is, or who is generally accepted as a white person, but does not include a person who although in appearance obviously a white person is generally accepted as a coloured person'. These somewhat loose definitions open the possibilities of confusion, hardship, and even fraud.

The 1959 amendments to the Act sought to make certain that no African would be able to take part in any deliberations under the Act. Section 21 now stipulates that 'No native shall be appointed as a representative of the employees or as an alternate to such a representative' on industrial councils, while section 37 now provides that, unless otherwise authorized by the Minister, 'no native shall be appointed to represent the employee parties' in connexion with disputes under the Act.

In addition to the express exclusion of Africans from the operation of the Act, the most significant manifestation of the group approach in the Industrial Conciliation Act is to be found in the relevant sections dealing with the elimination of inter-racial competition. The 1951 Industrial Legislation Commission had considered the position, but carefully avoided undue discussion by recommending 'that the task of finding a satisfactory solution in regard to protective measures in general is one which should be entrusted to an expert scientific body, which would require careful study before it could complete a general survey of the whole labour economy and submit concrete and sound proposals'. Nevertheless it had some definite views on the effect of racial protection on the optimum use of labour resources, mooting that such a body should 'take into account the relative youthfulness of the South African National Economy and the fact that any policy suggested should not have the effect of an *economic straitjacket*'[5] (my italics). Once again there was the expression of fear that racial discrimination would conflict with the needs of the economy. The 1951 Commission was in effect echoing the warnings of its 1935 predecessor that 'social aspirations and policies should be in harmony with economic realities and should not conflict with the economic policy of encouraging the expansion of employment and thereby of the national income, the source of all wage payments'.[6]

In spite of the already widespread artificial barriers to mobility it was nevertheless found necessary to carry matters a stage further. To understand this one must view the matter to some extent as a natural outcome of historical evolution. It would be too much to expect that with the growing political power of traditionally prejudiced white labour there would be any concession to the politically impotent non-white, handicapped in the labour market through inadequate trade union machinery. While for the economist it may be impossible to divorce the labour problem from the over-all economic problem, it became quite impossible for white labour to see the problem in any other light than as one of maintaining white supremacy; immediate advantage is thus preferred to conjectural advantage.

Job reservation and racial separation in trade unions were two radical concessions to this group first introduced by the 1956 Industrial Conciliation Act. The Act was amended in 1959 to give the Minister stronger powers to implement reservations and overcome the various legal difficulties which had arisen following the enactment of the 1956 legislation.[7]

[5] U.G. 62/51, p. 163, para. 1159.
[6] Report of the Industrial Legislation Commission, 1935 (U.G. 37/35), para. 153.
[7] For a discussion of attempts to implement job reservation and a general appraisal of the trade union viewpoint, see Ray Alexander and H. J. Simons, *Job Reservation and the Trade Unions*, 1959.

(b) *Job reservation*

The upholders of the traditional prejudice had long been thinking in terms of an extension of the conditions existing in the mining industry, under the Mines and Works Act, to the economy as a whole. During parliamentary discussion of the 1937 Wage Bill, attempts were made by prominent Nationalist M.P.s to have included in the provisions of the Act some form of statutory colour bar.

When introducing the 1956 Industrial Conciliation Bill, the Minister of Labour said:

> ... here we have a precautionary measure so that one race cannot set standards which make it impossible for another race to make a living, and to mention it specifically, Clause 77, which is a precautionary measure to safeguard the standards of living of the White workers of South Africa and to ensure that they will not be exploited by the lower standards of any other race.[7a]

In terms of section 17 of the 1956 Act, an Industrial Tribunal, consisting of five members appointed by the Minister of Labour, was established. It has, among other duties and functions, the power to make investigations, on the instruction of the Minister, into the desirability of making determinations which will reserve defined types of work for specified racial groups, whenever it appears to the Minister that such measures should be taken in order to safeguard the economic welfare of white, Coloured or African employees in any industry, trade or occupation.

In terms of section 77(1)(*a*), as substituted by the 1959 Act, however, the Minister's powers have been considerably widened and he may now initiate investigations whenever he deems it desirable to do so.

The Tribunal may be assisted, in an advisory capacity, if the Minister thinks it advisable, by assessors appointed from representatives of employers and employees (section 17(14)(*a*)), but these assessors may not be Africans (section 21(5)).

The Minister is thus given wide powers of discretion under section 77 with regard to the direction of inquiries and the scope of the terms of reference of specific inquiries made by the Tribunal in matters regarding the need to 'safeguard against inter-racial competition'; for purposes of job reservation, the Act is extended to include Africans in the definition of 'employees'.

[7a] *Hansard*, 23 January 1956, col. 276.

The Act directs the Tribunal to submit a report to the Minister setting out the results of its investigations and the reasons for its conclusions, but only after: (1) considering any representations which may be made by interested parties following an invitation to do so in the *Government Gazette*; (2) consulting with (*a*) any industrial council concerned, (*b*) any registered employers' organization, registered trade union or local authority which is concerned in the matter and which is not a party to any industrial council already consulted, and (*c*) the Central Native Labour Board if the interests of Native employees are affected; (3) making any other investigations it deems necessary (section 77(5)(*a*)).

It may either recommend that no further action should be taken or that a determination be made in respect of the whole, or part, of the area specified and in respect of the whole, or part, of the undertaking, industry, trade, occupation or class of work specified (section 77(5)(*b*)(i)). Furthermore, 'in defining any portion of an undertaking, industry, trade or occupation or class of work, the tribunal may use any method of differentiation or discrimination it may deem expedient' while 'different recommendations may be made in respect of different areas or different portions of an undertaking, industry, trade or occupation or class of work' (section 77(5)(*b*)(i) & (iii)).

Determinations recommended by the Tribunal under section 77(6)(*a*) may have any one or more of the following effects:

(1) Employers may be prohibited from engaging workers of one race for jobs at present undertaken by workers of another race; or

(2) from reducing the percentage of employees of a particular racial group in relation to the total number of employees of a specified class.

(3) Any 'specified class of work' may be wholly or partly reserved for 'persons of a specified race or class' and other persons prohibited from performing such work. Thus, in addition to racial distinctions, workers may be classified on the basis of age, sex, type of work, or any other criteria.

(4) Minimum, maximum, or average numbers of persons of a specified race who may be employed during a specified period, or generally, on 'work or any specified class of work' may be laid down, or percentages for members of one race who may be

employed in relation to the total number of employees for specified types of work may be fixed.

(5) The Tribunal may also recommend the regulation, *on any basis which it deems advisable*, of the number of employees of any specified race who may be employed in any defined class of work. This provision is general in scope and is not limited by the other provisions of this subsection.

(6) Any other relevant matter may be provided for.

These very sweeping powers are further supported by the provision that, in making a recommendation, the powers of the Tribunal shall not be affected in any way by the extent to which persons of any race are, at the time of the investigation, employed or available for employment, or are likely to be available for employment in the undertaking, occupation, industry or class of work specified in the terms of reference (section 77(6)(*b*)).

In effect, therefore, the Tribunal can begin investigations into an industry where the overwhelming majority of the workers are of one race, and can introduce recommendations which favour the minority group of employees and totally disregard the position of the majority. This was particularly the case in the clothing industry.

The Tribunal is not guided by any specific principles in making recommendations; even the present or future employment positions need not be taken into account. In effect, therefore, the fact that changes in the racial composition of a labour force have come about as a result of economic progress can be completely disregarded.

An adjunct to a determination is the provision that replacement of workers of one race by workers of another race may be specifically prohibited (section 77(*a*)(i) and (ii)). In other words, displaced non-white workers cannot in these circumstances, be given non-reserved jobs held by other whites — an expedient which might have been resorted to by employers in order to minimize the cost effects of job reservation in a particular occupation.

Furthermore, the Act contains yet another example of the present trend towards the granting of extensive Ministerial powers in that the Minister is allowed to 'correct any error or omission or clarify any provision in a determination' if he regards it as necessary, after the coming into force of the determination. Such changes will have the same effect as if they had been part of the original determination (section 77(8)).

In the 1959 Act, the provision which formerly excluded occupations covered by the Mines and Works Act from the imposition of job reservation was dropped, so that it would now be possible for job reservation to be extended to the mining industry.

Since the passing of the 1959 Act it has not been necessary to obtain the consent of an industrial council for a determination made during the life of an industrial conciliation agreement. This amendment followed the difficulties which arose after attempts were made to apply job reservation to the clothing industry in 1957. Consent was withheld by all the industrial councils in the trade, and non-white workers, who constituted the vast majority of employees, stayed away from work in November 1957. Later, the unions took the matter to court and in the case of *Garment Workers' Union, Cape* v. *Viljoen*, 1958 (2) S.A. 393 (C), the Cape Provincial Division of the Supreme Court set aside the determination on the grounds of a misconception of powers on the part of the Industrial Tribunal.

The 1956 Act and the amending Act of 1959 thus placed in the hands of the Minister of Labour sweeping powers which enable him to determine virtually arbitrarily the part which each race can play in the labour market or any sector or area of it at any given moment.

Whereas, on paper, job reservation can be applied for the protection of any race, the nature of existing circumstances in the labour market and the list of determinations which have already been published indicate that, in practice, determinations will be designed to afford the white group another legal barrier against non-white encroachment, thus further preventing the non-white from rising to higher and more responsible positions in industry and accentuating those frustrations of ambition which have in turn a profound effect upon the over-all efficiency of this group as a factor of production. From the economic point of view the waste which flows from this misuse of potential is obvious. Not only is the non-white prevented from the opportunity to rise in the job scale and consequently denied the chance of revealing his true capacity, but the efficiency of the white is reduced through lack of effective and healthy competition.

The entire concept of allocating jobs on a basis of racial selection has met with widespread criticism from employers on the grounds that it cuts across the principle of free choice of labour and creates conditions of great uncertainty. Employers argue that they will be unable to plan their labour policies in advance, while any projected training schemes would have to take into account the possibility that a particular sphere of employment might at any given moment be reserved for one race. The powers granted in the Act enable the Minister, for example, to reserve an occupation for a particular race even in cases where there may be no members of that race doing such work. While such extreme determinations may not necessarily be resorted to in practice, the power to make them nevertheless exists and uncertainty is consequently made greater. The fact that the Minister may in certain cases grant exemptions from the provisions of a determination (section 77(10)(*a*)), does not lessen the tensions generated, for the workers granted such permits are made aware that should the Minister deem it advisable he may revoke permission at any time.

In the building industry the powers conferred by the Act have already been used to remove non-whites from a large variety of jobs in the Transvaal and Orange Free State. Determination No. 6 in terms of section 77 (Government Notice No. 1428, *Government Gazette* 18.9.59) declared 'work in the Building Industry in urban areas of the provinces of the Orange Free State and the Transvaal' reserved for white persons. The determination defines the building industry in terms of all occupations associated with building and defines 'work' as all work excluding a carefully listed schedule of some ninety semi-skilled and unskilled jobs. The combined effect of this determination and the Native Building Workers Act is to give the white building worker complete protection against non-white competition, while the supplanted non-whites must either leave the provinces concerned or seek other occupations.

Determinations have also been made in the clothing industry, in Durban's municipal cleansing department, the iron, steel and metallurgical industries, the Cape Town municipality and for passenger-lift operators in Bloemfontein, Johannesburg and Pretoria.

In the clothing industry, in terms of Government Notice

No. 1656 of 25 October 1957, work of machinists, supervisors, cutters and choppers-out and table-hands was reserved for whites.

On 23 May 1958 the driving of motor transport vehicles in the Durban municipal cleansing department was reserved for whites for a period of five years (Government Notice No. 724).

Fifteen types of work have been reserved for whites in the iron, steel, engineering and metallurgical industries concerned with the manufacture of window and door metal surrounds (Government Notice No. 1066 of 25 July 1958); while on 30 October 1959 some 29 categories of work in the manufacture of kitchen equipment were also declared reserved (Government Notice No. 1771).

In November 1958, in municipal undertakings in Cape Town, the jobs of traffic policemen above the rank of constable, firemen, ambulance drivers and attendants were reserved for whites, while no further non-white traffic constables may now be employed (Government Notice No. 1659 of 7 November 1958). It is interesting to note that Coloured men were used as traffic police following difficulties in finding suitable Europeans for these jobs. The experiment proved a great success until objections were made that it was *infra dig* to have non-whites controlling 'white' traffic.

The operation of passenger-lifts in Bloemfontein, Johannesburg and Pretoria has also been reserved for whites (Government Notice No. 979 of 26 June 1959).

In all these cases, the services of non-whites had been used because of the general shortage of suitable whites. Thus, in recent years, as will be shown in a later chapter, non-whites have been filling the vacancies in the field of 'white' work left by Europeans who have risen in the work scale, or have filled those new openings created by technical progress and economic expansion for which no suitable whites are available. The reports of the Industrial Tribunal which have followed investigations into the desirability of making work reservations in particular sections of industry appear to support this view.

It is, of course, too soon to generalize or to draw definitive conclusions as to what circumstances will lead to job reservation in individual cases, or what reasons will be given for introducing it. Of the seven determinations made at the time of writing, three have been concerned with services and four with branches of industrial activity. The group approach is clearly reflected in the Industrial Tribunal's reports on these proposed reservations: despite the admission of a paucity of statistics and the difficulty of obtaining reliable information either from representatives of employers and employees or from replies to questionnaires sent to employers, the Tribunal has not hesitated to pronounce on the need for 'protection of the European' who may be threatened by the fragmentation of artisans' work into partly unskilled and semi-skilled work. (Report on work reservation in the building industry in the O.F.S. and Transvaal, 10 July 1959.) In the report on work reservation in a section of the iron and steel industry (dated 25 February 1958) the Tribunal stated '. . . that the economic welfare of those employees that are at present employed is being threatened . . .' and in the Report on job reservation in the manufacture of kitchen equipment (dated 10 September 1959) we read that the industry is one in which 'the European ought to have a greater share'.

Although technical progress and ever-increasing specialization and mechanization make inevitable a continuous reorganization and improvement of industrial technique, it would appear from the Industrial Tribunal's reports that this process 'cannot be allowed to exist unhampered at the cost of the *most important* body of employees'. (My italics—the quotation is from the report on reservation in the building industry.) In other words, the job security of the white worker cannot be threatened by actual substitution of non-white labour or by the splitting-off of less skilled jobs, or by the introduction of semi-skilled work: if circumstances show this to be a danger, the employment of the white worker can be assured by job reservation.

The guiding principle to which job reservation gives expression is, therefore, that where white workers feel they should have the monopoly of a particular class of employment, criteria of suitability or of established employment patterns will count for nothing, and its immediate application in a particular field is that employers may be forced to employ unsuitable Europeans whom they would not otherwise have included in their labour force or prevented from introducing programmes involving technical change.

If it comes to be widely implemented, this policy will constitute an extension into the fields of secondary and tertiary industry of a system of racial stratification akin to the colour bar restrictions which have been a feature of the mining industry since the enactment of the 1926 Mines and Works Act. The future effects on the economy of such a development, both as regards the disqualification of non-whites to undertake specified jobs, and the reservation of the same jobs for whites, simply on grounds of colour, could be very serious indeed.

The industrial economy as a whole would rapidly assume the characteristics of the mining industry where the better utilization of manpower through technical innovation is drastically hampered.

It is also likely that non-whites would be forced to bear the brunt of any spread of unemployment in the economy, for by using the machinery of job reservation, jobs could be rapidly reclassified in order to ensure the minimum of white unemployment.

(c) *The separation of mixed unions*

Section 4(6) of the Act provides that a trade union may not be registered in respect of both white and coloured persons; nor may it be registered if membership is open to white and coloured people, unless total membership is so small that separate unions are not practicable, in which case the Minister may give special permission for registration of a 'mixed' union.

If a mixed union is registered, section 8(3), as amended in 1959, provides that it must have separate branches for white and coloured members, hold separate meetings, and have an all-white executive body. Members of one race may not attend meetings of another racial group, and coloured people may only attend meetings of the executive body when giving evidence or being interrogated. The Minister is given power to grant exemptions from any or all of these provisions, if *he deems it expedient to do so*, on conditions and for periods which he may determine. It is also specifically laid down that 'no such union shall appoint or elect as an official or office bearer thereof any person who is a native'.

These sections constitute a direct implementation of recommendations made by the 1951 Industrial Legislation Commission which argued that mixed unions did not provide 'adequate protection for the economic interests of minority groups, particularly in times of economic depression', did not recognize racial differences which if suppressed may lead to eventual 'racial strife', and which, because of their mixed nature, could not promote 'solidarity of labour'. The Commission noted that although Europeans generally exercised leadership in mixed unions, there was an increasing tendency for non-Europeans to do so, which 'constitutes an economic threat to Europeans and consequently to industrial peace'. Furthermore, it considered that a central body, representing different trade unions, could be a satisfactory substitute for one, single union for purposes of negotiation.[8]

The feeling that racially mixed unions lead to racial strife is based not upon experience but rather conjecture. The Commission itself admitted that the evidence it received was 'overwhelmingly against the introduction of legislation compelling the segregation of the various races into separate unions, and the witnesses who advocated the retention of mixed unions included both employers and employees'.[9] The decision of the Commission to recommend the legal separation of the unions in spite of such evidence is clearly a case of bowing to particular political pressure groups.

The Industrial Conciliation Acts, of course, removed Africans from the trade unions recognized for the purpose of industrial conciliation, so that the so-called 'mixed' unions were made up of white, Coloured and Asian workers. The 1951 Industrial Legislation Commission reported that of the 199 unions registered in South Africa in 1949, 63 were genuinely multi-racial in membership, while a further 76 were registered as multi-racial of which 54 had white members only and 22 non-whites only. On the other hand 38 were registered for whites only and 14 for non-whites only, while 8 did not furnish clear information.[10] Research undertaken by the South African Institute of Race Relations in 1958 showed that of 159 unions reviewed, 68, with a total membership of 210,679, were all white; 18 were Coloured

[8] U.G. 61/51, p. 152, para. 1069.
[9] Ibid., p. 147, para. 1040.
[10] Ibid., p. 147, para. 1038.

10

and/or Indian, with a membership of 18,422; 22 were African (unofficial), with a membership of 20,175, while the remaining 51, with an over-all membership of 183,762, were 'mixed' unions.[11]

It is clear from the above figures that the changes made by the 1956 Act constituted a major disturbance of the pattern which was developing. Furthermore, one may legitimately express the opinion that, in the circumstances, the separation of the unions instead of reducing racial strife could create conditions of unpleasant rivalry and even rancour between the separate unions. Liaison is made difficult and negotiations with employers protracted. Generally speaking, employers prefer not to negotiate with more than one body, and there might also be the temptation to play off one union against the other.

The effectiveness of the labour force as a whole is thus reduced as a factor in collective bargaining, while an important bridge between the races is broken. It is perhaps in this direction that the reason may be found for the separation. According to the 1951 Industrial Legislation Commission, for example, some witnesses had explained that Europeans were in principle generally opposed to mixed trade unions, but where they accepted them, it was because they were compelled thereto by trade union leaders with leftist leanings who ignored differences of race and creed. Thus from the point of view of traditional prejudice, the mixed unions constituted an important barrier to the separation of the races and afforded the possibility that the whole labour force might eventually be united into a single, multi-racial labour movement. Any evolution along these lines would, of course, have run completely contrary to the separatist ideas of apartheid and therefore had to be prevented.

The exclusion of African trade unions from the scope of the Act is interesting in light of the fact that the 1951 Industrial Legislation Commission had recommended that these unions should be granted official recognition, though with 'special measures for their control and guidance'. In supporting its conclusion the Commission had this to say:

In the firm opinion of the Commission, it would be in the general interests of South Africa as a whole to grant Native trade unions

[11] Muriel Horrell, *Racialism and the Trade Unions*, S.A. Institute of Race Relations, 1959, pp. 34-5.

recognition under separate legislation, to subject them to a measure of reasonable control, and to give them sympathetic guidance. Such a course would enable the authorities to lead them into correct channels and to subject them to educational influence, which could only react to the advantage of the Natives and the community as a whole. It would also give Native workers generally, excluding of course those whose minds have been poisoned by leftist agitation, a sense of satisfaction, and it is likely to induce a greater sense of responsibility and reasonableness amongst the leaders and the rank and file. The proposal would ensure that justice is done to the reasonable, responsible and law-abiding Native workers without, the Commission is convinced, creating any danger of undermining European standards or civilization. It covers that extent of common ground which makes possible a sufficient degree of acceptance by European and Native public opinion and, as the Commission has fully explained, it does not do violence to any irresistible economic tendencies. Finally, the proposal accords with the constitution of the International Labour Organization and should, therefore, be acceptable to international opinion.[12]

(d) The Native Labour (Settlement of Disputes) Act, No. 48 of 1953, as amended

This Act was designed to remove Africans from the scope of the Industrial Conciliation Act and to establish special machinery for the settlement of disputes involving African workers on the one hand and employers of Africans on the other (section 1). It applies to every trade or section of trade but does not apply 'to natives in respect of their employment in farming operations, or in domestic service in private households, nor to natives employed by the Government of the Union (including the Railway Administration) or a provincial administration'; nor to the performance of unpaid work in charitable institutions, nor to work in any educational institution, maintained wholly or partly from public funds, which forms part of the education or training of the persons performing it (section 2(2)).

The Governor-General may, however, 'by proclamation in the Gazette, apply the provisions of this Act to natives in respect of their employment in the gold or the coal mining industry in any area with effect from a date to be specified in such proclamation, and may in like manner amend or withdraw any such proclamation' (section 2(3)).

The Act absolutely forbids strikes and lock-outs, and while

[12] U.G. 62/51, p. 226, paras. 1636-7.

not expressly forbidding African trade unions it withholds official recognition from them. It thus largely removes Africans from the ordinary sphere of collective bargaining.

Section 18 (as amended by Act No. 59 of 1955) stipulates that:

No employee or other person shall instigate a strike or incite any employee or other person to take part in or to continue a strike, or take part in a strike or in the continuation of a strike, and no employer or other person shall instigate a lock-out or incite any employer or other person to take part in or to continue a lock-out, or take part in a lock-out or in the continuation of a lock-out.

Anyone who takes any part in a strike or lock-out or in the continuation of a strike or lock-out, 'shall be guilty of an offence and liable on conviction to a fine not exceeding five hundred pounds or imprisonment for a period not exceeding three years', or imprisonment without the option of a fine, or in addition to a fine (section 18).

In terms of section 18, as amended by Act No. 59 of 1955 (section 1), a 'strike' is given the same very wide definition as in section 1 of the Industrial Conciliation Act, namely any one or more of a long list of acts or omissions by employees or former employees. These acts or omissions include partial or complete work stoppages, go-slow practices and obstruction of work performance. They also include the breach of employment contracts as the result of an agreement or understanding between workers, whether expressed or not, which aims at compelling or inducing employers (*a*) to comply with demands put forward by the workers with regard to conditions of employment; (*b*) to employ or dismiss any other employees; (*c*) to restore the *status quo* where the employer himself has introduced changes in the conditions of employment.

Special machinery is provided under the Act for the prevention and settlement of disputes concerning African employees. Regional native labour committees can be established by the Minister in any area (section 4(1)), with not less than four members, the chairman being the native labour officer for the area, who must be a *European* civil servant (section 8), and the other members being Africans appointed by the Minister to represent the interests of African employees (section 4(2)).

The regional committees are charged with the tasks of keeping in contact with African workers in the area and with their conditions of employment; of submitting reports from time to time both to the local inspector and to the Central Native Labour Board on disputes which may arise, or have arisen, and of assisting in the settlement of such disputes (section 6(1)). In pursuing these objects, a regional committee can make such inquiries as it deems necessary and can also hear representations from employers and African employees (section 6(2)).

Provision is also made for a Central Native Labour Board to be set up, with wholly *European* membership, after consultation with regional committees (section 1). It is the function of the Board to deal with disputes if the regional committee fails in its task of mediation (section 3).

As already mentioned when the Industrial Conciliation Act was under consideration, when an industrial council or conciliation board (in terms of that Act) is considering an agreement affecting occupations in which Africans are employed, representatives of the Central Board and the European chairman of the local regional committee are entitled to attend and join in the deliberations, but not to vote.

Section 7 of the Act provides that 'whenever in any establishment there are employed not less than twenty employees and such employees advise their employer that they are desirous of electing a works committee', the employer must notify the inspector who then makes the necessary arrangements for the establishment of such a committee under the chairmanship of the local native labour officer.

In actual practice little headway appears to have been made with the setting up of these committees and by April 1959 only eight were actually functioning, largely, it would appear, through lack of support on the part of African workers. It would seem that the antipathy of African workers towards the machinery created under the Act is widespread as is suggested by the following observations:

Africans maintain that the Labour Board officials generally have more sympathy for the views of the employers than for those of the workers. Various strikes have been prevented, they say, by making promises that are not fulfilled, or by intimidating the workers into accepting whatever conditions the employers may offer. When serious labour disputes threaten, detectives of the Special Branch often accompany the Labour Board officials who arrive to undertake investigations. The leaders of the dispute then fear that unless they capitulate, they may be required to leave the town concerned and be denied permits to work in any urban area. Much hostility is, naturally, engendered when the workers are intimidated in these ways.[13]

Besides being a further barrier to the community approach, the Act thus denies Africans two fundamentals of collective bargaining; the right to organize effectively and the right to strike. This fosters the danger that in the long run the Act might drive grievances underground, which has obviously unpleasant implications.

In spite of these drastic restrictions the Act has not prevented strikes; in 1957, 113 strikes involving 6,158 African workers were reported. In 20 of these cases the workers were prosecuted for striking illegally. Altogether during 1957, 539 Africans were charged and 274 were convicted, while in 1958, 588 were charged for illegally striking and 453 convicted.[14]

It is, of course, extremely dangerous to approach the problem of African labour from a purely paternal point of view. While it may have been possible to regard primitive, tribal Africans, in the stage of introduction, from this viewpoint, these conditions no longer apply to a large proportion of the African population in South Africa today. A fresh approach is now required in which Africans in the process of adaptation can be given every assistance and guidance to facilitate their smooth absorption into the industrial economy. The recognition of African trade unions should, therefore, be regarded as an essential part of this process, in order to give Africans the much-needed opportunity to gain experience in responsible citizenship and to develop sound leadership. In the modern society the trade union should represent an important cohesive factor among urban detribalized Africans; filling the vacuum caused by the necessary disappearance of tribal ties.

(e) The Wage Act

Act No. 27 of 1925 and its successors, the Wage Act, No. 44 of 1937, and the Wage Act, No. 5 of 1957, created machinery for the fixing of wage-rates and the regulation of conditions of work in industries employing *unorganized* labour.

[13] Muriel Horrell, op. cit., p. 10.
[14] *Hansard*, 24 January 1958, col. 206, and 30 January 1959, col. 209.

The Act, however, does not apply to (*a*) 'persons in respect of their employment in farming operations or in domestic service in private households'; (*b*) officers of Parliament and persons employed by the State; (*c*) the performance of unpaid work in charitable institutions; (*d*) work in or in connexion with any educational institution maintained wholly or partly from public funds, which forms part of the education or training of the persons performing it; (*e*) 'university students in respect of their employment in any trade as part of their university training, if such employment is required for the completion of their curricula' (section 2(2)). Employees falling within the scope of the Industrial Conciliation Act and apprentices subject to the Apprenticeship Act (section 2(3)) are also excluded and, as already noted, section 13(4) of the Native Building Workers Act removes Africans falling within the scope of that Act from the benefits of wage-determinations made under the Wage Act.

Section 3(1) of the Act sets up a Wage Board consisting of three members appointed by the Minister of Labour, with the object of investigating and making recommendations upon the general conditions of work and rates of pay in work spheres falling within the scope of the Act (section 3(10) and section 4). The Minister may, if he is 'of the opinion that it will assist the Board if employees and employers are represented on the board during any investigation in that trade' (section 4(8)), appoint 'one or more assessors to represent the employees and an equal number of assessors to represent the employers on the board during such an investigation'.

The 1957 Act embodied two important changes: (1) in the right to initiate an investigation, and (2) in the composition of the Wage Board.

Under previous legislation it was the duty of the Board to investigate and report to the Minister on any trade or section of trade 'on a reference to it by the Minister; or *on the application to it of any trade union or employers' organisation registered under the Industrial Conciliation Act* or where no such organisation exists, of a number of employees or employers'. The 1957 Act now leaves the matter entirely to the discretion of the Minister. On the other hand, the previous Wage Acts permitted a trade union or group of trade unions registered or deemed to be registered in terms of the Industrial Conciliation Act to nominate *any* person for appointment as an additional member of the Board, while the same right was extended to employers' and employees' organizations. This privilege is now removed, and section 4(8) substituted, which gives the Minister the power to appoint assessors.

Both these changes are important from the point of view of the present study, for while the Act itself expressly forbids differentiation or distinction on the basis of race or colour (section 4(3)), one may detect in the new provisions disguised discriminatory intent—to understand them it is necessary to consider some aspects of the history of the Acts. When the Wage Bill was first introduced in 1925 there was little doubt as to its purpose as a racial bolster. In making recommendations, the Wage Board was given the express instruction to fix wages at a level which would enable workers to maintain a *civilized standard of living*, with due regard to costs, both of living and production, and to the value of payments in kind. To this end, the then Minister of Labour (Colonel Cresswell) in introducing the Wage Bill had this to say:

In South Africa we have not got a homogeneous population. We have two races separated by a wide gulf of history and civilization; a gulf of difference in material wants which are considered necessary for life. The same process which leads to sweating in another country gives a tendency in this country to eliminate those who require the higher standard of life. . . . In the competitive wage-production system in a situation such as we have in South Africa the lower civilization will gradually drive out the higher civilization. I believe there is room in South Africa for all of us, but I cannot understand any man who can dream that it can be in the long run good for either the civilized or uncivilized inhabitants of South Africa that the civilized population of South Africa should fail to keep their end up and have fullest opportunities of expansion in the country, which is their own. . . . If our civilization is going to subsist we look upon it as necessary that our industries should be guided so that they afford any men desiring to live according to the European standards greater opportunities of doing so, and we must set our face against the encouragement of employment merely because it is cheap and the wage unit is low. This Bill is designed as one that will help in raising the status and efficiency of the worker.[15]

The 1925 Economic and Wage Commission saw clearly the dangers of this procedure and commented:

[15] Hansard, 1925, cols. 1589-90.

While definite exclusion of the Natives from the more remunerative fields of employment by law was not urged upon us, the same result would follow a certain use of the powers of the Wage Board under the Wage Act of 1925, or of other wage-fixing legislation. The method would be to fix a minimum rate for an occupation or craft so high that no Native would be likely to be employed. Even the exceptional Native whose efficiency would justify his employment at the high rate, would be excluded by the pressure of public opinion, which makes it difficult to retain a Native in an employment mainly reserved for Europeans. The significance of such a policy is that it would extend still further, to all skilled and responsible work, the conditions we observed in the mining industry and some other industries where there is a skilled white class, receiving a relatively high rate of pay for their work accompanied by the payment of a low rate for all other work.[16]

With the structural changes in the Union's economy which have taken place since 1925 and particularly since 1937, the Wage Act has, however, become largely applicable to non-whites who today form by far the greater part of the unskilled labour force falling within the scope of the Act. The rigid interpretation of the concept of 'civilized labour' has been modified and more attention has been paid to the question of unskilled wage-rates generally.[17]

The changes in the racial composition of the labour force are of significance when one considers the right under the Act to request investigations, for while in the past there had been, in fact, few requests for investigations from interested parties, there was always the possibility that with the growing sophistication of the non-white there would be an increased demand for these rights. During the second reading debate on the 1957 Bill, one Opposition member had this to say about the removal of the right of interested parties to request an investigation:

A comparison between 1937, twenty years ago, and now, shows that conditions are vastly different. In 1937 there was a large number of Europeans who were unorganised and whose conditions of employment had to be taken care of. That situation has been largely remedied in the last twenty years as a result of boom conditions that have existed in South Africa. But there is another very important factor, and that is that the number of non-Europeans in private industry in South Africa multiplied two and a half times. The number has

[16] U.G. 14/25, p. 124, para. 221.
[17] For a full discussion of the Wage Act and its effects, see S. T. van der Horst, *Native Labour in South Africa*, 1942, p. 252 et seq.

increased from 145,000 in 1938 to 363,000 in 1952. There is a further important consideration, namely that the non-European workers of 1937 were mostly illiterate workers, workers who were unable to know what their rights under the laws were and who were unable intelligently to make use of a law like the Wage Act. But the position is quite different in 1957. The number of articulate non-European workers who are anxious to use this machinery has grown very rapidly, and such workers would, from this point onwards, make increasing use of the Wage Act, and they would do so in spite of the clumsy provisions of the Native Labour (Settlement of Disputes) Act, which almost prevents them from making proper use of the Wage Act. It virtually blocks their access to the Wage Act excepting through officials of the Department of Labour. It prevents their autonomous use of this machinery.[18]

While it might be possible to debate the merits of the decision to remove the right of interested parties to request investigations, the purpose behind the changes in the composition of the Board is clear. There was, under the old system of nomination, the real possibility that employees would nominate a non-white as their representative on the Board, and as the Board's deliberations would most likely embrace both white and non-white workers, it raised from the government's point of view the possibility of a serious conflict with the accepted basis of apartheid. In fact, the Minister of Labour made it clear during the second reading debate that he would not consider appointing non-white assessors:

because the white man is the guardian of the non-white in this country, and because it is part of the policy of this Government not only to apply apartheid and not only to care for the welfare of the non-white in the white areas where the non-white finds himself, but to take pains to do so and to protect his interests thoroughly.[19]

One cannot minimize the importance of the granting to the Minister of far wider powers of discretion than existed previously. Thus, for example, the important decision to make a determination on the basis of the Board's recommendation is left to the Minister 'if he deems it expedient to do so' (section 14(1)), while the same discretion is left with him in regard to amendments or suspensions (sections 15 and 16).

[18] *Hansard*, 1957, vol. 93, cols. 375-6.
[19] Ibid., col. 399.

The Growth
of Legal Rigidity
in the Labour Market

THE CONTENT OF
LEGISLATION (continued)

THE GENERAL REGULATION OF EMPLOYMENT:

THE MINES AND WORKS ACT

THE ORIGINAL Mines and Works Act, No. 12 of 1911, had been passed to control general conditions of work on the mines. Amending Act No. 25 of 1926 regularized and legalized the colour bar on the mines. The present Act, No. 27 of 1956, is in effect a consolidation of all previous legislation. A mine is defined by section 1(ix) as 'any excavation in the earth, whether abandoned or being worked, made for the purpose of searching for or recovering any mineral and any place where any mineral deposit is being worked'.

The Mines and Works Act of 1911 had permitted the Governor-General to promulgate regulations governing the issue of competency certificates for certain categories of work in which it was regarded essential to maintain some control for interests of safety (section 4(i)). The mining regulations, in fact, went further than the Act and stipulated that for a variety of tasks certificates of competency were required which, under Regulation 285, were not granted to 'coloured persons' in the Transvaal or the Orange Free State, while certificates issued in the Cape or Natal to 'coloured persons' were invalid in the other provinces.

There was from the beginning some doubt as to the legality of introducing a colour bar by means of such regulations. The Chamber of Mines for instance had this to say, in evidence presented to the 1913 Economic Commission:

It has been the custom of white men in immediate supervision to place greater responsibility upon their natives as these gradually became

158

more skilled, with the result that the white man long ago arrived at the position of overseer, and now exhibits no inclination to do work which he was formerly accustomed and content to perform. It ensued, naturally, that the white man, owing to his practice of relegating work, often unlawfully, to the native, came to regard manual labour more and more as 'kaffir work', with the result that the opportunity was thus opened to the native to progress in skill in the actual work of the mining, and the overseer, from want of practice, became less efficient in such work. The majority of the white miners now employed by the industry acquired their knowledge of underground work here, and, on account of the native being the labourer, their practical knowledge of mining work is inferior to that of men trained in other mining centres. Consequently, the curious and unsatisfactory position has arisen of underground overseers supervising the work of natives who are frequently more skilled than themselves. . . . There is also the anomaly that in two provinces of the Union of South Africa (Cape Colony and Natal) coloured persons are allowed to hold positions from which they are expressly debarred in the Transvaal and Orange Free State. The opinion is held by many that these regulations are *ultra vires*, though the matter has not been tested at law.[1]

The 1920 Low Grade Mines Commission estimated that the regulations prescribed 32 occupations, embracing 7,057 persons, which could only be filled by whites, while there had been a further *de facto* extension of this situation, as a result of trade union influence and force of custom, to 19 other occupations, embracing 4,020 persons.[2]

Matters were brought to a head as regards the legality of the position following an attempt by the Department of Mines, in 1923, to compel Crown Mines Limited to dispose of the services of an efficient African driver on underground rock-haulage. The magistrate's court decision went in favour of Crown Mines and it was upheld on appeal, so that the colour bar regulation was declared *ultra vires*.[3]

Following the election of the Pact Government, a Bill was introduced in the 1925 session of Parliament to regularize the position and make the colour bar legal in the mining industry. This became the Mines & Works Amendment Act, No. 25 of 1926. The true motives behind the Act had been clearly stated by the 1925 Mining Regulations Commission as being, in

[1] Chamber of Mines Annual Report for 1913, Statement 14 presented to the Economic Commission, p. 478.
[2] U.G. 34/20, p. 27, para. 164 et seq.
[3] *Rex* v. *Hildick Smith*, 1924 'T.P.D. 69.

addition to securing 'to mine workers an adequate measure of protection against accident and disease', to 'go some way towards effecting . . . not only safety and health generally *but also of counteracting the force of the economic advantages at present enjoyed by the native*[4]'. There is thus once more a blatant dualism of purpose: the passing of legislation ostensibly for the community interest but in reality for the benefit of the privileged group. The attitude of the mining industry was that all the needs of protection could be safely left to custom.

Sir Ernest Oppenheimer as member for Kimberley and leading spokesman for the mining industry, besides reiterating these views, said in the second reading debate:

I am strongly opposed to class legislation of any kind. It is an evil to impose class legislation, and the curse of the evil deed is that one must continue to do evil. Once we have passed a measure of this kind we would be forced into more and more class legislation. This is not the means to protect the European worker. It is only by efficiency and application to work that the Europeans can maintain the position which we now occupy in South Africa.[5]

General Smuts, then Leader of the Opposition, had expressed similar misgivings:

Do not pile on the agony and do not make the position of the white man in South Africa impossible.

Do not ring-fence him in with the hatred of all the other races. I would suggest to the Government—I am not going to move an amendment—but I would suggest that we discharge the Order for the second reading and put our heads together to see if some other way out cannot be found. If we do not do that there is not a person here who will not regret it, whose children and grandchildren will not regret the evil results which will arise, evil results beyond the foresight of any man here today to perceive. I have spent my life with these difficulties and I know that this sort of thing is making the life of the white man in South Africa impossible. I hope, therefore, it will be possible for us to find some other way of meeting this difficulty which will help this country on to a saner and sounder policy than we have followed hitherto.[6]

After thirty years, increased inter-racial animosity and a maze of racially biased legislation stand as an increasingly pointed reminder of these warnings.

[4] Mining Regulations Commission, 1925 (U.G. 36/25), para. 119.
[5] *Hansard*, 1925, col. 1922.
[6] Ibid., col. 285.

The colour bar is retained under Act No. 27 of 1956, whereby the Governor-General is given the right to make regulations as to (among other matters): 'certificates of competency required for employment in any particular occupation in, at or about mines, works or machinery, the grant, cancellation and suspension of such certificates and the prohibition of employment of persons not in possession of the required certificates of competency' (section 12(1)(*n*)). Section 12(2)(*a*) specifically excludes Africans and Asians from holding such certificates:

> Any regulation under paragraph (*n*) of sub-section (1) may provide that in any Province, area or place specified therein, certificates of competency in any occupation likewise specified, shall be granted only to persons of the following classes;
>
> (i) Europeans;
> (ii) persons born in the Union and ordinarily resident therein who are members of the class or race known as Cape Coloureds or of the class or race known as Cape Malays; and
> (iii) the people known as Mauritius Creoles or St. Helena persons or their descendants born in the Union.
>
> (*b*) The regulations may also restrict particular work to, and, in connection therewith, impose duties and responsibilities upon, persons of the classes mentioned in sub-paragraphs (i), (ii) and (iii) of paragraph (*a*) of this sub-section, may apportion particular work as between them and other persons, and may require such proof of competency as may be prescribed.

The law enacting the colour bar on the mines remains substantially the same as set out in the 1926 amendment to Act No. 12 of 1911, with the result that non-whites are effectively debarred from any avenues for worth-while advance.

As has already been shown in chapter 3, the mining companies are largely precluded from introducing schemes of reorganization which would, on the one hand, result in the more efficient use of their over-all labour force and, on the other hand, would enable them to utilize African labour in more advanced jobs. The policies of fragmentation, or splitting up of jobs as a result of mechanization or other improvements, which have been put into effect on the Copperbelt of Northern Rhodesia, and which allow Africans to advance smoothly along the job scale, are thus made virtually impossible in the gold-mining industry of South Africa. Furthermore, any loopholes which may have existed can be effectively closed by the extension of job reservation to the mining industry permitted in the Industrial Conciliation Act. Should any attempt be made to fragment a job held at present by a European, with the intention of handing part of its function to a non-white, the Minister would be able to step in and utilize the powers available to him under section 77 of the Act to prevent it.

It should be remembered, however, that the legislation in this regard merely adds legal effect to a situation which is well controlled by the powerful European Mineworkers' Union, which has in recent times showed no preparedness to grant concessions to the non-whites.

THE FACTORIES, MACHINERY AND BUILDING WORK ACT, NO. 22 OF 1941*

The first Factories Act in the Union was passed in 1918. It was revised and re-enacted in 1941 and provides for the control and administration of factories, the hours and conditions of work, supervision of machinery and prevention of accidents and method of excavation works.

In terms of section 51(3), the Governor-General is empowered to make regulations for different classes of persons on the basis of race or colour in respect of accommodation facilities and conveniences to be provided in factories for employees while they are working, resting or eating therein, and this provision has an important bearing on the numbers of a particular race which factories will employ. The expense entailed in providing separate facilities for each race, for example, may influence smaller factory owners to limit their payroll to a particular race.

THE PASS LAWS

None of the laws in South Africa showing racial bias have caused as much hostility among Africans as the so-called 'Pass Laws' while their importance in the labour market as a

* Since this book was written, the Factories Act has been amended by Act No. 31 of 1960 which *inter alia* gives the Minister wider powers to separate 'persons of different sexes, races and classes' in any factory and to make 'separate provision in or at any factory for persons of different sexes, races and classes *in regard to any matter*' [my italics] (section 21 (6) of the amending Act).

whole has become paramount. It is, however, difficult to define in precise terms what constitutes a 'pass'. The Native Laws Commission felt that

it would be correct to say that in the mind of the Native a document is a pass, to which they object, if it is a document—

(a) which is not carried by all races, but only by people of a particular race; and which either

(b) is connected with restriction of the freedom of movement of the person concerned; or

(c) must at all times be carried by the person concerned on his body, since the law lays the obligation on him of producing it on demand to the police and certain other officials and the mere failure to produce it is by itself a punishable offence.[7]

Pass laws in one form or another have been in operation in South Africa since the eighteenth century. The first law requiring slaves to carry passes when moving between urban and rural areas was enacted in 1760. Similar passes for Hottentots became obligatory after 1797, while registration of service contracts was introduced in 1809.

Broadly speaking one may classify documents of this nature as either (a) permits of movement, (b) proofs of employment (i.e. labour contracts etc.), (c) poll-tax receipts.

The resentment engendered among Africans by the system cannot be minimized and is due largely, on the one hand, to the feeling that the laws blatantly discriminate on racial grounds and, on the other hand, to the way in which the system is administered.[8] The fact that failure to produce a pass on demand is a punishable offence means that Africans are constantly being called upon to produce their reference books by the police or other officials, and failure to do so renders them liable to arbitrary arrest and imprisonment.

From the point of view of the present study, our main concern must be the attempts to use the machinery controlling movement as part of a general plan for the mobilization of African labour; the cornerstones being the Natives (Urban Areas) Act and the various influx control measures. Nevertheless, one cannot ignore the economic effects of the Pass laws as a whole; the resulting economic waste is immense and incalculable—the

[7] Report of the Native Laws Commission, 1948 (U.G. 28/48), para. 39.

[8] See, for instance, the comments of Prof. D. D. T. Jabavu in *The Black Problem, papers and addresses on various Native problems*, Lovedale, 1920.

administrative and other direct costs flowing from the system, the continuous immobilization of a large proportion of the labour force through imprisonment; the indirect effects upon productivities flowing from the uncertainties and resentments engendered by the system.[9] In 1955, for example, over 300,000 Africans (100,000 more than in 1950) were convicted under Pass and allied laws while it has been estimated that twice this number spent at least one night in prison during the same year.[10]

In 1952 an attempt was made to co-ordinate the various laws relating to the carrying of passes by Africans through the issue of reference books which would serve as a means of identity and incorporate the various other documents which had formerly to be carried separately.

The title of the Act (No. 67 of 1952) is somewhat of a misnomer (*Natives (Abolition of Passes and Co-ordination of Documents) Act*), for the provisions objected to in the past are retained. Section 13, for example, stipulates that 'any authorized officer may at any time call upon any native who has attained the age of sixteen years to produce to him a reference book'. Furthermore the definition of 'authorised officers' has been progressively extended to include a wide range of officials.

CONTROLS ON THE MOVEMENT OF AFRICANS AND ATTEMPTS AT LABOUR MOBILIZATION

The influx control regulations promulgated in terms of the Natives (Urban Areas) Act and allied laws have two broad aims: in the first place, the control of the townward movement of Africans and in the second place the mobilization of African labour. Both have vital consequences for the economy and their significance must be carefully evaluated.

The character of these laws is predominantly restrictive and their administration is closely linked with the desire to maintain the migratory system and to preserve the tribal nature of the so-called 'Bantu areas'. It is essential, therefore, that the nature of the Reserves be briefly considered before further examining the problem of influx control.

[9] The problems of the Pass laws have occupied the attention of numerous commissions. See particularly the Report of the Native Laws Commission, op. cit.; and the Report of the inter-departmental Committee on the Native Pass Laws (U.G. 41/22). See also ch. XII in the *Handbook on Race Relations in South Africa*, 1949.

[10] Source: Director of Census and Statistics—quoted in *Hansard*, 1957, col. 8386.

11

THE NATIVE RESERVES

The consolidation of areas exclusively for Africans resulted partly from historical evolution and partly from design, stemming from the interplay of the pressure of liberal feeling, administrative convenience, and the desire of Europeans to see the bulk of the African population excluded or 'segregated' either partially or wholly from the white spheres.

Up to the time of Union each of the four provinces pursued independent and widely differing land policies towards Africans. In the Cape and in Natal, Africans could buy land anywhere, but in the Free State and Transvaal land purchases were restricted and could only be effected through the agency of the authorities who held Native land on trust for the Africans concerned.

After Union, in 1910, an attempt was made to introduce a measure of uniformity in the Native land laws; consequently in 1913, the Native Land Act (No. 27 of 1913) was passed under which all existing mission Reserves, tribal locations and tribal and privately owned farms were declared 'scheduled Native' areas. Sales of any such land to whites were expressly forbidden, with the object of protecting the African from encroachment by Europeans and others. On the other hand, these benefits were perhaps more than counterbalanced by the provision which forbade any African from buying property outside of the areas except in the Cape.

There is no doubt that there were some worthy motives behind the passing of the 1913 Act, the intention being to prevent the further diminution of the already restricted area of land available to the African. On the other hand, the restriction of land ownership to the scheduled areas meant that the Africans were being permanently forced into a land space already proving inadequate for their needs. It was estimated that in 1936, compared with the average population density of 20·3 to the square mile for the entire Union, in the case of the scheduled areas the density exceeded 50, and in some cases even reached 100.[11] The seriousness of this state of affairs is exacerbated by the extensive land-use requirements of Bantu pastoral subsistence farming.

[11] Report No. 9 of the Social and Economic Planning Council, 1946 (U.G. 32/46), p. 9.

Commenting on the matter, the Social and Economic Council said in 1946:

Some of the principal obstacles to progress are lack of foresight or consideration for posterity, lack of education, superstition, custom, prejudice, an ingrained fear that improvements may lead to Europeans desiring their land, and sheer inertia. It has been suggested that cause and effect are inseparably linked to one another; poor agricultural methods lead to low productivity, which leads to inadequate food supplies, and the consequent malnutrition in turn leads to poor methods of cultivation. It must be remembered that Native peasants are not alone in this respect, as rural communities the world over are noted for their conservatism. The Natives' scale of preferences is after all different from the Europeans. . . .[12]

The writer himself has at times heard Africans say that they were afraid of developing their lands for fear that this would encourage European desires to take them over; how important such opinions are in influencing behaviour is, of course, a matter for conjecture, although similar attitudes are discernible among urban Africans who are conscious of their lack of secure tenure in the urban African townships.

The restriction on land ownership outside the scheduled areas meant that the growing proportion of Africans who were permanently domiciled in the urban or other European areas in fact constituted a permanent landless element without any assured tenure on property they occupied. The shortcomings of the 1913 legislation did not pass entirely unnoticed; following the report of the Beaumont Commission in 1916,[13] which recommended the 'release' of some 8 million morgen, the government introduced the Native Affairs Administration Bill of 1917, but not for the last time in South African history the provisions covering land met with considerable European opposition. The Bill, which embodied the Beaumont recommendations, did not pass the second reading and was dropped after being referred to a select committee. In fact, in spite of the laudable motives behind the Native Land Act, the concept it embodied of setting aside specific areas for African occupation paved the way for the more rigid policies of segregation, apartheid and separate development.

Following a fusion of part of the South African Party (led

[12] Ibid., p. 12, para. 50.
[13] U.G. 19/16.

by General Smuts) and a section of the Nationalist Party (led by General Hertzog) to form the United Party in 1934, new compromise legislation governing Native areas was introduced in 1936 to carry the separationist ideals a stage further. The Act formed part of the 'civilized labour' segregationist policies of General Hertzog who led the United Party Government until 1939 and who had attempted to introduce similar legislation in 1926, but by this time the long-mooted idea of a permanent separation between the whites and the Bantu had gained ground and had become an important political factor. It was now hoped that a permanent solution to the South African dilemma could be found by allowing each race to develop separately in its own area.

It was in this spirit, therefore, that Act No. 18 of 1936, known as the Native Land and Trust Act, extended the restriction of the purchase of land by Africans outside Native areas to all provinces. It was hoped that this new restriction would be compensated for by making provision for the extension of the Native areas through 'released areas' within which land could be bought either by individual Africans or by the newly formed South African Native Trust, which derived its finances from a Trust Fund made up of parliamentary grants, African rentals, trading rentals, prospecting and licence fees and certain fines. Parliament undertook to vote a sum of £10 million for this purpose over ten years. Clearly the amounts contemplated for the extension of the Reserves were low in comparison with the needs, but finance was not the only limiting factor; the European section of the population who owned farms bordering on the Native areas were not easily disposed to part with their rights.

During the following years land was in fact purchased under these arrangements, and added to the Native areas. By 1945, for example, the Trust had purchased 1,592,814 morgen of land at a cost of nearly £5,000,000. Yet, in spite of this, the problem of population pressure was not solved; by 1951 the over-all Native areas comprised some 58,000 square miles with a population of 3,633,259 and a density of 63 persons per square mile, thus constituting the most densely populated portion of the Union, outside of the major cities. Furthermore, contrary to popular notion, not all of these areas fall within the best climatic regions of the Union; 47 per cent are desert or semi-arid. On the other hand, there is the compensating factor that 33 per cent of the Native areas enjoy a temperate rainy climate compared with only 8 per cent of the entire Union.

It has been calculated that the income of the Native areas for 1950-1 was £48,878,000, to which different sectors made the following percentage contributions: agriculture 62·1, services 19·1, government 9·2, secondary industries 9·6. Of the total, wages and salaries constituted only 11·7 per cent while the over-all figures represented a mere 3·7 per cent of the total geographical (adjusted) income of the Union.[14] There was thus a *per capita* income of £12·9, compared with £99·4 for the Union as a whole in the same year, or (approximately) £623 for the United States and £260 for the United Kingdom.[15] Remittances from migrant workers and others raised the over-all figure to £87,616,000, or £24·3 *per capita.*[16]

It is clear, therefore, that the areas provided by the 1913 and 1936 legislation in which permanent African occupation and ownership of land are permitted, are quite inadequate for this purpose, are unable to support their population without outside help, and, even with this 'assistance', are only able to afford support at a bare subsistence level.

THE MOVEMENT TO THE TOWNS AND THE NATIVES (URBAN AREAS) ACT

In spite of the obvious deficiencies of the Reserves, Africans are prevented, to a great extent, from migrating permanently as family units to the urban areas by government policy implemented through legislation, administrative action and the influx control regulations framed under the Natives (Urban Areas) and other Acts. Dr. Eiselen, then Secretary for Native Affairs, in an article already quoted in an earlier chapter, comments on:

the tendency (*under the previous Government*) to accept this redistribution of the Bantu population [*i.e. the migration to the towns*] as both inevitable and permanent. The present Government . . . has made it quite clear that this runs counter to the principle of separate communities by reaffirming that the Bantu have no claim to permanency

[14] Summary of the Report of the Commission for the Socio-Economic Development of the Bantu Areas within the Union of South Africa (Tomlinson Commission) (U.G. 61/55), p. 99.
[15] Ibid. and the Economist Intelligence Unit.
[16] Tomlinson Commission Report, op. cit., p. 99.

in the European areas, that they are in these areas as workers, and therefore own no real estate and can claim no political rights outside of the Bantu reserves.[17] [The phrases in italics are mine.]

The first Natives (Urban Areas) Act was introduced in 1923 (Act No. 21 of that year):

for improved conditions of residence for natives in or near Urban Areas and for the better administration of native affairs in such areas; for the registration and better control of contracts of service with natives in certain areas and the regulation of the ingress of natives into and their residence in such areas.

The 1923 Act was replaced by Act No. 25 of 1945, the Natives (Urban Areas) Consolidation Act, which has in turn been subject to numerous important amendments. The Act is long and complicated and in addition to creating the machinery for the control of African migration from the rural areas and the control of African urban employment, it governs the establishment of African urban townships and the administration of urban African affairs generally including the 'restriction and regulation of the possession and use of Kaffir beer and other intoxicating liquor' by Africans in certain areas.

From the point of view of the present study the most important sections are sections 23 and 10.

Section 23(i) permits the Governor-General to proclaim areas in which urban local authorities are given wide powers for the control of Africans including:

(a) 'the registration by the employer of every contract of service entered into by a male African and the payment by the employer in respect of such registration of a monthly fee not exceeding 2s. per month';

(b) the requirement that every male African entering the proclaimed area, unless exempted, must report his arrival within a prescribed period and must obtain 'a document certifying that he has or has not obtained permission to be in the proclaimed area, and to produce that document on demand to an authorized officer';

(c) the right to refuse permission to be in the proclaimed area to any African unless otherwise exempted (under section 10 or by virtue of being granted the right to take up employment). He must in any event be in possession of a valid

[17] W. M. M. Eiselen, 'Harmonious Multi-Community Development', *Optima*, March 1959, pp. 3-4.

reference book issued under the Natives (Abolition of
Passes and Co-ordination of Documents) Act;

(*d*) the right to exclude any African female from entering the
area for the purpose of residence or employment without
prior approval;

(*e*) the right to prohibit any male African who is not in
possession of a contract of service from remaining in the
area for a period beyond fourteen days unless otherwise
authorized.

Section 10, on the other hand, deals with the general right of
Africans to enter and remain in urban or proclaimed areas for
periods exceeding seventy-two hours and is extremely important
in curtailing the townward migration of Africans. The section
applies to every African unless:

(*a*) 'he has, since birth resided continuously in such area';

(*b*) 'he has worked continuously in such area for one employer
for a period of not less than ten years or has lawfully
resided continuously in such area for a period of not less
than fifteen years, and has thereafter continued to reside
in such area and is not employed outside such area and has
not during either period or thereafter been sentenced to a
fine exceeding fifty pounds or to imprisonment for a period
exceeding six months';

(*c*) 'such native is the wife, unmarried daughter or son under
the age at which he would become liable for payment of
general tax under the Native Taxation and Development
Act, 1925 (Act No. 41 of 1925), of any native mentioned in
paragraph (*a*) or (*b*) of this sub-section and ordinarily
resides with that native'.

In the case of workseekers, authority must be given to seek
work in the form of a permit issued by an official labour bureau,
and the African may be restricted to particular classes of
employment or to a particular employer. In such cases:

(*a*) 'where a native has been permitted to remain in any area
for the purpose of taking up employment, the period of
validity of the permit shall be limited to the period during
which he remains in the service of the employer by whom
he has been engaged';

(*b*) 'where a native has been permitted to remain in any area
for the purpose of seeking work, the period of validity of

the permit issued to such native shall be not less than seven or more than fourteen days, unless before the expiration of his permit such native finds such work, in which case the permit shall remain valid until the expiration of the period during which such native remains in the service of the employer by whom he is engaged'.

It will be seen from these provisions that an African may not obtain or change his job without recourse to the registration office where he must obtain the necessary permission.

It is further laid down that contravention of any of the provisions of section 10 shall constitute an offence, and the burden of proving that an African has not, in fact, been in an urban area without a permit for more than the permitted seventy-two hours rests on the African himself.

Section 11 of the Act makes it an offence to introduce Africans into the proclaimed areas without authority, while section 13 provides that 'notwithstanding the provisions of section 10' no African who was not born in the Union or South West Africa shall enter or remain in any urban area, whether employed or not, unless written permission has been obtained from the Secretary for Bantu Administration and Development.

The Act thus places in the hands of the local authorities charged with its administration very wide powers in regard to the entry of Africans into urban areas, and their subsequent employment there. As will be seen in a later chapter, the provisions of section 10 have been particularly rigorously applied in the western Cape, both to African men and women, where it is declared government policy to encourage employers of non-European labour to dispense as far as possible with Africans, and use Coloured people in their place. In all urban centres, however, the Act is in force and the machinery of permits and prohibitions regulates all aspects of the working lives of the migrant worker and of the settled town dweller and his family.

THE EFFECT OF THE NATIVES (URBAN AREAS) ACT
ON THE LABOUR MARKET

The implementation of the Urban Areas legislation in the framework of official policy is often at variance with the needs of the urban industrial employer. In the preceding section it was

shown how the machinery of influx control is used to circumscribe the movement of Africans, and this in itself constitutes
a serious hindrance to employers in meeting their labour
requirements readily and/or satisfactorily. What is of more
significance, however, is the attempt to graft a system of labour
mobilization on to the general machinery of influx control.
The Natives (Urban Areas) Act is essentially concerned with
the control of the African in the urban areas and with the
exclusion of 'rural' Africans from such areas, but, in addition,
by creating a network of labour bureaux throughout the
country, charged with the control of African employment, the
authorities have sought to extend control to the supply of and
demand for African labour. Thus in 1952 the Department of
Native Affairs introduced, under regulations framed in terms
of the powers granted by the Native Laws Amendment Act
(No. 54 of 1952), a national scheme for the establishment of
labour bureaux with the purpose of eliminating the 'appalling
wastage and uneconomic employment of Native labour'.

The Department set as its objectives:

(i) The reduction of the high turnover of labour and the
extension of the length of service and duration of employment.

(ii) A proper and expeditious distribution of labour according
to the needs of each area.

(iii) An assessment of the labour requirements of each area.

(iv) The placing of labour in jobs on the basis of a workman's
experience, training and physical and mental attainments,
thus reducing the desire to change employment and, at
the same time, meeting the needs of employers.

To achieve these objectives, a system with four distinct, but
interrelated types of labour bureaux was set up:

(a) A central bureau in the office of the Secretary for Bantu
Administration and Development to co-ordinate and
control the activities of regional, district and local bureaux
and to equate the supply and demand for labour on a
national basis.

(b) Regional bureaux, in the offices of each of the chief Bantu
commissioners, to co-ordinate and control the activities
of district and local bureaux and to equate the supply and
demand for labour within their areas of jurisdiction.

(c) District labour bureaux, in the office of each Bantu commissioner or magistrate, which function within the area of jurisdiction of such Bantu commissioner or magistrate.

(d) Local Bantu labour bureaux which are established and controlled by some local authorities within a defined area of jurisdiction.[18]

Little has been done to assess the workings of the entire system along scientific lines, though research undertaken in Cape Town would suggest that in many respects it does not represent a great advance from the previous haphazard attempts at labour placement, largely because of the absence of effective means of selection and because officials are overburdened with the purely restrictive tasks involved in movement control.[19]

Workers' reference books must be signed monthly by employers, and vacancies reported to the local labour bureau within three days. In theory an employer may not engage labour other than directly through an appropriate labour bureau. In practice, however, employers are usually free to engage labour from a pool of workseekers registered, in terms of the Act, with the local labour bureau, and in possession of reference books endorsed with permits to seek work. It is probable that most employers prefer this system for a number of reasons. With the exception of one or two bureaux (of which Germiston is a notable example) there is no system in operation which would bring about any form of scientific selection of workers, so that in most cases, if selection is left to officials at the bureaux, the procedure followed is based on the assumption that as all Africans are basic manual labourers there is small need to make distinctions between the requirements of individual employers. Furthermore, the employers are often given little latitude in their final selection and they are compelled to make fresh application for workseekers should they be unable to satisfy their requirements from the Africans sent from the bureaux. The waste of valuable time is obvious.

Even where employers make their own selection, the fact that they are limited to the 'official' pool of registered work-

[18] Regulations for the establishment and control of Native Labour Bureaux, Government Notice No. 2495 of 31 October 1952, and explanatory memorandum.

[19] See G. V. Doxey, 'Fabcor', unpublished thesis, University of Cape Town, 1956, ch. VI.

seekers can prove a significant bottleneck. The officials at the labour bureau are charged with the unenviable task of using the influx control machinery to supply labour to employers as and when required. This matching of supply and demand, in addition to the difficulties created by the lack of an effective means of judging short-period future demand, is made more complicated by the fact that the two are balanced numerically rather than qualitatively. Thus, in Cape Town for instance, the author found that seasonally unemployed ice-cream hawkers were directed during the winter months to work in quarries in spite of the fact that such workers had no experience of 'heavy' labour.

In terms of Government Notice No. 63 of 9 January 1959 (issued in terms of the Native Labour Regulation Act of 1911 as amended), Africans may only enter urban areas as work-seekers if they have permission from the labour bureau in their own district. They must register with the local labour bureau immediately and obtain a permit to seek work or to take up employment. If an African is qualified in terms of section 10 of the Urban Areas Act to remain in the urban area, he may, at the discretion of the labour bureau, be given an extension of time in which to find a job, but if he refuses available vacancies he may eventually be treated as an 'idle or undesirable person' and sent out of the urban area. If he is not qualified to remain, and refuses a job offered to him, he may be sent out of the area forthwith.

'Open' permits to seek work of any type are not frequently issued and the more usual practice is for the reference books of the workseekers to be endorsed for one type or class of work in a specified industry, or even in some cases, for a specific employer. The workseeker is given the choice of taking such employment or leaving the area. As the selection of employment opportunities is based on the state of demand for labour and not upon the type of labour needed, it is very likely that employers will often find themselves with unsuitable or unwilling workers. Furthermore, it is usually the practice to confine a worker to the same occupation he was permitted to undertake on entry to the area, irrespective of whether he subsequently proved unsuitable and would have been of more use in another job.

The whole system of labour bureaux is thus open to the criticism that, instead of ensuring that the right person is placed in the right job, it merely adds to the problems of employers and workseekers and costs a great deal both in time and money. One cannot avoid the conclusion that the root of the trouble lies in the fact that influx control and direction of labour, as operated today, are not primarily or even chiefly concerned with the needs of the economy, but are regarded as an effective means of excluding as many Africans as possible from the urban areas and of perpetuating the migratory system. Once again, there would appear to be a serious divergence between official policy and the needs of economic development, and more will be said about this in the next chapter.

The attitude of the authorities towards any growth in the stabilized African labour force, which would mean a corresponding diminution in the number of migrant workers, is well illustrated by their reaction to an attempt by the gold-mining industry to solve some of its labour problems in this manner. Over the years, Africans in the Union have shown less inclination to work on the mines, and as the 'regulars' become more sophisticated, the tendency has been for them to drift into other and more lucrative fields of employment. To meet this problem and to make a start in overcoming some of the undesirable features of the migratory system, the mining companies decided to institute on the new Orange Free State mines a programme for the stabilization of a portion of their African labour force—married quarters were to be provided, and it was hoped that the nucleus of a permanent body of employees could be built up. The scheme was initially regarded as experimental, and it was hoped to accommodate up to 10 per cent of the workers and their families.

The scheme was, however, brought to an abrupt end in 1952 by the intervention of the then Minister of Native Affairs, Dr. Verwoerd, who made it clear that the government would not tolerate innovations of this kind, which ran counter to its stated policies. Subsequently, the Department of Native Affairs ruled that stabilization would only be permitted up to a maximum of 3 per cent of the labour force, that it could only be introduced for absolutely essential personnel, and that no foreign Africans could participate in the scheme. The mining companies were thus compelled to refrain from any attempt, however modest in scope, to build up a settled labour force and could do no more than introduce improvements in the facilities provided in the mine-hostels for migrant workers.[20]

OTHER LEGISLATION

The Native Services Levy Act (No. 64 of 1952), as amended

Mention should be made of the Native Services Levy Act of 1952, as amended by the Native Transport Services Act, No. 53 of 1957, in terms of which employers of African labour are required to pay 2*s.* per week to the local authority for every male African over 18 years of age who is employed by them (excluding domestic servants), and an additional levy, which may not exceed 1*s.* per week, to the National Transport Commission. The local authorities use the funds raised in this way to provide and maintain essential services, such as roads, lighting, etc., in African townships, and the other portion of the levy is used to subsidize the cost of transport services for Africans who, as a result of the siting of their townships at considerable distances from the centres of towns and places of employment, would otherwise have to incur expenditure on fares which their earnings would not enable them to meet.

The only exemptions from this levy are for employers who provide housing for their employees.

The main significance of the Act is the addition to cost which it entails for employers of African labour: there is also the possibility, in Natal and the western Cape, that it might lead to a certain amount of substitution of Indian and Coloured workers for Africans by employers who wish to avoid the burden of the levy.

The Group Areas Act (consolidated as Act No. 77 of 1957)

To conclude this brief survey of legislation which has direct bearing on conditions in the industrial labour market in South

---

[20] In the Free State and elsewhere the mining companies introduced radical changes in hostel accommodation, recreational facilities and in feeding methods. There were also major improvements in medical services; for example, the Ernest Oppenheimer hospital for Africans in Welkom, which cost nearly £1 million, is regarded as being one of the best equipped in Africa. See Edgar H. Brookes, 'New Outlook on Mine Native Housing', *Optima*, March 1950.

Africa, it must be noted that the Group Areas Act (originally enacted in 1950, but amended many times and now consolidated on the statute book as Act No. 77 of 1957) seeks to segregate members of each racial group into separate residential areas, and ownership and occupation of property by a member of one group in an area designated for another group will not normally be permitted.

The effects of this Act on the lives of those affected and on the property market are not under consideration in this context, but it is clear that the pursuit of business and professional activities, and the provision of personal services will be stringently regulated on racial lines when the Act is implemented by the proclamation of full group areas. The group whose interests are particularly affected are the Indians who trade extensively in what are, or are likely to be proclaimed, 'white' areas. To what extent a system of permits will enable them to continue their business activities in these areas is not yet clear.

It is further provided that in the case of trading and business concerns in specified non-white areas, whites will not be allowed to work as employees for non-white employers, that the owners of a business must appoint a manager who belongs to the same racial group as they do, and that disqualified persons will not be granted exemption from the Act if they hold senior positions, such as charge-hands, executives, supervisors, and so on. Domestic servants are exempt from disqualification if they are employed in white group areas, but not otherwise: in other words, in an Indian group area, African or Coloured servants would not normally be permitted.

It is clear that if the provisions of the Act are strictly enforced, it will further circumscribe freedom of income-earning activity of an independent nature and will effectively limit the market available to whites and non-whites for the sale of their services on a personal basis.

THE IMPLICATIONS OF OCCUPATIONAL APARTHEID

A close examination of labour legislation in South Africa brings into focus the potential dangers stemming from officially endorsed policies of racial discrimination.

As is evident from the foregoing discussion, Parliament has increasingly abdicated its authority by granting extensive

Ministerial powers, with the result that the state, as represented by the government in power, has become the virtual arbiter of non-white destiny.

Deprived of direct political action, the non-white must therefore depend upon the arbitrary decisions of government for his status in society and his stake in the economy. The resulting frustration and increasing restlessness among non-whites appear to have little effect upon the firm conviction of those in authority, encouraged by growing electoral majorities, that it is possible, in the circumstances surrounding a modern industrial society, to control successfully the pattern of African advance and to dictate permanently the occupational patterns of the various inhabitants of South Africa.

In fact, as will be seen in the next chapter, apartheid is now more than ever firmly founded upon the belief that even if economic losses are incurred, or force becomes necessary, the absorption of the African into the modern economy must be slowed down and eventually arrested by the resuscitation of decaying tribalism. The concepts of Bantustans, of tribal authorities and of controlled education thus become the latest additions to a legal apparatus designed to halt the competitive advance of the non-white which is seen as a threat to the privileged position of the white.

The Contemporary Scene

THE ADVENT OF APARTHEID

THE DECADE FOLLOWING the declaration of war in 1939 saw the consolidation of the industrial economy, and the return to political power of the champions of traditional white prejudice. In 1948, Dr. D. F. Malan, the leader of the National Party, was able to form a government in coalition with the small Afrikaner Party led by Mr. N. C. Havenga.[1] The new government had as its main platform the policy of apartheid, which could be broadly regarded as an extension of the Hertzog-Cresswell segregationist platform of a generation earlier. Henceforth, as has been shown in the last three chapters, the labour market was to become more rigid and the inequalities between white and non-white more blatant. While traditional attitudes remained largely unchanged, the economic scene had become vastly different; expanding industrialism had enveloped the Poor White problem and had provided new and wider opportunities for non-whites.

Yet the economic progress which took place was constantly bedevilled by the conflict of views on the permanent role of the African in the industrial sphere. Even before the advent to power of the Nationalist Government, and in spite of colour bar relaxations to meet the exigencies of war, there remained a clash between the needs of industrial development, which called for a stable and settled labour force, and those influences stemming from the traditional prejudice which refused to allow African townward migration to follow the same pattern as that of the whites. The need for additional African labour for wartime industries forced a lessening of control over African townward movement and settlement, but once hostilities ended, there were

[1] In May 1948, the Malan-Havenga coalition had an over-all majority of 5 in the House of Assembly. The two parties soon merged and in the 1953 General Election the National Party majority was increased to 29. In 1958, their majority was increased to 47. By this time Mr. J. G. Strydom had succeeded Dr. Malan as Prime Minister and upon the former's death, Dr. H. F. Verwoerd assumed this office in August 1958.

growing calls for a tightening up of influx control. The Natives (Urban Areas) Act of 1945 was largely a concession to these pressures.

On the other hand, throughout the years from 1936 until 1948 little was done to relate the problem of the Native Reserves to the over-all economic pattern.

THE IMPACT OF WAR

With the outbreak of hostilities in September 1939, it was necessary to organize South Africa to meet the requirements of a war economy and to offset as far as possible the curtailment of overseas sources of supply. Before the war the country was greatly dependent upon imports, and the wartime shortage of shipping, with consequent shipping priority ratings, meant that it was doubly necessary to encourage local industries. Production generally underwent considerable expansion. Steel output, for example, increased from 344,700 tons in 1939 to 520,000 in 1945, while clothing output almost trebled in value from £8,160,000 in 1938-9 to £22,530,000 in 1944-5, with an increase in the number of employees of all races from 22,222 to 31,077.

Similar advances were recorded in other branches of secondary industry, as well as in mining.[2]

In the labour market the most pressing problem was soon to become the shortage of skilled labour; the armed forces made considerable inroads into the country's manpower, while the colour bar made it difficult to utilize fully the reserve of non-white labour. Nevertheless, some 'dilution' did take place, particularly by using Coloured and Indian males as skilled workers.[3]

THE POST-WAR EXPANSION

The accelerated growth of the economy continued in the years immediately following the war, and this can be largely attributed to the following factors: a very high level of investment; increased exploitation of mineral reserves; an accelerated shift to more intensive agricultural methods with more advanced

[2] Official Year Book of the Union of South Africa, No. 29, ch. XXIV, p. 809 et seq.
[3] Ibid., p. 858 et seq.

12

techniques; improved entrepreneurship; improved ancillary services; and a wider utilization of manpower.

The real national income increased in the decade 1946-56 at an average annual rate of 4·8 per cent, while the number of persons employed in secondary industry doubled in the same period and the value of industrial output more than trebled. Investment averaged 26 per cent of gross national production during the same period.

Secondary industry was, of course, afforded a sheltered position during the war years because of the cutting off of traditional overseas sources of supply, and after the imposition of import control in 1948 there was the added factor of artificial protection; in addition to the stimulant this gave to local enterprises, many overseas exporters found it expedient to establish factories in the Union itself. Overseas investors were also influenced to some degree by the uncertain immediate post-war conditions in Europe and elsewhere, while the particularly attractive prospects of the new Orange Free State gold discoveries acted as an added inducement to new investment.

Favourable export markets were a further influence: the high world prices of primary produce not only meant that the terms of trade shifted in the Union's favour but farmers, in consequence, were encouraged to improve their farming methods and engage in more intensive cultivation. The index of the physical volume of agricultural production rose from a 1937-8 base of 106 to 176 in 1956-7.

THE EFFECT ON THE LABOUR MARKET

All these developments were not to leave the labour market untouched. Conditions of full employment were experienced, while serious shortages of administrative and clerical workers, technicians and artisans became evident. It was estimated that by May 1956 the shortage of European artisans was 7·4 per cent; the shortage of apprentices 11·5 per cent and the shortage of clerical workers 5·5 per cent males and 4·1 per cent females.[4]

The expanding requirements of secondary industry also led to an acceleration of the shift of population from primary to

[4] See Report of the Commission of Inquiry into policy relating to the protection of industries (U.G. 36/58), p. 31, para. 251.

secondary and tertiary industry and there was a general widening of opportunities for all races, with a vertical movement of whites from semi-skilled and labouring jobs to more responsible positions.

The shortage of skilled artisans and 'white-collar' workers could not be alleviated by the wider use of non-whites owing to the erection of legal barriers to their advancement. Nor has white immigration proved adequate to meet these needs, largely because of the absence of positive official policies in this direction.

The Commission of Inquiry into policy relating to the protection of Industries (Viljoen Commission), reporting as late as 1958, was of the opinion that 'immigration on a very considerable scale is necessary in order to strengthen the European section of the community—the section that is very largely responsible for providing the initiative and organising ability . . . of the country'; it stated further that 'support for the policy of immigration on a very considerable scale was forthcoming from all the organisations which gave evidence before it—organisations representing organised industry, finance, commerce, the mining industry and agriculture, and representing both the main language groups of the population'.

To obtain immigrants of the right calibre and in sufficient numbers—the Commission suggested 25,000 per annum as a suitable intake—it was recommended that the government should 'adopt a positive and effective immigration policy, with the appropriate financial assistance of the State'. Failing this, the Commission considered that the country's industrial expansion would be jeopardized.[5]

How far actual immigration figures have fallen short of this target can be judged from the fact that in 1954, net immigration totalled 5,080; in 1955, 3,684, and in 1956, 2,038.[6] Apart from the absence of a full-scale campaign to attract immigrants, with assisted passages etc., conditions in Europe were now so prosperous—in contrast to the immediate post-war years—that a widespread desire to emigrate was unlikely to be found.

The acute shortage of higher-grade workers has resulted in a situation similar in many respects to that which existed during

[5] Ibid., p. 64, para. 522, and p. 33, para. 280.
[6] Official Year Book, op. cit., p. 724.

the early stages of diamond- and gold-mining in which Europeans could command salaries and wages based more upon their scarcity value than upon productivity[7] and were therefore able to extend the wage gap between non-whites and themselves.

In this respect, interesting figures appear in the censuses of industrial establishments covering wages paid in private manufacturing industry. For instance, in 1944-5, the average wage received by white male workers in this type of employment was £389 per annum, and in 1953-4 £706 per annum. The average Coloured man's wage in 1944-5 was £168 per annum (43% of the white wage) and in 1953-4 £264 (37% of the white wage). Indian average wages corresponded closely to those calculated for the Coloured workers: that is, for the latest date, less than half that of the white wage, but African wages were very much lower. The average wage received by Africans in 1944-5 was estimated at £92 per annum (24% of the white wage) and in 1953-4 at £139 per annum (20% of the white wage). These figures show that although all races have enjoyed considerable increases in wages since the last war, the disparity between white and non-white wages has, in this case, actually grown.

Another interesting comparison is between the average wages received by white building artisans, which, for example, were estimated in 1956 at approximately 7s. an hour, while those paid to Africans doing the same work in African townships and rural areas (in terms of the Native Building Workers Act) were about 2s. an hour.

In the gold-mining industry, the widening of wage disparity was reinforced by the continuance of the colour bar which acts as a formidable barrier to a more effective use of non-white labour. The problem of matching costs to a fixed price of gold which beset the gold-mining industry since its inception has become more acute in recent years: it has been estimated that in the six years 1950-6, the wage-bill, which represented half the total costs, had increased by 50 per cent, while the remaining items had increased by 70 per cent.[8] In contrast, the price of gold has remained fixed at $35 per oz. since 1934.

In 1956, Europeans constituted 12 per cent of the labour force

[7] The term *productivity* is used throughout the text in its most general sense as referring to the average standard of output per worker.
[8] See Chamber of Mines Annual Report for 1956, p. 62.

on the gold-mines and received 71 per cent of the wages paid, the average wage being £1,000 a year. For non-whites, who represented 88 per cent of the labour force, the average wage was £70 per annum and their share of the total wage-bill was 29 per cent. It must, of course, be stressed that comparisons of wages paid in the mining industry are very far from being exact, because of the non-monetary benefits received by African workers in the form of accommodation, food, etc., and by the European workers in the form of subsidized housing and other amenities. Nevertheless, the disparity in wages revealed by these figures is striking.

There is thus a repetition of the paradoxical situation shown in chapter 2 in which, on the one hand, the country possesses a large basic labour force cheap in terms of wages and, on the other, a small skilled labour force earning wages comparable with those paid in the most affluent societies. But while the nineteenth-century situation was brought about as a result of a genuine scarcity of skilled miners at a time when non-whites were largely primitive and unsophisticated, the present state of affairs has been allowed to develop in spite of the fact that there are now many sophisticated non-whites who would be capable of undertaking skilled work.

The restrictions placed upon the upward movement of non-white labour have meant that, with the broadening of the economy, members of the white group have enjoyed relatively greater freedom from competition with the consequence that, in the absence of significant immigration, their incentive to provide continuous effort or to improve their efficiency to give optimum productivity has been weakened. The white group has, in fact, been expected to carry a burden beyond its capacity, both quantitatively and qualitatively, and as the economy expanded, this state of affairs had a very real effect upon over-all productivity: with fewer workers available in relation to the jobs to be filled, standards of efficiency fell off, not only because of the easing of competitive conditions but also because employers were compelled to utilize the services of less well-qualified and consequently less efficient workers.

In contrast, the frustrations which non-whites suffer as a result of being largely prevented from participating in the labour market at higher levels, or from improving their position through the normal avenues of collective bargaining, have had very real effects upon their productivity as a group.

In addition, general restrictions upon employment and mobility in the labour market, the retention of the migratory system and the increasing network of legal restrictions combine to prevent the non-white from giving of his best.

Furthermore, in the case of basic labourers, it may well be that the payment of wages which are largely inadequate to maintain a reasonable standard of living is an extremely important factor in reducing their effectiveness. It is clear, for instance, that a large part of the African population suffers from malnutrition, particularly protein and vitamin deficiencies, and associated diseases such as tuberculosis.[9] One may quote as an example of the low level of unskilled wages, determinations made under the Wage Act in the Witwatersrand and Pretoria districts in 1959 which set minimum wages paid by local authorities at £11 4s. 3d. and £10 9s. 1d. per month. (Determinations Nos. 186 and 187 of 24 July 1959.)

The migratory system has widespread effects on the productivity of African workers. Even in unskilled tasks a modicum of instruction or training will be required and proficiency will largely come with practice, probably to be lost at the end of the migrant worker's spell in the towns when he goes home. There is no guarantee that on his return to the town for a further period of employment he will be taken on by his former employer, who may not have a vacancy for him, although it does often happen that workers return more than once to the same employer. Even in this case, however, it is unlikely that what the worker learned in his previous contact with the advanced economy will have been wholly retained after a sojourn in the primitive environment of his tribal home. The writer found, for instance, in the induction centres on the mines of Southern Rhodesia that it was necessary to re-instruct many returning migrant workers in the most elementary functions. On the other hand, a survey of productivity sponsored by the University of Natal in the Durban factory of Dunlop Limited revealed that there was a much higher turnover during the first three months of service than during longer

[9] See J. C. Carothers, *The African Mind in Health and Disease*, W.H.O. Monograph Series No. 17, Geneva, 1953.

periods, and that the average productivity of workers who stayed for a short time was very much lower than that of employees of longer standing.[10]

It has been authoritatively estimated that a migrant African worker, who works until he is 60, fills at least eight posts and participates in about five different occupations, and that Africans whose homes are in the Reserves are occupied in wage-earning employment for only 38 per cent of their working lives.[11]

The waste of time spent in the rural areas, the waste of effort in re-training workers—these are direct products of the migratory system. The influx control machinery may add to these wastes and increase the rate of labour turnover. For instance, having been directed to a particular job by the labour bureau, with a permit issued in terms of section 10 of the Natives (Urban Areas) Act, an African will probably take the job in order to avoid being ordered out of the urban area, but if he does not like the work he will soon leave and seek permission to take other employment. Stability is thus lessened and turnover further increased. Alternatively, an African may be unsuitable for the type of work to which he has been directed and the employer will then have to dismiss him and recruit another worker in his place. Again there is a waste of time, a waste of such instruction as has been given, and an over-all loss of productivity.

Taking all these factors into consideration, the apparent savings made as a result of comparatively low wage-rates for non-whites are very likely to be at least partly offset by their low productivity, while any net saving may be more than negated by a failure on the part of whites to match their high wages with compensatingly high standards of work performance.

From the employer's point of view, there is little inducement to embark upon extensive training schemes for non-whites. Quite apart from notions of inherent non-white inefficiency, it is a fact that very little justification for such schemes exists

[10] See University of Natal Dept. of Economics, *The African Worker: a sample study of the Life and Labour of the Urban African Worker*, 1950.
[11] Summary of the Report of the Commission for the Socio-Economic Development of the Bantu Areas (Tomlinson Commission) (U.G. 61/55), p. 95, para. 19; p. 96, para. 26.

at the present time. What use would it be to spend time and money on training a worker for a particular job if at some future unspecified date the job is 'reserved' for a member of another race. Or to spend time on training Africans who in a few months will return to the rural areas.

AFRICAN MIGRATION AND THE RURAL AREAS

The rapid expansion of manufacturing industry since 1939 meant that Africans were drawn into the exchange economy in increasing numbers. It was thus imperative that some long-term plan should be devised to cope with the situation.

It was evident that the new industrialism would be better served by a stable and permanently settled labour force than by a continuation of the migratory system under which male workers commuted at regular intervals between the urban and rural areas.

If stabilization and urbanization had been allowed to continue unhindered, it would have represented a radical departure from what was now generally considered the natural and traditional order of things and would have required not only a drastic change in policy, but also a fundamental reorientation of the outlook of most whites. The crux of the problem was whether the African was to be looked upon as an essential and permanent element in the urban industrial society, in which he could be encouraged and helped to develop away from primitivism towards modernity, or whether he was to be forced to retain or to revert to tribalism and have contact with the advanced economy only through intermittent periods of migratory work.

The emergence of a truly urban African population, sophisticated and unhindered by archaic tribalism, would have constituted a serious affront to traditional prejudices which refused to admit the need to encourage advance on these lines or (which is of greater consequence) refused to believe that the African was capable of such advance, at least within the foreseeable future.

The fact that, prior to 1948, official policy did little positively to encourage or prevent the process of change was important, in that it permitted the expansion of the urbanized African *élite* who had no ties with the rural areas, who were to become increasingly restive in the role allotted to them, and upon whom, with the Coloured and Indian peoples, the brunt of the colour bar inequalities was to fall.

The problem did not, of course, escape official attention. The Smuts Government appointed a commission under a distinguished jurist (the Hon. H. A. Fagan) to inquire into the operation of laws relating to Africans in urban areas, the Pass laws and the employment in mines and other industries of migratory labour. In its Report, published in 1948,[12] it took the firm view that the Reserves must be regarded as an integral part of the South African economy and advocated a policy of encouraging stabilization of Africans in urban areas. It stated that 'the conclusions to be drawn from the facts . . . cannot be otherwise than that legal provisions or an administrative policy calculated to perpetuate migratory labour and put obstacles in the way of the stabilisation of labour are wrong, and have a detrimental effect'. Furthermore, the Commission went into great detail to show that 'in South Africa's industries, Europeans and non-Europeans are not in each other's way but complement each other' and that total segregation, or separate, self-contained areas for whites and blacks was virtually impossible to achieve.[13]

Nevertheless, these forward-looking ideas were not destined to be implemented as shortly afterwards the concept of apartheid was accepted by the South African white electorate and the country saw once again a return to the expedient of separate development as a solution of the race problem.

Inevitably, the new government repudiated the opinions of the Fagan Commission and in 1950 it appointed a new commission, under an agricultural economist, Dr. F. R. Tomlinson, to 'conduct an exhaustive enquiry into and to report on a comprehensive scheme for the rehabilitation of the Native areas with a view to developing within them a social structure in keeping with the culture of the Native, and based on effective socio-economic planning'. The Commission's terms of reference thus presupposed two basic aims: (1) the setting up of separate areas for white and African, and (2) the development of the African on the basis of tribal culture as opposed to western culture.

[12] Report of the Native Laws Commission, 1946-8 (U.G. 28/48).
[13] Ibid., p. 46, para. 61; p. 7, para. 8; p. 13, para. 18 et seq.

All suggestions that the Africans and their tribal areas (and, indeed any non-whites) should be regarded as an integral part of the wider economy were rejected in favour of the idea of separation in one form or another. In its narrowest sense, this of course involved regarding the town-dwelling working African as merely a temporary visitor. The illusory nature of this attitude is perhaps best borne out by the Tomlinson Commission itself which predicted that, by the end of the century, even with the implementation of its far-reaching recommendations for separate development, there would be a greater number of Africans dependent for their livelihood on employment in the European areas than there are now.[14]

The very lengthy Report of the Commission was published in summary in 1955 and much of what had been said by earlier commissions on the state of the Reserves was repeated, but their development was now looked upon as the essential pre-requisite to the implementation of the separate development ideal.

The government's attitude to the Report, outlined in a White Paper (F-56) published shortly afterwards, revealed many fundamental differences of opinion between it and the Commission and consequently there has been no significant attempt to implement its proposals.

A major point of difference centred on the question of land tenure in the Reserves. The Commission's recommendation that the present outmoded system of restricted land tenure should be drastically revised in order to permit a full-scale programme of agricultural development was rejected by the government, chiefly on the ground that it would *completely undermine the tribal system*. This has meant that such progress as has been made, in soil conservation and other improvements, can only have a limited effect.

With regard to possible industrial and commercial development, the Commission's recommendation that £30 million should be spent on such projects over a ten-year period was considered by the government to be excessive, as indeed were all the Commission's financial proposals totalling £104,486,000.[15] Furthermore, the government rejected outright the proposal

[14] Summary of the Report of the Tomlinson Commission, op. cit., ch. 50, sec. VIII.
[15] Ibid., ch. 50, sec. X.

that white entrepreneurship should be permitted to assist in development inside the Reserves; this meant that any industrial activity sponsored by whites, with private capital, would have to be sited on the borders of these areas.

By the middle of 1959, State expenditure on internal development of these areas had reached a total of only £3,500,000: of this, £500,000 made up the capital of the Bantu Investment Corporation, established by Act No. 34 of 1959 with the object of promoting industrial development. The Corporation is managed by a board appointed by the Minister of Bantu Administration and Development and its powers, resources, and capacity for risk-taking are obviously very limited. Some mining projects are in operation within the Reserves, but it does not seem likely that these areas are rich in minerals.

Economic factors are, on the whole, not favourable to the siting of industry on the borders of the Reserves: transport costs, even where transport is available, must be very high for raw materials must be conveyed to the factories and the product distributed in distant markets. The Africans, who would be used as basic labour, would not provide a worthwhile market, at least in the foreseeable future. Skilled white labour, power and water, and capital resources might be difficult to obtain although, of course, some financial assistance might be provided by the government.

The low wages which can be paid to unskilled workers in these areas, which fall outside the jurisdiction of industrial council agreements, appear to offer some inducement, and certain clothing factories did move to sites near the Reserves during 1958. This low-wage advantage may not prove permanent, however, for it became apparent that the new factories might be able to undercut existing enterprises and so threaten white employment. To meet this possibility, the Minister of Labour stated in the House of Assembly that the relevant industrial agreement would be applied to any area, if the industrial council made representations which appeared justified.[16]

Some diversion of appropriate industrial activity to the border areas may prove possible and advantageous, but only if it is linked with full-scale agricultural development of the

[16] *Hansard*, 1959, vol. 12, cols. 4241-2.

Reserves. The danger is that the existing economic pattern may be disturbed and scarce resources diverted to uneconomic uses. Official spokesmen have indeed referred to the possible sacrifices involved in such parallel development, but consider it justified in the interests of the apartheid ideal and the transference of 'the centre of gravity of African interest from the European homeland'.[17] Economic considerations must take second place.

It is therefore clear that although policy rests upon the concept of total apartheid, little of real note has, in fact, been accomplished, and the ultimate goal remains a distant prospect. In the political sphere, however, the government's proposals for the separate development of the African envisage the creation of a complicated series of local and territorial authorities in eight Bantu areas, which will eventually enjoy some degree of autonomy. Expression has been given to these policies by the Promotion of Bantu Self-Government Act (No. 46 of 1959) which provides for the gradual development of Bantu national units—Bantustans—and for direct consultation between the government and tribal authorities on matters affecting their development. The emphasis, as in economic policy, is on the re-creation and maintenance of tribal structure.

INTERIM APARTHEID

With total apartheid as the ultimate goal, in the interim period some flexibility has been permitted. This has been due either to the fact that the colour bar had not been extended to cover all occupations, and notably those in the semi-skilled range, or to the policy of allowing non-whites temporarily to do 'white' jobs.

The services of non-whites can therefore be utilized temporarily in order to alleviate conditions of marked, over-full employment, while at the same time they (the non-whites) are prevented from becoming competitive to whites. Their position thus does not constitute a threat or a directly competitive force and the existing circumstances in South Africa mean that any spill-over of non-whites into the 'white' sectors has to be regarded in this light.

It would appear that this principle is to be applied even in

[17] See for instance report of address by the Minister of Bantu Administration and Development to the Federated Chamber of Industries which appeared in the *Cape Times* of 6 November 1959.

the case of purely labouring jobs. It will be recalled that in government service it was official practice, stemming from the civilized labour policy, to replace non-whites by whites in labouring posts. It would seem, however, that the position is now being reversed and non-whites are being used in those jobs formerly occupied by whites, who are now no longer available —but only as a temporary measure. For instance, in reply to a question in the House of Assembly in March 1959, the Minister of Transport stated that: 'on the 28th February, 1958, 14,642 Bantu, 407 Coloured and 4 Indian workers were employed purely as labourers on work previously undertaken by European railworkers', while 'in addition, 457 Bantu, 13 Coloured and 52 Indian workers were employed on unskilled or semi-skilled work perviously performed by Europeans in positions such as stokers, crossing attendants, messengers and so on . . . *sufficient Europeans are not at present available* for appointment to the graded positions. However, no Europeans have been *replaced* by the temporary use of non-European labour.'[18] (My italics.)

Job reservation also permits concessions to be made without arousing white opposition. In other words, whites can be persuaded to accept 'temporary competition' from non-whites, on the understanding that, should the need arise, the machinery of job reservation created by the 1956-9 Industrial Conciliation Acts could be invoked in their favour. This reasoning is not dissimilar from that which underlies the machinery of influx control: the African is permitted to enter the industrial environment within a framework of laws which creates machinery by which he can be ejected should the necessity arise.

It has also been possible to create further outlets for the alleviation of some of the pressure in the white sectors by the provision of separate facilities in public services, such as transport. This is, of course, part of official policy to limit inter-racial contacts and supplements action where, in some cases, existing amenities have been reserved exclusively for whites.

Between 1948 and 1957, for example, the number of African police increased from about 6,000 to 10,144 and non-whites have largely taken over 'foot-patrol' duties from Europeans. The Post Office has also increased the number of its non-white employees, while the expansion of the Department of Bantu

[18] *Hansard*, No. 7, 1959, cols. 2466-7.

Administration and Development has led to the opening up of a considerable number of salaried posts for Africans, as well as an increase in the extent of unskilled employment. 'White-collar' outlets have also been provided on the Railways where the provision of separate railway facilities has led to the employment of non-whites as ticket-examiners, booking clerks, and so on.[19]

In the Cape, the compromise between the aim of total apartheid and the needs of economic growth has been noticeable. During the years following the war, in common with the rest of the country, greater Cape Town enjoyed rapid industrial expansion, with the Europeans on the whole moving progressively towards higher occupations and the Coloured people moving into less-skilled occupations vacated by Europeans. As has been shown earlier, these circumstances led to a situation in which the needs of the time were matched by a degree of flexibility in the labour market which benefited all races.

Many of the Coloured people thus became stabilized at a higher level, leaving a gap in the labouring categories which was filled by increased migration of African workers. This state of affairs is illustrated by the fact that in a sample of 185 firms examined in 1954, it was found that 71·5 per cent of the unskilled labourers were African, against 27·9 per cent Coloured workers and only 0·9 per cent European.[20]

It would also appear that in a wide variety of jobs which custom reserved exclusively for whites, particularly those of a 'white-collar' nature, such as factory office workers, shop assistants, and cinema attendants, 'passing' as white for employment purposes enabled many Coloured people to raise their employment status. It should be stressed that in many cases this form of 'passing' was restricted to the employment sphere and was not comparable with 'passing' in its widest sense, which involved becoming a full member of the white group.[21] Work

[19] See Muriel Horrell, *South Africa's non-White Workers*, S.A. Institute of Race Relations, 1956, p. 76 et seq., for a resumé of these trends. The Department of Native Affairs became the Department of Bantu Administration and Development and a new Department of Bantu Education was established by administrative order in October 1958.

[20] See G. V. Doxey, *Racial Stratification in the Labour Market in relation to Labour Turnover among non-Europeans in the Cape Peninsula*, op. cit., Durban, 1956.

[21] Ibid.

'passing' will of course become more difficult when the Population Registration Act is fully implemented. In terms of this Act (No. 30 of 1950, as amended) the entire white and non-white population will be classified according to race, and whites, Coloureds and Asiatics will be compelled to carry identity cards which specify the racial group under which the owner has been classified by the official Race Classification Board. A great deal of suffering has already been caused in 'borderline' cases, where persons who have believed themselves to be white have suddenly been reclassified as Coloured, and have been forced to change an entire way of life, which in many cases included jobs in the white sphere.[22]

It is perhaps a further example of the paradoxical situation in South Africa that, while more and more barriers have been erected to block the advancement of non-whites generally, and while the impact of job reservation has so far fallen largely upon the Coloured group, concern should have been expressed in official and semi-official circles on the need to protect Coloured people from African competition.

Addressing the South African Bureau of Racial Affairs (S.A.B.R.A.) in 1955, the Secretary for Native Affairs (Dr. Eiselen) outlined the official attitude towards African migration to the Western Cape as follows:

(a) All foreign Natives are gradually to leave the Western Province, and no more of them are to be permitted in this region.
(b) The influx of Natives is strictly controlled.
(c) The Union Natives already in the region are being screened with a view to repatriating the more recently arrived families.
(d) The legally admitted remainder are to be housed in good rented quarters for families and single workers.[23]

In some respects there appeared to be a projection of the attitudes underlying job reservation in particular and 'white protection' generally. Dr. Eiselen argued in the course of his address that:

. . . For the Coloured Community, this integration with the Natives in the economic and social fields constitutes a serious danger. Far

[22] On this whole subject, see Muriel Horrell, *Race Classification in South Africa: its effect on Human Beings*, Fact Paper No. 2, 1958, published by the S.A. Institute of Race Relations.
[23] W. M. M. Eiselen, 'The Coloured people and the Natives', *Journal of Racial Affairs*, S.A.B.R.A., April 1955.

less attention is being paid to the former's rehabilitation and to their development into good trustworthy workers than should be the case, or would be, were it not for the existence of this huge source of Native labour, from which the necessary workers can conveniently be drawn, while the weaker elements of the Coloured population are pushed aside.

While it may be true that a percentage of the Coloured people have become demoralized by addiction to drink or the drug 'dagga', it is surely unwise to base policy for the whole community on the needs of this small proportion. Existing competition is largely between the Africans and the weaker elements of the Coloured population who, like the Poor White, would be better served by rehabilitation than by schemes of artificial bolstering which stifle competition.

CHAPTER 10

The Triumph
of the
Traditional Prejudice

IT HAS BEEN SHOWN how, from 1870 onwards, both the traditional prejudice and the cultural gulf between the races played an important role in the economic scene. Europeans had the monopoly of skill, capital and know-how, and the artisans possessed the organizational power necessary to exploit their scarcity. However, whereas originally the cultural gulf between the races was an important factor in assisting white artisans to entrench themselves in the better-paid jobs and in strengthening their bargaining position, by the mid-twentieth century this was no longer the case.

In the twentieth century it became increasingly necessary to create barriers to the occupational advancement of non-whites in the face of their growing sophistication. Viewed in the light of historical evolution, therefore, the industrial colour bar as it exists today must be regarded as the ultimate expression of the process begun in the latter part of the nineteenth century, which has slowly given overt expression to the traditional prejudices of white South Africans.

Whereas the diamond-fields from the 1880's onwards saw the genesis of white artisan entrenchment, the very nature of gold-mining in South Africa called for special conditions which were to remain a persistent influence in the labour market. The crux of the matter was the fact that, in the absence of advanced mechanization, the mines were largely dependent upon a reservoir of cheap labour. It is, in the circumstances, understandable that until comparatively recently the mining companies should have looked upon the migratory system as an essential prerequisite to operating the mines at a profit, while, of course, their post-war efforts to stabilize part of their labour force in the Orange Free State were checked by official intervention.

The fact that from 1918 onwards they were more or less

totally prevented by the colour bar from using their non-white labour more effectively and from introducing schemes designed to create openings for non-whites, only served to ensure the permanence of the migratory system.

It was possible to obtain workers, limited in their range of wants, who looked upon their earnings as a subsidy to their rural incomes and therefore did not need wages comparable with those which would have had to be paid to stabilized, urban manual workers. In addition, of course, the companies fed and housed their workers during their employment on the mines.

In the course of time, with the spread of competing demands for local African labour, the mining companies had to extend their recruiting to territories outside the Union, thus complicating further the difficulties of doing away with the migratory system.

It is clear therefore that one of the enabling factors for early South African industrialism was the existence of a considerable number of unsophisticated people who could undertake basic labouring work at wages lower than those which would be necessary to maintain more advanced urban manual workers.

Although these circumstances sped South Africa's industrial development, the adverse effects of the state of mind which they encouraged cannot be discounted in a discussion of this sort. Clearly, once the unsophisticated non-white worker had been introduced and partly absorbed into urban industrial society, the old premises which underlined the system upon which gold-mining had been based were no longer wholly applicable.

However, white opinion had now come, more than ever, to look upon the African as exclusively the provider of unskilled labour. The fact that the majority of Africans were still unsophisticated, together with the delaying effects of the migratory system on African advancement, reinforced this notion. The idea of the African being only fit for manual work was, of course, strongly reinforced by the traditional prejudice which looked upon non-whites as inferior and which could not easily tolerate permanent African urban settlement where such settlement was likely to lead to closer social and cultural contact between the races.

While it was true that those Africans making their first

contact with the industrial environment (i.e. in the stage of introduction), and those in the process of becoming acquainted with it (i.e. in the stage of adaptation) were, as yet, largely incapable of performing more complicated tasks, extreme white opinion tended to regard any total absorption of Africans into the civilized society as threatening the very existence of that society.

The labour organization of the gold-mining industry thus provided a convenient pattern for the labour market in general; it was possible, by accepting these circumstances, not only to avoid disrupting the existing order of things, but also to accommodate those prejudices and fears common to all sections of the white group.

Although the extensive use of basic labour inherent in the migratory system was adopted by industry as a whole, there were, nevertheless, strong influences militating in favour of higher wages in secondary industry. The gold-mining industry had, of course, to contend with the problem of the legal colour bar far earlier than secondary industry, but it should also be borne in mind that secondary industry did not have to feed and house its workers and therefore had, in any case, to pay compensatory higher wages. Furthermore, the wage-regulating machinery set up in the 1920's did not discriminate on grounds of colour and so non-whites were able to enjoy the advantages flowing from the enforcement of minimum wage-rates in occupations where such rates were laid down. In the case of the Coloured and Indian workers, particularly, the development of semi-skilled jobs meant that new avenues were opened for them which had not existed previously.

The most significant legal development reinforcing the powers of artisan trade unions was, perhaps, the Apprenticeship Act of 1922 which, by raising entry qualifications to trades denied many non-whites the opportunity to qualify for skilled work.

The circumstances surrounding the Poor White problem, on the other hand, created the need to extend the colour bar to occupations other than skilled, but if whites were to undertake unskilled tasks, prejudice was such that they would only do so if non-whites were prevented from undertaking the same occupations. In addition, the situation was complicated by the notion that all manual work constituted 'Kaffir work' and was therefore beneath the dignity of a white man.

The idea of spheres of white and non-white industrial work thus became firmly accepted, and was gradually to grow in importance in determining the inflexible pattern of the South African labour market. It followed that the problem of urban white unemployment could only be permanently solved once the economy had expanded sufficiently to provide all whites with skilled or 'white-collar' jobs. Any encroachment by non-whites on these spheres was henceforth only to be tolerated in the face of economic necessity.

It was not surprising that policy became geared to the maintenance of a white supremacy line encouraging a growing intensity of colour bar restrictions. Clearly, as more non-whites grew in sophistication, their ambitions for better jobs also grew, and although it was possible by legislative action to deny them opportunities for advance, the widening scope of economic activity increased the strains in the preserved spheres. In the absence of significant white immigration, the problem thus presented itself as to how white exclusiveness in the upper employment brackets could be maintained while, at the same time, the need for more skilled and 'white-collar' workers could be met.

The ultimate attempted solution was based on two main props. On the one hand, the pace of African absorption was to be slowed down, through the retention of the migratory system and the re-creation of tribal societies in paternally controlled Bantustans; on the other hand, a cumbersome and intricate network of laws was created to enable the services of the non-white to be used in the advanced economy for as long as the needs of industrialism required, but with the safeguard that control could always be maintained over occupational distribution and over the stake of the non-white in the so-called white society.

The hoped for solution was thus one in which the doors to non-white advance and competition had been closed and all opportunities for inter-racial co-operation drastically reduced and controlled. Yet in spite of this triumph of the traditional prejudice, it is true to say that white South Africans are beginning to feel less secure and less certain of the future than they felt a half-century ago. For although the industrial colour bar and, for that matter, the colour bar as a whole, has now been firmly drawn, it is clear that after fifty years of Union, South Africa is further from solving its wider race problem than ever before. The illusion of a white society permitted an undue political preoccupation with inter-white quarrels, while the general fear of non-whites has reinforced Afrikaner nationalism in its present position of political supremacy. Ultimately, no substantial non-Nationalist section of the white electorate will wholeheartedly challenge this entrenchment, for fear of upsetting the established order of society as drawn by the traditional prejudice.

There is thus created in the minds of white non-Nationalists a split political attitude which, while opposing the growth of Afrikaner nationalism, has largely tolerated extreme racial policies that, in essence, refuse to admit non-whites on a common basis in any aspect of the life of the country.

Even if we could disregard the presence, in the so-called white areas, of the Coloured people, the Indians and the urban Africans, and thus visualize the ultimate ideal of a racially partitioned South Africa—as do some imaginative upholders of apartheid—in reality it is now apparent that apartheid has achieved little else than the creation of a vicious circle of restriction, frustration and fear, with an ever-widening cleavage between white and non-white South Africans, and has made more, not less remote the attainment of a peaceful solution of the South African dilemma.

It would seem that this state of affairs will continue so long as the vast majority of white South Africans of both language groups are unable to visualize life in a multi-racial society, inspired by the community approach, without at the same time thinking in terms of the disintegration of that society and the inevitable destruction of western civilization.

Neither the realities of substantial non-white sophistication, nor the blatant injustice of discrimination, nor the sting of informed criticism seem likely to alter a racial prejudice which has, through the centuries, slowly hardened into a national tradition.

INDEX

A

Acts:
Act 40 of 1894, 137
Act 34 of 1959, 190
Apprenticeship, 1922, 198; 1944, 131–3, 154
Asiatic Land Tenure, 1946, 104
Diamond Trade, 1882, 26, 27
Group Areas, 1957, 176–7
Factories, Machinery and Building Work, 1941, 162
Immigration Legislation, 1913, 10, 104
Industrial Conciliation, 11 of 1924, 135; 36 of 1937, 135; 28 of 1956, 135–50; 41 of 1959, 136 et sqq.
Mines and Works, 1911, 117, 125, 143, 158–62; 1926, 147.
Amendment, 1926, 127, 159
Native Building Workers, 1951, 133–5, 154
Native Labour Regulations, 1911, 129–31, 137, 174
Native Labour (Settlement of Disputes), 1955, 150–3
Native Land, 1913, 165
Amendment, 1952, 172
Native Land and Trust, 1936, 167
Native Service Levy, 1952, 176
Native Taxation and Development, 1925, 170
Native Transport Services, 1957, 176
Native (Abolition of Passes and Co-ordination of Documents), 164
Natives (Urban Areas), 1923, 137–8, 163, 168–9
Natives (Urban Areas) Consolidation, 1945, 138, 169–71, 180, 186
Population Registration, 1950, 194
Promotion of Bantu Self-Government, 1959, 191
Regulation of Wages, Apprentices and Improvers, 1918, 126
Wage, 1957, 126 et sqq., 135, 153–7
Union, 2
African convicts, 35
African labour for war-time industries, 179
Africans: see under various headings
Afrikaners and secondary industry, 67–84
Afrikaner Party, 179
'all-white policy', 60
Agar-Hamilton, 47
Amery (Mrs.), 63
Anglo-Boer War, 1 et sqq., 57, 61, 72, 77

Angove, J., 16, 19, 25, 26, 36
apartheid, 5, 191–4; advent of, 179; implications of, 177–8.
Apprenticeship Act: generally, 131–3; African, 134; Cape Coloured, 132, 133, 134; civilized standards, 131; criticism of, 132–3; effect on non-white, 133; minimum entry requirements, 131–2; poor whites, 131; purpose of, 131.

B

Baines (traveller), 39
Bantu Areas, 164
Bantu Investment Corporation, 190
Bantustans, 178
Barkly, 15
Barkly, Sir Henry, 19, 40
Basutoland, 1
Basutos, 16
Batlapins, 16
Baynes, Bishop Hamilton, 61
Bechuanaland, 1
Beit (Mr.), 42
Bethlehem v. *Min. of Labour*, 1943 A.D. 75, 137
Boer Republics, 1, 2, 27, 61–2, 74, 116, 128
Boksburg, 42
Brakpan, 42
Brookes, Dr. Edgar, 50
Building industry, 144
Building workers, 144, *and see* Native Building Workers Act
Bultfontein, 15, 21, 28
Burgers, President, 40
Bushmen, 7, 8

C

Cape Masters and Servants and Apprentices Ord., 1856, 128
'Cape Smoke', 16
Cape Town traffic police, 145
Central Native Labour Board, 152–3
Chamberlain, 60
Chamber of Mines, 52 et sqq., 93, 124, 125, 158
Chinese labour, 8, 17, 58, 61, 62–4
civilized labour policies, 121, 122, 126; *and see under various Acts*
Clay, Prof. Henry, 80
closed-shop principle, 23, 126
clothing industries, 143, 144–5
coal, 42, 58
Coetzee, Prof. J. H., 83
Colesberg Kopje, 21

201

Colonialism, 2
Coloured: miscegenation between whites and, 9; population, 3; skilled craftsmen, 10; stigma of slavery, 6, 9; *and see under various headings*
Commissions:
  Asiatic Enquiry, 102–3
  Beaumont, 166
  Cape Labour, 1893, 55
  Com. of Enquiry, 1958, 67
  Carnegie, 1932, 76n., 78, 81n
  Cape Coloured, 1937, 79, 80n., 97, 98
  Diamond Report, 1882, 20
  Dominion Royal, 1914, 92n., 117, 118
  Economic, 1913, 66n., 158–9
  Economic and Wage, 1925, 76, 77n., 78, 79, 82, 86n., 92, 122, 155
  Industrial Com. of Inquiry, 1897, 49n., 92
  Industrial Legislative, 1935, 77n., 80n.; 1951, 101, 105, 130, 136, 138, 139, 148, 149–50
  Industrial and Agricultural Requirements, 1940, 82
  Low Grade Mine, 1920, 120–1, 159
  Martial Law Enquiry Judicial, 1922, 126n.
  Mining Regulation, 1925, 159–60
  Native Economic, 1930–2, 86n., 88n., 91
  Native Laws (Fagan), 1948, 94, 163, 164n., 188
  National Transport, 176
  State Mining, 1917, 35, 117, 119–20, 121–2
  Select Committee, 1890, 55
  Transvaal Labour, 1904, 64n., 62n.
  Transvaal Indigency, 1906–8, 56n., 74n., 77n., 81
  Tomlinson, 1955, 70n., 88n., 168n., 186n., 188–90
  Unemployment, 1921, 1922, 77n., 121
  Viljoen, 1958, 132–3, 182
  Witwatersrand Mine Native Wages, 1944, 130
Committee of Consulting Engineers, 57
Company, The (Dutch East Indian), 7, 8
compound system, 32–6
Cresswell, F. H., 59, 60, 64, 112, 126; *and see* Pact Government
Crown Mines, Ltd., 159
Currey, J. B., 16

D

Daily Independent, 28, 33
Danckert, Jan, 39n.
De Beers Consolidated Mines, Ltd., 23, 34, 36

Diamond Diggers Mutual Protection Association, 20
Diamond Fields Advertiser, 29n., 31
diamonds and diamond-mining: generally, 12–38; African convicts, 35; African migration to, 14–15; bonuses, 35; 'Cape Smoke', 16; character of early diggings, 17 et sqq.; closed-shop principle, 23; compound system, 72–6; debris-washers, 13, 36–7; Diggers' Committees, 19, 20, 27; 'diggers' right fee', 20; discovery of, 11, 12; impact of, 12; effect of amalgamation of claims, 20–4, 23, 37; emergence of white artisans, 36; guns, sale of, 16; illicit diamond buying, *see under that heading*; importation of professional miners, 32; influence of liquor, 16, 34; Kaffir-work, 38; poor whites, 13–14, 36; 'Star of Africa', 12; trade unionism, 23–4; wages, 18, 19–20, 38
Dunn, 942
Dunlop, Ltd., 185
Durban, 69, 101, 104
Durban riots, 104
Dutoitspan, 12, 15, 21, 28

E

Economist, 22, 26
Eiselen, Dr., 168, 169n., 194
Engelbrecht, Dr. S. P., 40
European liquor, 17
European Mineworkers' Union, 162

F

Fagan, Hon. H. A., 188
fear of White debasement, 111, 114
Fish River, 8
First World War, 1, 68, 77, 117, 123–4
'flat' contract, 124
Frankel, Prof., 42
French Huguenot settlers, 7

G

Garment Workers' Union v. *Viljoen*, 1958 (2) S.A. 393 (C), 143
gold: generally, 39–64; Africans, molestation of, 53–4; 'all-white policy', 60; Anglo-Boer War, 57; Boer interests, 61–2; Chamber of Mines, 52 et sqq.; Chinese labour, 88, 62–4; Committee of Consulting Engineers, 57; cost of living, 42; cost of materials, 42–3, 44; death-rate, 57; discovery of, 39 et sqq.; Indians, 58; 'Kaffir-work', 62; labour, other sources of, 55 et sqq.; labour market—factors in, 43–55—

gold (*cont.*)
African, impulses behind, 46–52 —
competition for, 45–6 — liquor, 48, 49
— *lobolo*, 48 — pass system, 53–4 —
poll-tax, 48, 49 — unpopularity of
Rand, 52–4; methods of procuring
workers, 54–5; migration to, 40–1,
43; Native Labour Supply Association, 55; price of, 124; poor whites,
51; problems of mining, 41–3, 123–4;
Transvaal and O.F.S. Chamber of
Mines, 52–3; wages, 42, 44, 51, 52;
Witwatersrand Chamber of Mines,
52; Witwatersrand Native Labour
Supply Association, 55
Goldman, C. S., 49n.
Gorgas, Gen. W. C., 92
Government Notices: 1656 of 1957,
144–5; 1066 of 1958, 145; 1659 of
1958, 145; 63 of 1959, 174; 979 of
1959, 145; 1428 of 1959, 144;
1771 of 1959, 145.

H

Hartley (traveller), 39
Havenga, N. C., 179
Hertzog, Gen., 59n., 79, 167; *and see*
Pact Government
High Commission Territories, 1
historical background prior to 1870, 6
Hobart Houghton, Prof., 90
Hopkinson, T., 94n.
Hottentots, 8, 73, 163
Huguenots, 7
Hutt, Prof. W. H., 99

I

Illicit Diamond Buying: generally, 24–
32; effect on labour market, 25;
Kaffir 'eating-house' proprietors, 25;
kopje-walloping, 26; lynching, 26;
Mechanics and Artisans Protection
Association, 29; penalties, 26;
searching, 26, 27–32; 'soup' diamonds, 25; strike of 1884, 31;
stripping, 28, 29, 31–2; white
leadership, 30; white prejudices,
25, 27
immigrant miners, 116
immigration from overseas, 182
Indians: arrival, 10; population, 3;
stigmas of slavery, 6; sugar-cane
cultivation, 10; *and see under various
headings*
Industrial Conciliation Act, 1956:
generally, 135–50; Africans, 137,
138, 140, 148; application of, 136;
building industry, 143, 144–5; clothing
industry, 143, 144–5; Coloured, 138,
140, 145, 148; definitions: Coloured

Industrial Conciliation Act, 1956 (*cont.*)
138 — Native, 138 — white, 138; industrial councils, 136 et sqq.; industrial tribunals, 136 et sqq. — determinations of, 141–7 — powers of, 140–2;
job-reservation, 139, 140–7; Ministerial powers, 142–3, 144; mixed
unions, 147–50; racial discrimination, 138–9; strikes, 136; trade
unions, 139, 147–50; wages, 136;
work-reservations: building industry, 144 — clothing industry, 143,
144–5 — iron, steel and metallurgical
industries, 144, 145 — motor transport, 145 — passenger lifts, 145 —
traffic policemen, 145
industrialization, spread of: Africans,
85–95; Coloureds, 96–101; Indians,
101–4; Whites, 67–84.

J

Jabavu, Prof. D. D. T., 163
Jennings, H., 92
job-reservation, 135, 139, 140–7
Johannesburg, 43, 54

K

Kaffir eating-house proprietors, 25
Kaffir Wars, 4, 5, 9, 38, 77, 81
'Kaffir-work', 38, 58, 62, 78, 81
Kimberley, 15, 36, 37, 38, 40 et sqq.,
45, 48, 49, 50, 52, 116
Klipdrift, 12
kopje-walloping, 26
Kruger, 53n.

L

Labour Party, 35, 119, 121; *and see*
Pact Government.
Limpopo River, 15
liquor, 8, 17, 25, 34, 117
lobolo, 48
Lydenburg, 40
lynching, 26

M

Malan, Dr. D. F., 179
Malays, 9–10
manufacturing industry, growth of,
108–9
Marais, Prof. J. S., 73
Mashonaland, 39
Mashonas, 16
Masters and Servants Laws: generally,
55, 128–9; influence on later legisla-
tion, 128; offences by servant, 129;
racial discrimination, 129; 'servant'
defined, 129; slavery, 128
Matabele, 15, 16
Matthews, Thomas, 117, 118 et sqq.

Mauch, Carl, 39
Mauritius, 10
Mechanics and Artisans Protection Association, 29
Merriman, J. X., 28
migratory system of labour, 91–5
Milner, Lord, 2, 60, 61, 62
Mines and Works Act: generally, 158–62; Chamber of Mines, 158; Coloured, 158, 161; Crown Mines, Ltd., 159; European Mineworkers' Union, 162; 'mine', definition, 158; Pact Government, 159; racial discrimination, 160–1
mining industry and colour bar, 116–26, 127
miscegenation, 9

N

national income, 68, 120, 181
Nationalist Party, 4, 125, 167, 179
Native Building Workers Act: generally, 133–5; Africans, 133–4; Coloured, 134; job-reservation, 135; Native Building Workers Advisory Board, 134; powers of Ministers, 134–5; skilled work, definition, 134; wage-regulations, 135
Native Labour Regulation Act: generally, 129–31; embraces mining industry, 129; offences under sec. 14(1), 129–30; trade unionism, 130
Native Labour (Settlement of Disputes) Act: generally, 150–3; Africans denied collective bargaining, 151, 153; Central Native Labour Board, 152–3; regional Native labour committees, 151–2; strike, defined, 151; strikes and lock-outs, 150–1
Native Labour Supply Association, 55
Native smelting industry, 50
Native (Urban Areas) Act: generally, 168–76; Africans, 170; Coloured, 171; labour bureaux, 170, 172–3, 174–5; labour market, effect on, 171–6; 'open' permits, 174; reference books, 170, 173; urban local authorities, 169–70; workseekers, 170–1, 173–4
New Rush, 20
N.Z.A. Railway Co., 53

O

Old De Beers, 21
Olifants River, 42
Oppenheimer, Sir Ernest, 160
Orange River, 12
Ordinances:
    Cape Masters and Servants and Apprentices, 1856, 128

Ordinances (cont.)
    10 of 1874, 20
    12 of 1876, 20, 21
    11 of 1880, 28n.
    17 of 1904 (Labour Importation), 58, 63
    17 of 1907, 64
O'Reilly (trader), 12

P

Pact Government, 79, 82, 115, 118, 126–7
pass laws: generally, 162–4, 188; permit of movement, 163; poll-tax, 163; proof of employment, 163; racial discrimination, 163; reference books, 163; slaves, 163
pass system, 52–3
Paterson, 39n.
Payton, C. A., 13n., 14, 17
Phillips, Sir Lionel, 123
Pietermaritzburg, 101
Pinetown, 69
Pistorius, H. F. E., 43n.
poll-tax, 48, 49, 163
poor whites, 13–14, 36, 38, 51, 59, 76–84, 111, 122, 126, 198; attempted solution, 78–80; impact of on economy, 71–80; 'Kaffir-work', 77, 81; skilled and unskilled work, 80–4; underlying causes, 76–7
population figures, 3, 69–70, 104–7
Port Elizabeth, 69, 101
Port Elizabeth Telegraph, 32
post-war expansion, 180–1
Post Office, non-white employees, 192

R

Race Classification Board, 190
Rand Daily Mail, 83n., 94n.
Retief Manifesto, 45
Reserves: generally, 9, 50, 67, 90, 91, 164, 165–8, 189, 190; areas of, 165, 167; buying of property outside, 165; civilized labour, 167; income, 168; internal development, 190; mission reserves, 165; policies of the provinces, 165; 'scheduled native areas', 165; segregation, 165; South African Native Trust, 167–8
Rhodes, C., 42
Roan Antelope Copper Mine, 48
Rousseau, J. J., 9
Rudd (Mr.), 42
rural areas, 187–91

S

S.A. Bureau of Racial Affairs, 194
S.A. Industrial Federation, 124, 125
S.A. Institute of Race Relations, 148

S.A. Native Trust, 167–8
Sadie, Prof., 70
Sauer, Hans, 24
Sauer, J. W., 24
Schreiner, Mr., 29, 30 et seq.
Schreiner, W. P., 29
searching, 26, 27–32
Second World War, 72, 179–81;
    impact of, 180; effect on labour
    market, 181; post-war expansion,
    180–1
secondary industry, 67 et sqq.
Settlers, 1820, 24
Sivewright, Sir James, 54
slavery, 8
Smuts, Gen., 111, 112, 119, 126, 160,
    167
Social and Economic Council, 166
Springs, 42
'Star of Africa', 12
status quo agreement, 1918, 25
Strachey, John, 61
strikes, 111, 125, 126
Struben Bros., 41
Strydom, J. G., 179n.
subsistence farming, 88
Suez Canal, 11
sugar industry, 11, 58
Swaziland, 1

T

Tati, 39, 40
Taylor, J. P., 16
Theal, G., 39
Tomlinson, F. R., 188; and see Com-
    missions
trade unionism, 24, 115–16
traditional way of life, 4
training schemes for non-whites, 186–7

Transvaal Grondwet, 45
Transvaal and O.F.S. Chamber of
    Mines, 52–3

U

Uitenhage, 69
United Party, 167
University of Natal, 185

V

Van Bruggen, J. R. L., 72
Van Riebeeck, 8, 39n.
Verwoerd, Dr., 175, 179n.
Victoria Diamond Mining Co., 31
Village Main Reef Mine, 59
Von Weber, 15 et sqq., 18
Voortrekkers, 9, 39, 45, 128

W

Wage Act: generally, 153–7; applica-
    tion of, 153–4, 156; exemption from,
    154; racial bolster, 155; Wage
    Board, 154–6, 157; wage determina-
    tions, 154 et sqq., 185
Wage Bill, 1924, 111–12
wage rates, 15, 19, 20, 35, 36, 44, 52,
    81–2, 111–13, 122, 124, 160, 176,
    183–4, 185, 186
white supremacy line, 114–15
Williams, Gardner, 21
wine industry, 11
Witwatersrand Chamber of Mines, 52
Witwatersrand Native Labour Asso-
    ciation, 55
wool industry, 11
Wrench, J. E., 63

Z

Zulus, 15, 16